Environmental Marketing

Environmental Marketing

Positive Strategies for Reaching the Green Consumer

Walter Coddington
President, Coddington Environmental
Management, Inc.

McGraw-Hill, Inc.

New York   San Francisco   Washington, D.C.   Auckland   Bogotá
Caracas   Lisbon   London   Madrid   Mexico City   Milan
Montreal   New Delhi   San Juan   Singapore
Sydney   Tokyo   Toronto

Library of Congress Cataloging-in-Publication Data

Coddington, Walter.
    Environmental marketing : positive strategies for reaching the
    green consumer / Walter Coddington.
            p.   cm.
    Includes index.
    ISBN 0-07-011599-0
    1. Green marketing.   2. Product management—Environmental aspects.
    I. Title.
    HF5413.C63   1993
    658.8′02—dc20
                                                            92-35217
                                                            CIP

1 2 3 4 5 6 7 8 9 0   DOC/DOC   9 8 7 6 5 4 3 2

ISBN   0-07-011599-0

*The sponsoring editor for this book was Betsy N. Brown, the editing supervisor
was Mitsy Kovacs, and the production supervisor was Suzanne W. Babeuf. It was
set in Palatino by McGraw-Hill's Professional Book Group composition unit.*

Printed and bound by R. R. Donnelley & Sons Company.

This book is printed on recycled, acid-free paper containing a
minimum of 50% recycled de-inked fiber .

Contents

Preface

Environmental marketing is more rewarding than any other corporate marketing practice. When *you* "win," you win big—spiritually, socially, and professionally. When your company wins, so do all those who have a stake in the environment—employees, vendors, regulators, environmentalists, consumers, and shareholders—in short, everyone.

Environmental marketing is complex. And, laying the corporate, organizational, and cultural groundwork for it is comparable in difficulty to setting up a quality management process in a company that has never had one. The playing field is riddled with potholes and inconsistencies—differences in state regulations and federal guidelines, the absence of green-product development standards, consumer confusion, and a disunified scientific community.

People who want to play this field are many, their motivations as varied as themselves; some want to gain a competitive advantage, stay ahead of the regulatory curve, or simply "do the right thing."

As a child, I played for hours at a time in our neighbor's cornfield. As a teenager, I would occasionally hunt deer and pheasant for food in the woods surrounding our home. I don't really remember when it was that *I* lost touch with the natural environment. I assume it was when I entered college or when earning a living became a preoccupation. I moved to New York City shortly after I graduated from college. It was big-city living from then on. My reference point for nature came from the wildlife specials on public broadcasting stations.

For nearly 20 years I worked as a marketing consultant to large corporations, helping them position and promote hundreds of products and services. The 1970 Earth Day celebration didn't make much of an impression on me. And, quite frankly, the aspect of the 1990 Earth Day that got my attention was not the "let's-care-more-about-the-wellbeing-of-our-planet" message. It was the half-hearted, transparent, and embarrassing way in which many major consumer goods and services companies tried to capitalize on the environmental movement to promote quasi-green products, processes, or packaging initiatives.

I immediately recognized two things: (1) that the environmental movement had touched mainstream America and was, therefore, here to stay; and (2) as business cleaned up its act and its products, there would be a need for a new breed of marketing management consultants, ones who were as knowledgeable about environmental management as they were about business growth management.

The more my company practiced the developing art of green, or environmental, marketing, the more deeply we became involved with our clients' entire business management operations, from environmental policy determination and environmental-improvement process design to green-product and packaging development, and even to environmentally-related regulatory lobbying support. We couldn't in good conscience design environmental marketing programs without first helping to ensure that our clients' intentions and deeds were as sincere and correct as their communications would have their customers believe.

It soon became clear that a "total" environmental management orientation was the requirement for a sound environmental marketing platform. Everything a business does has some impact on the environment and vice versa.

Eldon Enger and Brad Smith in their book, *Environmental Science: A Study of Interrelationships*, inform us that "environmental science is an interdisciplinary area of study...[one] that must also deal with areas of politics, social organization, economics, ethics, and philosophy." And so it is with environmental marketing. The environment has an impact on every business cost decision area from raw material, pollution prevention, and waste management to research and development, administration, and marketing. A company's environmental marketing initiatives are, therefore, usually accompanied by—if not driven by—a gradual change in corporate culture and the way in which the company does business, a shift from compliance-oriented environmental management to proactive environmental management and marketing planning.

It should be evident by now that environmental marketing is not comparable in scope and practice to cause-related marketing or sports marketing. Not one of these disciplines is so sensitive or complex an exercise that it must involve the planning participation of representatives of every business operating area. Environmental marketing is not only an end in itself, but it is also a new perspective from which to approach everyday marketing planning and business decision making.

This book will help you to appreciate environmental marketing for the remarkable new business-building tool that it is and may motivate you to engage in the practice for the good of your business. But this book will not instill in you a desire to practice environmental marketing for the good of the planet. For that inspiration you must reacquaint yourself with nature. Look at your children's faces as they enjoy running through the tall grass or playing hide-and-seek in the woods. Take a walk in a heavily polluted city and ask yourself about the air and water you want to bequeath to your grandchildren. (And, speaking of children, a recent study has pointed to environmental pollutants as the cause of an apparent 50 percent drop in the sperm count in healthy men worldwide over the last 50 years!)

I don't mean to be an alarmist, although I am convinced that the time to act is now. But it is not the planet that I am *most* concerned about. The planet survived whatever wiped out the dinosaurs and it would even, over time, regenerate life after the worst of all imaginable scenarios—a nuclear holocaust. It is actually my daughter and her friends and her friends' friends that I am most concerned about. They are infinitely more fragile than the planet earth; and they, like all of us, depend upon a healthy environment for their survival and their quality of life.

Acknowledgments

I would particularly like to thank Carl Frankel, editor and publisher of Green MarketAlert, for his substantial assistance in preparing this manuscript. He has helped considerably in the difficult task of translating my ideas into tolerable prose. In addition, by granting permission to reproduce a number of charts which initially appeared in Green MarketAlert, he has kept me from having to reinvent the wheel.

I must also express my sincere appreciation to Katrina Coddington and Yee W. Chan for their patience and support, and to Bryan Thomlison and Paramahansa Yogananda for their ongoing inspiration.

Finally, a book about environmental marketing would be incomplete without a chapter on the environmental advocacy and conservation groups—champions of the environmental movement and our collective environmental conscience. Richard Wiles, Director of The Environmental Exchange based in Washington, D.C., contributed Chapter 4—an overview of the nature and roles of national, state, and local environmental organizations including profiles of representative leading groups.

Walter Coddington

Environmental Marketing

1
Introduction

Under fire from environmentalists for its disposable diapers, Procter & Gamble pledges to spend $20 million per year to help develop a composting infrastructure.

L'Eggs, a subsidiary of Sara Lee Corp., redesigns its famous plastic egg, making it far more environmentally benign.

Coca-Cola starts using recycled plastic in its 2-liter soda bottles.

McDonald's makes a $100 million recycling commitment to its consumers.

We have entered the age of environmental marketing.

Environmental Marketing Defined

Business growth in modern times has been managed largely by marketers who depend upon market research, scientific and technical breakthroughs, quality and financial controls, trade relations, and promotion to accomplish their mission.

Today, however, another major influence acts on the marketing planning and implementation process—the environment. More specifically, I am referring to the environmental impacts of the manufacturing, management, and marketing processes as measured by scientists, regulators, grass-roots environmentalists, investors, and the consuming public. Marketing activities that recognize environmental stewardship as a business development responsibility and business growth opportunity are what I mean by *environmental marketing.*

In response to regulatory and activist pressure for corporate environmental stewardship, some businesses are doing the bare minimum required by the law. This is legally adequate but strategically regressive.

More forward-thinking managers are identifying and seizing new environmentally related business opportunities ranging from pollution prevention and more efficient technologies to environmental education and green-product promotion.

The environmental marketer adds the environment to the standard mix of decision-making variables. But it is a unique variable, for it is omnipresent, serving as a backdrop against which all strategic decisions are made. No matter what the specific subject is—product and packaging design and development, labeling and advertising, or promotional strategies—the environmental marketer takes environmental considerations into account.

Thus environmental marketing is also about a change in perspective. But it is even more than that. It demands a new set of procedures for implementing the strategies that arise out of environmental-impact consideration, resulting in a fundamental change in how we do business.

For most consumers, altruistic concern about the contamination and degradation of their natural physical environment is accompanied by personal and practical worries about the impact of this environmental damage on their health and safety and on that of their loved ones. The highly charged nature of consumers' environmental anxieties makes it doubly important for marketers to exercise extreme care when they incorporate the environment into their business decisions. There are clear do's and don'ts in environmental marketing. In short, environmental marketing involves both *perspective* and *know-how*. Many perspective issues are addressed throughout this book, but the primary focus is on providing hands-on, *how-to* advice for creating and implementing effective environmental marketing strategies.

Environmental marketing programs must be managed carefully, but not defensively. Environmental marketing makes it possible to establish alliances that can benefit a business not only in terms of its environmental credibility but, as we will demonstrate, across a broad range of other business fronts. Environmental marketing offers enormous opportunities.

Environmental Marketing and Environmental Management

Paradoxical as this may sound, environmental marketing is about more than environmental marketing. It's not enough to make environmental claims about a product or a package, even if they are truthful, if the manufacturer has a negative or suspect environmental record. Environmental messages will inevitably be viewed as attempts to deliver a message about the manufacturer's overall environmental commitment. If the two communications are perceived by consumers as being inconsistent, even apparently innocuous environmental product or packaging claims run the risk of backfiring.

Issues of environmental *marketing* thus track back to issues of environmental *management*, i.e., to issues of overall corporate environmental commitment and responsibility. It is absolutely essential that a commitment to total quality environmental management be in place before an environmental marketing program is launched. Otherwise, the marketing program will be neither credible nor sustainable.

This does not mean that a company's environmental performance must be perfect prior to environmental marketing. Performance needs time to catch up with policy. Not every process and product design will reflect the highest standard of environmental sensitivity. Still, before an environmental marketing program is launched, a corporation has to have begun the process of incorporating environmental considerations into the length and breadth of its management operations.

Environmental marketing's umbilical connection to environmental management broadens the role of the marketing executive. In addition to targeting the consumer, the marketer must also aim his or her messages inward to ensure that the company's internal management practices are in sync with its environmental marketing messages.

Marketing executives who practice environmental stewardship often find themselves actively participating in internal management decision making through such activities as membership on the corporate environmental management task force. Typically, this involves functioning in the dual role of (1) scout who reports back to the corporation on relevant external factors and (2) advocate who promotes higher levels of environmental understanding within the organization.

The Ubiquitous Environment

The environment surrounds us; it is part of us—it is all-encompassing. We are enveloped by air, water, and other natural resources. Everything we do is affected by and has an impact upon the environment.

Naturally, this is as true in our business lives as in our nonbusiness lives. If we examine the life cycle of the typical product, we find that at every stage, from research and development (R&D) through product disposal, there are clear and significant environmental impacts.

The Research Stage.   Animal-rights issues as they relate to product testing are often a factor here. In addition, much R&D consumes natural resources and results in polluting by-products.

The Manufacturing Stage. Here, too, natural resource depletion and pollution are common. The environmental costs associated with manufacturing are enormous. And, even the most efficient manufacturing operations produce at least small amounts of waste. Most manufacturing operations produce extensive by-products, many of them toxic.

Many industries which at first glance would seem to have relatively clean manufacturing processes are actually environmentally problematic. The computer industry, for instance, which is based in Silicon Valley, California, has been cited for causing substantial environmental contamination to the area. Historically, hazardous waste stored by Silicon Valley industries have leaked, giving the area the largest concentration of Superfund sites in the country. In addition, heavy metals are used in the manufacturing of printed circuit boards, and lethal gases such as phosphine and arsine are used in chip production.

The Distribution Stage. Shipping products to retailers consumes energy—lots of it. And if refrigeration is required, as is often the case, the energy cost is that much more severe. Pollution is an inevitable concomitant of the need to distribute products.

The Disposal Stage. Solid-waste disposal is a major problem in this country, with landfills becoming rapidly filled and incinerators encountering strong resistance from consumers who are concerned about toxic substance emissions. And even if toxic materials are captured in incinerator residue ("fly ash"), they still have to be gotten rid of somehow.

Figure 1-1, from the Elmwood Institute, presents a schematic of the relationship between the environment and standard industrial processes.

Complex cause-and-effect relationships, coupled with the new and therefore inexact science of environmental-impact assessment, make environmental management and marketing difficult tasks.

Difficult but not impossible. In this book, we describe what we have found to be the best strategies for developing, evaluating, and implementing environmental marketing plans. The entire process begins with the *right approach*.

The Right Approach

Let's look briefly at the elements of the right approach to environmental marketing. The pursuit of profits and prosperity without destroying the very environment that makes life on the planet possible is part of the new equation commonly referred to as *sustainable development*. A sus-

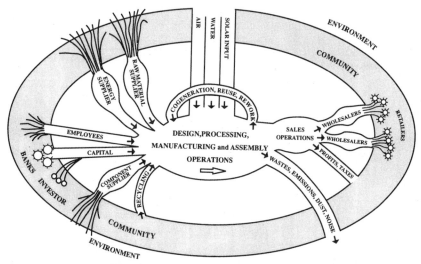

Figure 1-1. Simplified "metabolic" chart of a prototypical company. [*Reprinted by permission from* Eco Management: The Elmwood Guide to Ecological Auditing and Sustainable Business (*San Francisco: Berret-Kohler, 1993). Copyright 1991 by The Elmwood Institute.*]

tainable development management philosophy has two main features: (1) perspective and (2) commitment.

- *Environmental perspective.* An appreciation of the effect of corporate actions on the environment and of actions taken (and not taken) in response to the environmental crisis

- *Environmental commitment.* The corporate resolve to become an environmental steward and to reflect that posture in all its actions

    The elements of the right approach are laid out in Figure 1-2.

Perspective

Having the right perspective requires an understanding of both the severity and breadth of the environmental crisis. *The Green Consumer*, a business study published by the New York–based information company FIND/SVP, has identified three general categories of concern:

- Clean air and water
- Solid-waste management
- Animal rights and species preservation[1]

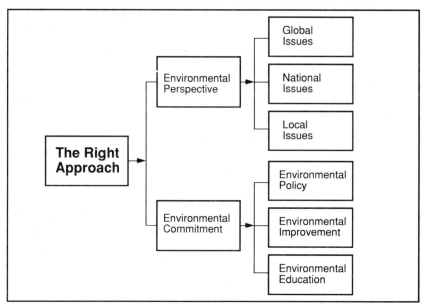

Figure 1-2. The right approach to environmental marketing.

Clean Air and Water.   The FIND/SVP study includes four sub-categories under this domain.

1. *Air pollution.*   The EPA registers releases of well over 2 billion (billion!) pounds of toxic chemicals into the air annually in the United States—and many more toxic chemicals are released which are not tracked by the Agency. In addition, some 23 million tons of smog-causing chemicals, mainly hydrocarbons and nitrogen oxides, are released in the United States each year. Most major cities in the country violate federal clean-air requirements on a regular or infrequent basis. The air we breathe is hazardous to our health.

Nor should another critically important area be overlooked. A continent-sized hole has opened up in the earth's protective ozone shield, placing millions of people at risk of getting cancer. This has been widely attributed to the use of chlorofluorocarbons (CFCs) in a variety of industrial processes and commercial and consumer products.

2. *Groundwater contamination.*   Groundwater contamination results from pesticide usage, faulty hazardous-waste disposal, and leaking underground storage tanks. The causes are largely industrial and agricultural.

3. *Ocean contamination.*   Perhaps the most obvious evidence of ocean contamination comes from a stroll on a beach, which more often than

not is littered with plastic and other debris. A far more serious and potentially life-threatening example of ocean contamination is the widespread concern about the health effects of eating fish, which contain increasingly high levels of heavy metals and other contaminants. The oceans and rivers have served as sewers for decades, receiving both toxic and nontoxic wastes on the assumption that the water system could somehow purify and clean up the waste. We now know that this is not the case!

4. *The greenhouse effect.* There is general agreement that the earth's atmosphere will get warmer in the years ahead, due largely to extensive carbon dioxide emissions. While scientists disagree on how and to what extent this will affect climatic conditions, there has been speculation that entire coastal populations could be threatened and currently fertile areas could become barren.

Although some greenhouse gases have natural causes, most greenhouse gases are the by-product of industrial processes. Deforestation also contributes to the greenhouse effect by reducing sources of oxygen and stimulating the production of carbon dioxide. The world's forests are being destroyed at the rate of one football-field-size area every second.

Solid-Waste Management. The FIND/SVP study notes that between 1960 and 1988, the volume of refuse discarded in the United States climbed from 78 million to nearly 150 million tons, an annual average of about 3.5 pouds per household per day—and an amount twice that of most other industrialized nations. Every year, about 450 million cubic yards of trash, or enough to bury 26,000 football fields in a layer of garbage 10 feet deep, are generated.

Half the landfills in the United States are filled, and it is projected that the other half will be filled by 1999. In response to this crisis, most states and many local governments have enacted recycling regulations and established recycled material and recycling participation and volume goals. It is these recycling programs—some mandatory, some voluntary—that will keep the environment a major concern to growing numbers of consumers.

Animal Rights and Species Preservation. According to FIND/SVP, this area has four basic categories:

- *The use of animals for laboratory testing.* This raises a host of difficult ethical questions. Do we have a right to kill animals for the sake of product safety? Does the answer depend on the type of product involved? Activists have come down hardest on animal testing for health and beauty aids and other personal care products.

- *Factory farming.* FIND/SVP writes, "This practice consists of confining animals in small spaces so that farmers can raise as many animals as possible.... Because the conditions breed disease, a side effect of factory farming is the routine spraying of the animals with pesticides and the introduction of antibiotics and other drugs into their diet."

- *Fur.* Consumer concerns about killing animals for their pelts has had an enormous impact on the fur industry. The FIND/SVP study, which was published in 1990, predicted that sales of furs in the United States would decline over 60 percent between 1987 and 1995.

- *Species preservation.* Our living species are dying out at the rate of 100 per day, a thousand times faster than at any time during the last 65 million years.

Some of these problems are global in nature, while others have a primarily national or local character. For instance, problems relating to the greenhouse effect and ozone layer depletion can only be addressed on an international, collaborative level, while solid-waste management issues often wear a local face. But even mostly local issues have more widespread ramifications. Leaking landfills, for instance, can contaminate rivers which proceed to spread the problems far and wide.

Those who believe that these problems are abating or may be self-correcting should bear in mind that the world population has doubled in the last 50 years and will do so again by the year 2050, putting even greater pressure upon our already overburdened and contaminated environment.

Figure 1-3 sets forth the relative risks posed by a variety of environmental problems, as measured by the U.S. Environmental Protection Agency (EPA).

The Political Dimensions. Having the right perspective also calls for familiarity with the political dimensions of the environmental crisis at both the national and local levels.

In the United States, environmentalism has been gathering steam since it first emerged in the 1960s. Each succeeding decade has expanded the ranks of the environmentalist camps, making the movement that much stronger. In the 1960s, industrial pollution and resource depletion served as the launchpads for environmentalist protests. The 1970s were ushered in by Earth Day, an idea proposed by Senator Gaylord Nelson of Wisconsin and brought to life by Denis Hayes. The EPA ws formed soon after the first Earth Day, and a wide range of federal and state environmental laws were enacted. The 1980s saw industry join the environmental movement with many voluntary CFC reductions and other environmental protection initiatives. And in the

> **High-Risk Problems:**
> • Destruction and alteration of habitats (rain forests and wetlands)
> • Species extinction
> • Stratospheric ozone depletion
> • Global climate change
> **Medium-Risk Problems:**
> • Herbicides and pesticides
> • Toxic chemicals and other pollutants in surface water
> • Acid rain
> • Airborne toxics (factories, vehicles)
> **Lower-Risk Problems:**
> • Oil spills
> • Groundwater pollution (from landfills and toxic-waste sites)
> • Airborne radioactive particles
> • Acid runoff from farms and industry
> • Thermal pollution (human activity that artificially heats the air and water)

Figure 1-3. Setting priorities. (*Environmental Protection Agency*)

mid-1980s to early 1990s, the public awoke to its apparent helplessness to prevent or avoid disasters such as those that occurred in Bhopal, Chernobyl, and Prince William Sound.

Cognizance of environmental politics at the local level is also important. If CEOs want to site new factories in a community, they'll increase their chances of approval and acceptance if they know the area's environmental history and sensitivities.

Commitment

Perspective must be backed up by *commitment*. Many companies are reluctant to make a wholehearted commitment to environmental management in part because they are worried about airing their corporate dirty (or polluted!) laundry. It is true that implementing the right managerial approach requires them to be open about their environmental performance, but this is not necessarily a bad thing.

Case Study: 3M. The track record of the 3M Company provides a case in point. According to data from the EPA, 3M is the nation's largest emitter of chemicals that are suspected of causing birth defects. According to 1988 data, the company emitted 61.3 million lb of toxics, 52.8 million lb of which are linked to birth defects. In 1989, 3M's total emissions jumped to 72.6 million lb. Talk about dirty laundry! Yet, the Franklin Research and Development Corporation, which tracks companies' social and environmental responsibility, has given 3M its highest rating. The company's "3P" (originally *Pollution Prevention Pays*, now *Pollution Prevention Plus*) program is endorsed by the EPA. And, the Council on Economic Priorities in its book *Shopping for a Better World* gives 3M the benefit of a mixed-record rating, somewhere between positive and poor public record.[2]

Despite its distressing emissions levels, 3M has become a corporate role model in environmental management because it has been straightforward about its environmental record, and because it has made a serious commitment to improve it. Representatives of 3M often lead off public interviews by discussing company practices that have damaged the environment. This then becomes a believable platform from which to discuss what the company is doing to clean up its act. The company's evenhandedness allows it to promote environmentally sensible processes and products without too much fear of getting caught up in a business-crippling backlash.

Another concern for companies is that commitment to environmental management may be premature. This is not correct: environmental management is a concept whose time has come. Throughout the industrialized world, enlightened companies are starting to examine how best to integrate environmental awareness and protection into their business processes and planning. The company that embraces total environmental management isn't stepping out onto the gangplank: it's walking onto the boat.

Once these threshold uncertainties have been overcome, a company's in-depth commitment will manifest itself in three basic ways:

- Through a formal corporate environmental *policy*
- Through a corporate environmental *improvement process*
- Through environmental *education*

How to incorporate these expressions of corporate commitment into a total quality environmental management program is the subject of Chapter 6.

A Sound Business Strategy

The environment needs the help of businesspeople and consumers alike. But that's not the only reason for businesses to get involved. It's also the smart choice from a strictly business point of view.

Environmental commitment is *anticipatory* in the most positive sense of the term:

- It anticipates the concern about the environment that is growing among consumers, regulators, and company employees.
- It anticipates increasing shareholder pressure on companies to behave in an environmentally appropriate manner.
- It anticipates the fact that a company may want to locate in new communities. Having an advance reputation as an environmentally responsible company can make a big difference.

A company's environmental reputation precedes it on a myriad of fronts. Carefully conceived, sincere environmental management and marketing programs can significantly improve a company's goodwill and success in the marketplace.

Why Not Keep Silent?

In recent years, a number of environmental marketing and public relations campaigns have received heavy criticism from the press, regulators, and environmental advocacy groups. This spate of bad publicity has made many people cynical about companies that claim to be environmentally responsible.

In 1992, I received anecdotal information about an informal poll of green-business experts on the environmental performance of a number of major U.S. corporations. Reportedly, a surprising number of them responded to inquiries about specific companies in the following way: "They have a very active environmental public relations program, so they must be doing something wrong . . ."—and then gave the company a low rating!

If the experts are having this sort of cynical reaction, then what about consumers? It's enough to give pause for thought.

But only pause. Environmental communications campaigns typically go awry in one of two areas. The first is product labeling or advertising, where problems tend to arise because product claims are made that are either untruthful or so vague as to be meaningless or at worst misleading.

The other area where environmental communications tend to backfire is image communications. Sentimental, banal ads don't play anymore—not in Peoria, not anywhere—yet many advertisers don't seem to have gotten that message yet.

In both of these situations, the solution doesn't lie in avoiding environmental communications, but in doing it right. In the product claims domain, that involves using extremely specific language and obeying all the regulatory requirements. In image advertising, that means avoiding banality in favor of stating the facts without *kitsch* or hyperbole.

It is better to have an active environmental management program and no visible environmental marketing program than the reverse, i.e., an active environmental marketing program with nothing to back it up. But a program in which environmental marketing and environmental management are closely coupled is the best strategy of all.

Why Not Image for Image's Sake?

Many businesspeople take a "me-first" approach to doing business. If they see a competitive edge and it's not illegal, they think, why not go ahead and do it?

In the domain of environmental marketing, this attitude translates into trying to cash in on consumers' environmental concerns without being truly concerned about the environment. Image is everything, isn't it?

The answer is no. I happen to think that such an attitude is ethically wrong, but leaving values aside, the plain truth is that such an approach to environmental issues simply won't work. Not any longer. For a long time, if something was stated in the media, it was assumed to be true. That is no longer the case. A succession of events in the last quarter-century, starting with Vietnam and proceeding through Watergate and Iranscam, has made people deeply skeptical about the assertions of people in positions of authority. A 1992 poll found that a startling 75 percent of Americans believe there was a cover-up in John F. Kennedy's assassination. That says a great deal about the credibility of our mainstream authority structures. Today's consumers believe that they have to look beyond what the public relations firm or corporate-communications representative says about a company.

Nor is it only a matter of credibility. Multiple systems for overseeing are in place that make it more difficult for a company to get away with misleading image-making operations. For one thing, there are formal legal requirements, such as the powerful Community Right-to-Know Law, which require companies to disclose toxic storage and emissions. In addition, there are a host of environmental organizations and investigative journalists whose main charter is to get behind the corporate curtains and find out what's really going on.

And Good for the Environment, Too

There are also important public policy reasons for companies to implement environmental marketing campaigns.

To the extent that the environment figures in corporate marketing campaigns, companies are inspired to compete environmentally, i.e., on the extent to which their products are environmentally benign. In this way, environmental marketing can bring about improvements in the environmental performance of consumer products and packages.

We have also seen how environmental marketing ties in to overall corporate environmental performance. For this reason, competition waged at the marketing level can "work backwards" to bring about improvements in corporations' nonproduct or package-related environmental performance.

Environmental marketing offers a third benefit, too. In addition to selling products, marketing has—or can have—another important function: consumer education. To the extent that environmental marketing raises the environmental awareness of the consuming public, it is intrinsically proenvironmental.

The time has come to make the public good a central consideration in business decision making. Unbridled capitalism created our environmental crisis. Acting for the public good is one way to get us out of it. Businesspeople have no real choice other than to mend their environmental ways.

The right approach to environmental management and environmental marketing implies a fundamental change in the traditional definition of what it means to be in business. As businesspeople, we haven't given enough thought to the aftereffects of our approach to resource management. Our priorities have been skewed.

In product packaging, for example, one of our main objectives has been to get more exposure on the shelf. For years the challenge has been how to take a small product and justify putting it into a package big enough to make it more conspicuous than the packages of our competitors.

Now that the environment has become a factor, a different approach to packaging is called for. More packaging means more resources consumed and more waste created. Minimal packaging is now the design rule. (Needless to add, this also often results in savings at the production end!) This is only one example of how the environment requires a fundamental change in business priorities and, more specifically, in marketing strategies.

How This Book Is Organized

This book is divided into three general sections. Chapters 2 and 3 focus on two areas that are of central importance to environmental managers—the relationship between environmental *marketing* and environmental *management* (Chapter 2), and the role of environmental intelligence in environmental marketing (Chapter 3).

Chapters 4–7 examine the current business environment for environmental marketing. Chapter 4 discusses the role of environmental organizations. Chapter 5 analyzes the nature and extent of green consumerism. Chapter 6 focuses on regulatory issues and on third-party certification of products' environmental assets. Chapter 7 provides an overview of other participants in the environmental marketing infrastructure, including retailers, industry and trade associations, policy and educational institutions, and scientific and technical organizations.

Chapters 8–11 provide a closer look at environmental marketing and related business strategies. Chapter 8 concentrates on green-product development, Chapter 9 examines green-product positioning, Chapter 10 analyzes strategic alliances and environmental marketing–partnership planning, and Chapter 11 discusses environmental communication strategies.

2

The Marketer and Environmental Management

Introduction

In Chapter 1, we identified the two basic components of what I called the "right approach" to environmental management: (1) perspective and (2) commitment. In that chapter, we discussed the question of perspective at some length, and deferred until later—specifically, until this chapter—the discussion of commitment.

Attitude and *actions* are words I might have used instead of *perspective* and *commitment*. Why? Because perspective is about the mindset—the attitude—from which management strategies flow, and commitment is about how that perspective manifests itself in terms of business policies and practices, i.e., in terms of concrete management actions.

For those marketers who are unclear about the connection between environmental management and environmental marketing, I ask for a little forbearance. There is a strong connection between the two, and the nature of that relationship shall be made clear later in this chapter.

It is important to note at the outset of this chapter that I am a strong advocate of *quality management* and its applicability to environmental management. Others have also related environmental management to quality management. In late 1991, the journal *Total Quality Environmental Management* appeared, published by New York–based Executive Enterprises.

The Global Environmental Management Initiative (GEMI) in Washington, D.C., which is the creation of environmental and safety professionals within the business community, is credited with having created the marriage of *total quality and environmental management* (TQEM). George D. Carpenter, director of environment, energy, and safety systems at the Procter & Gamble Company and chairman of the Global Environmental Management Initiative says of GEMI:

> We believe that through our knowledge of corporations, free market economics, and the environment, we can become a center of critical, leading edge thinking on the subject of how corporations can improve their environmental and safety performance.[1]

A GEMI primer identifies four basic elements in TQEM:

- *"Identify your customers.* Total Quality is based on the premise that the customer is always right. In fact, quality is defined by what the customer wants. Customers can be external (i.e., consumers, regulators, legislators, community and national environmental groups) or internal (such as other departments within the company, higher management levels)."

- *"Continuous improvement.* The systematic, ongoing effort to improve business processes, continuous improvement changes the entire corporate perspective. The staff is motivated to seek innovative alternatives to outdated processes and policies. With continuous improvement there is no endpoint, only progress along a continuum."

- *"Do it right the first time.* In TQEM it is essential to recognize and eliminate . . . problems before they occur. The best cure for a pound of . . . crises is an ounce of prevention."

- *"Take a systems approach to work.* TQEM teaches us to look at each part of . . . management as a system. The system includes all of the equipment and people who must work together to achieve the desired objective. Total quality causes us to work across organizational boundaries, forming teams that represent all the functions involved in making a system work as intended. . . . Interactions of people and decision-making procedures can be flow-charted and analyzed as a system. This focuses attention on what is wrong with the system, instead of forcing blame on an individual."

Figure 2-1. Total Quality Environmental Management. (*Global Environmental Management Initiative.*)

	1970s →	Late 1980s →	1990s →	
ERA	Compliance	Pollution Reduction	Pollution Prevention	Environmental Strategy
Key Drivers	Regulation	Regulation Cost	Regulation Cost reduction Efficiency	Market satisfaction Regulation Competition Global Change
Focus	Control effluents outside plant	Manage process on plant floor	Redesign process at manufacturing	Competitive positioning Product and package development Capture revenue Measure performance
Parts of Firm Affected	Environment	Environment Operations management	Environment Manufacturing management Supplier management	Marketing Distribution Product development TQM Finance

Figure 2-2. Evolution of environmental management. (*Abt Associates, Inc. 1990 study of 41 +3 billion companies*)

Figure 2-2 provides a timeline for the evolution of environmental management prepared by Abt Associates, Inc. Notice how the role of environmental management becomes more extensive with the passage of time. Marketing issues such as market satisfaction, competitive positioning, and product design are now important considerations in the development of corporate environmental strategy. Figure 2-3 expands on this point, showing the full scope of a comprehensive environmental management system as outlined by ENSR Consulting & Engineering.

This chapter is divided into three sections. The first contains a brief overview of quality management. The second consists of a case study which examines how these principles have been incorporated in the environmental management philosophy of Church & Dwight Co., Inc., the maker of ARM and HAMMER® brand products. In the third section, the role of the environmental marketer in environmental management is examined.

Quality Management Defined

Every period has its hot management concepts, but for the last three decades several quality management systems have grown in popular-

---

1. Protection policy and procedures programs
2. Regulatory program (existing and pending) awareness
3. Health and safety programs
4. Emergency preparedness and response planning
5. Pollution prevention and reduction programs
6. Risk communication programs
7. Product and packaging stewardship
8. Acquisition and divestiture programs
9. Development and training programs
10. Long-term strategic business and marketing planning and capital budgeting

---

Figure 2-3. A total environmental management system. (*Halley Moriyama, ENSR Consulting & Engineering*)

ity and in application. Quality management generally calls for changes in management attitude as well as behavior. Once attitudes have been changed—at a deep level, as it were (and it's no easy task to do that!)—they tend to stay changed. Quality management promises to have a long-term impact on how business is done in this country.

Quality management is a unique amalgam of a dedication to the ideas of personal responsibility and unwavering commitment, a holistic mindset, and a nuts-and-bolts approach to business management—all the requirements for corporate environmental stewardship.

The Importance of Personal Responsibility

In his book *Quality Without Tears*, quality management guru Philip B. Crosby (whose works we rely on heavily in our following discussion) has much to say about personal responsibility, including the following comment (made in the context of a business case study): "They (senior management) needed to realize that they as individuals, and as the thought leaders of the company, were causing most of the problems."[2]

According to Crosby, shopworn excuses like shoddy workmanship simply don't cut the mustard: responsibility for quality starts at the top of the management chain.

Quality management's call for senior managers to take personal responsibility for the quality of their company's products has a corollary. Personal responsibility must be made universal within the organization, i.e., it's not enough for senior managers to demand it for themselves alone. They must also require all corporate employees at all levels to accept responsibility for the quality of their company's products—and then they must clear the decks so that the employees can actually exercise that responsibility. Crosby uses the terms *de-hassling* and *empowering*. You can't have one without the other.

The Need for Unwavering Commitment

Quality Management also calls for practitioners to translate the awareness that comes with the acceptance of personal responsibility into a degree of commitment that never flags or wavers. There can be no exceptions, no excuses. If senior management even once blinks at a shortfall in quality, its credibility is gone forever. The senior manager who says "Well, just this one time it's okay to fall short" is like the recovering alcoholic who thinks just one little drink won't matter.

Personal responsibility, a focusing of the will, and an unwavering commitment to consistency of approach are the main characteristics that senior managers must bring to quality and environmental issues. Without them, quality management becomes nothing more than a hollow phrase, and goals like zero-waste and zero-pollution become impossible to achieve.

New-Paradigm Intuitions

Perhaps the easiest way to explain what I mean by the *new paradigm* is to quote from *The Elmwood Guide to Eco-Auditing and Ecologically Conscious Management* by Ernest Callenbach, Fritjof Capra, and Sandra Marburg:

> Our starting point is the recognition that the world's ecological problems, like all the other major problems of our time, cannot be understood in isolation. They are systemic problems—interconnected and interdependent—and need a new kind of systemic, or ecological thinking to be understood and solved. Moreover, this new thinking must be accompanied by a shift in values from expansion to conservation, from quantity to *quality* [italics added], from domination to partnership. The new value system and thinking, together with corresponding new perceptions and practices, are what we call the "new paradigm." ... The new paradigm may be called a holistic world view—seeing the world as an integrated whole rather than a dissociated collection of parts.[3]

Interdependence, process, flow—concepts like these gain ascendancy in the new-paradigm worldview. And as that scale goes up, the one containing *old-paradigm*, mechanistic, dualistic, thinking goes down.

One might expect science to buttress old-paradigm thinking rather than the new paradigm. However, that is not the case. Much subatomic behavior, for instance, can be explained by new-paradigm theorems but not by old-paradigm ones.

From this grounding in contemporary science, new-paradigm thinking is beginning to infiltrate other disciplines. Its tenets are increasingly being incorporated into a wide variety of seemingly inapposite intellectual constructs—including quality management. Here are two ways in which quality management reflects new-paradigm thinking.

Process, Not Programs.   In *Quality Without Tears*, Crosby writes:

> Quality improvement also has a profile. The companies that don't get much improvement, even though they appear to be determined, have common characteristics:
>
> 1.   *The effort is called a program rather than a process.* This reflects the idea management holds in its secret heart—that this quality business is one of finding the proper set of techniques to apply to the proper people. A "program" lets people know that if they wait and go through the motions, it will soon be replaced by something else. Governments call everything programs. A "process" is never finished and requires constant attention.

Crosby is saying that it's not enough to install a mechanistic set of procedures. To be effective, there also has to be a dynamic underlying core, a sense of ongoing vitality, that animates the operation. People have to do more than simply go through the motions. They have to be engaged, involved—participants, not observers, in the continuous improvement process. Crosby's preference of process over programs is new-paradigm.

Quality Is Organic.   Another central tenet of quality management is that quality is both macrocosmic and microcosmic, i.e., it arises out of a corporate (macrocosmic) commitment as well as the commitment of each individual employee (microcosmic). When Crosby makes comments like, "When all the employees are determined to conform exactly to the requirements and to offer feedback when the requirements are inadequate or impossible to achieve, then hassles will begin to die out and quality improvement will become a fact of life," he is basically saying that quality is organic.

This attitude is premised on the notion that the business organization itself is organic—and the organic nature of things is at the heart of the new paradigm.

Kinder, Gentler Management

There's another aspect to quality management which, while not quite new-paradigm, is decidedly not old-style management. It assumes that people have the ability and desire to contribute positively to a collective enterprise, and that they will do so if given the opportunity. Another management model makes much harsher assumptions about the proto-typical employee. It assumes that workers are basically like mules, and that they will do only as much as the whip demands of them. Quality management assumes that the corporate dynamo is driven by the un-leashed energies and aptitudes of all its employees. This is a far cry from the do-as-you're-told-and-be-grateful-you've-still-got-a-job attitude of much old-style business management.

The popularity of quality management is only one of the signs that we are entering a period of gentler, kinder management. Robert Welch, CEO of General Electric, recently created a stir when he declared in GE's annual report, "(I)n an environment where we must have every good idea from every man and woman in the organization, we cannot afford management styles that suppress and intimidate." Although Welch's comments were covered on the front page of business sections around the country, he was not breaking new ground. Welch's perception that business success comes from unleashing people rather than from driv-ing them has its origins in the new paradigm, which gives central im-portance to the role of personal empowerment. In addition to being im-portant for GE and for other companies that choose to follow GE's lead, Welch's remarks are important because they indicate the degree to which new-paradigm thinking is beginning to permeate the main-stream.

Pragmatic Business Considerations

But quality management is more than a combination of motivational thinking and new-paradigm constructs. It also has a solid business grounding, with a rigorous insistence on high standards and measur-able results. Consider Crosby's "Four Absolutes of Quality."

1. *"The definition of quality is conformance to requirements."* It is senior management's job to establish requirements (i.e., quality standards), and then to insist that those requirements are met—every time.

2. *"The system of quality is prevention."* One doesn't achieve quality by fixing things after they go wrong, or by fixing the symptom rather

than the cause. One achieves quality by making sure things don't go wrong in the first place. The mantra: Do it right the first time (DIRFT).

3. *"The performance standard is zero defects."* Tolerance for error? No. Flawlessness is the goal.

4. *"The measurement of quality is the price of nonconformance."* Quality is not an abstract concept involving vague notions of goodness. It is *measurable*. And the standard for measuring quality, as per the fourth absolute, is the price of nonconformance. How much does it cost to repair those defects? What is the impact on sales of reduced quality? One of the fundamental principles underlying quality management is that the price of conformance (POC) is less than the price of nonconformance (PONC), i.e., it costs less to achieve high quality than it does to fall short.

Quality at Parity

In the non–quality-management–oriented business, strategists assert, costs and schedule have priority over quality. If it would take the project over budget or put it behind schedule, it's okay to let a product with a minor defect go out the door. In a quality-management-oriented shop, however, if quality fails to meet the requirements, the problem must be fixed, even if it pushes a project over budget or behind schedule.

With quality management, quality is at parity with costs and schedule.

In the above pages, we've provided an overview of quality management. Quality environmental management (QEM), in turn, involves the application of the principles of quality management to environmental management. Now let's examine how one company has incorporated quality environmental management into its quality management process.

Church & Dwight and QEM

Church & Dwight Co., Inc. focuses much of its environmental management attention on pollution prevention or "front of the pipe" environmental issues. It is our observation that "end of the pipe" companies oriented toward pollution cleanup and control spend more money over time on waste-management (versus waste-prevention) technology and compliance than those companies that invest in clean technologies and processes to start with.

Getting Started

Let's say I'm a smoker. For me to become a nonsmoker, three operations are necessary.

First, I have to decide that I want to quit. This decision must be in earnest, or it will not last long. If I make a public pledge to stop smoking, that reinforces my sense of obligation. It will put that much more pressure on me to carry out my pledge. I need a *statement of commitment*.

Second, I must maintain my resolve. Resisting the temptation to smoke is a constant process. Nonstop vigilance is a must. Whether I'm going cold turkey or cutting back with a view to eventually eliminating smoking entirely, I must keep my sights on where I've been and on where I'm headed. I need a *continuous improvement process*.

Finally, there's this funny thing about stopping smoking: sometimes my will stays strong, but my fingers lose contact with my will. I look up, and there I am with a lit cigarette between my fingers!

It's not enough to decide not to smoke—I must also make sure that every part of me, fingers included, is in constant accord with that decision. I need a *communication system* to ensure that my requirement of nonsmoking is adhered to throughout my "organization."

These three requirements—a statement of commitment, a continuous improvement process, and an effective communication system—are captured in three separate Church & Dwight documents:

1. A corporate environmental policy statement
2. An environmental improvement process statement and guidelines
3. Environmental communications guidelines (Of course, in the corporate context, the communication system must be two-way. It's not enough for senior management to issue edicts about environmental improvement. Input from even the lowest levels must be solicited and accepted, as eagerly as if it came from the CEO. This is why one of the effects of quality management is to flatten traditional corporate hierarchies.)

Corporate Environmental Policy

Church & Dwight's corporate environmental policy (see Figure 2-4) was issued by CEO Dwight Minton in late 1991. Quality management is pervasive in the company's thinking:

- The preamble establishes the corporate goal as the production of quality products, which "in the totality of their life cycles, have minimum impact on the environment."

Church & Dwight Co., Inc.

I. Corporate Environmental Policy

Our corporate environmental policy is to produce quality products which, in the totality of their life cycles, have minimum impact on the environment. We will be a model of corporate environmental responsibility in this regard. Our carbonate-based technologies and products enable us to be a leader in toxics reduction and source reduction programs, especially as they relate to our nation's air and water resources.

To fulfill this policy, we make the following commitments:

1. We will understand the environmental impact of our technologies and products, and take scientifically sound steps to minimize them.

2. We will implement, as part of our Quality Improvement Process, an Environmental Improvement Process which will help ensure that minimization of environmental impact' continues to be part of our corporate culture.

3. We will develop products and processes which can be demonstrated to have a more favorable impact on air and water quality than most existing products and processes by focusing on the toxics reduction and source reduction capabilities of carbonates.

4. We will help educate our consumers and customers on environmental issues and the environmentally responsible distribution, use and disposal of our products and packaging.

5. We will assist environmental stakeholders in the development of environmentally responsible policies, programs and communications.

6. We will measure and regularly review our environmental performance against these commitments.

Figure 2-4. (*Church & Dwight Co., Inc.*)

- Paragraph 1 reads, "We will understand the environmental impact of our technologies and products and take scientifically sound steps to minimize them." This reflects a quality-management-oriented emphasis on *measuring* the impacts of nonconformance.

n Paragraph 2 states, "We will implement, as part of our Quality Improvement Process, an Environmental Improvement Process which will help ensure that 'minimization of environmental impact' continues to be part of our corporate culture." This paragraph specifically addresses the role of quality management in environmental management. In addition, it underscores an emphasis on integrating continuous improvement and zero defects in the corporate culture.

- Paragraph 6 declares, "We will measure and regularly review our environmental performance against these commitments." Like Paragraph 1, this paragraph emphasizes the need for ongoing measurement against quality management requirements.[4]

Figure 2-5 is a conceptualization of the objectives of Church & Dwight's environmental management policies and practices. As Figure 2-5 indicates, the company's internal environmental management objectives are twofold: (1) compliance and (2) prevention.

These internal objectives are to be realized via quality management, for the four listed strategies are actually the "Four Absolutes of Quality":

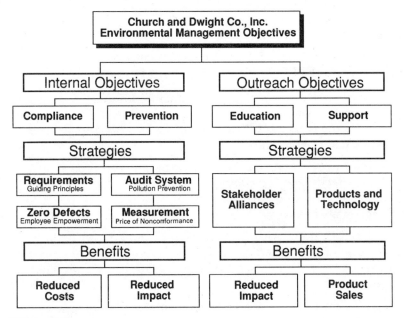

Figure 2-5.

- *Requirements* refers to the first absolute of quality: "The definition of quality is conformance to requirements."

- *Audit system* refers to how the second absolute of quality is effected: "The system of quality is prevention."

- *Zero defects* refers to the third absolute: "The performance standard is zero defects."

- *Measurement* refers to the fourth absolute: "The measurement of quality is the price of nonconformance."

The benefits of such an approach, as laid out in Figure 2-5, are twofold: (1) reduced costs, i.e., an improvement in the company's bottom line, and (2) reduced impact, i.e., environmental benefits.

The company's outreach objectives also reflect Church & Dwight's quality management orientation. Collectively, their goal is to empower consumers, customers, and others to participate in the same sorts of continuous environmental improvement activities that characterize the company's internal operations. And empowerment is, of course, a core quality management concept.

Continuous Environmental Improvement

Figure 2-6 presents a schematic of Church & Dwight's continuous environmental improvement process.

The program has two major tiers. The first, which it calls the *foundation*, involves managing for compliance and has four components. In Church & Dwight's words, here is what they are:

- *Commitment.* "Our corporate Environmental Improvement Process begins with the commitment of our Chairman and CEO, Dwight C. Minton and the company's Board of Directors to on-going corporate environmental stewardship."

- *Accountability.* "This commitment to corporate environmental stewardship demands that key company managers assume responsibility for corporate environmental impact improvement and that they be held accountable for same."

- *Compliance.* "Along with the health and safety of our employees, consumers and customers, compliance with government environmental laws and regulations must be our primary environmental improvement imperative."

- *Alliances.* "To keep abreast of environmental regulations, issues, debates, technology and attitudes, we must form *information and resource*

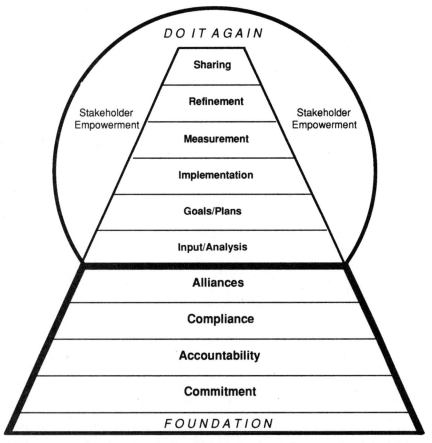

Figure 2-6. Church & Dwight Co., Inc. environmental improvement process.

exchange relationships with a variety of stakeholders, including legislators, environmentalists, educators, industry associations and media representatives."

The second tier in Church & Dwight's continuous environmental improvement program builds upon this foundation of managing for compliance. Church & Dwight calls this second tier managing for assurance.

Managing for assurance has six components as described in Church & Dwight's environmental improvement process statement.

1. *Input and Analysis*

   Environmental management for assurance requires the participation and involvement of all company employees. As such, each and every employee is empowered by our Chairman and our corporate environmental policy to practice conservation, waste reduction and pollution prevention measures at all times and bring to the attention of the corporate environmental task force all ideas and recommendations regarding same.

2. *Goals and plans*

   Based upon the recommendations of all employees and regular audits and assessments, the environmental task force develops environmental impact improvement plans and establishes goals for each company department.

3. *Implementation*

   Each department environmental improvement process manager will be responsible for overseeing the implementation of the plans developed [with their input] by the environmental task force.

4. *Measurement*

   On a quarterly basis, the environmental task force will measure the progress of all environmental improvement initiatives. On a semiannual basis, company senior management will review the progress of the corporate environmental improvement process. All employees will be regularly informed of the environmental improvement initiatives of each company department through our corporate newsletter. Measurement will be in terms of achievement of goals or standards and the costs or savings associated with compliance conformance and proactive "prevention" measures.

   Measurement of QEM varies from company to company. For perspective, Table 2-1, developed by Chris FitzGerald, editor-in-chief of *Total Quality Environmental Management* magazine, indicates the measurement parameters of six other organizations. Notice that Xerox Corporation includes as a parameter the gaining of market share via environmentally responsible positioning.[5]

5. *Refinement*

   Regular evaluation and measurement of our environmental improvement initiatives will lead to refinements in our objectives and our methods for achieving those objectives. The acts of "doing" and "refining" are the basis for our environmental education.

6. *Sharing*

   The lessons we learn from doing and refining will be shared within the company (across departments) and outside the company—with all those who have an interest in sustainable economic development or increased prosperity without the destruction of our environment.

Church & Dwight's environmental improvement process statement concludes as follows: "There is no end to corporate environmental stewardship; like quality control and our Quality Improvement Process, the

Table 2-1. Selected TQEM Measurement Systems

Company	Purpose of measures	Parameters
AT&T/Intel Joint Project	Develop benchmarks for corporate pollution prevention (PP) programs	• Weightings of program elements • Evaluation of "best of class" • Design of generic PP program • Gap analysis
Sandoz Corporation	Monitor plant and corporate S & E (safety and environmental) performance	Key indices reported at all facilities: • Lost time and workday accident rates • Totals: energy, water, waste • S & E investments, expenses, personnel • Total production, personnel
Niagara Mohawk	Track effectiveness of corporate environmental protection programs	Weighted index comprised of: • Compliance incidents (NOV's etc.) • Emissions and wastes • Enhancements (dollar value)
Xerox Corporation	Integrate environmental issues to core company values	Economic Incentives • Gain market share via positioning • Cost savings reporting • Reduce risks, future costs
3M Company	Track continuous improvement in Pollution Prevention Pays (3P) and production efficiency	Waste quantities reflect 3P, efficiency • Absolute values • Reductions over time • As percentage of inputs
US EPA	• Publicize polluters • Economic incentives • Recognize "good citizens"	• SARA 313/TRIS • Clean Air Act 1990 pollution market • 33/50 • Green lights

SOURCE: Chris Fitzgerald, *Total Quality Environmental Management.*

Environmental Improvement Process must be a permanent part of our operating procedure. Conservation, waste reduction and pollution prevention are practices we *do again and again.*"

Environmental Communications Guidelines

Communication is the lifeblood of an effective environmental management program. Figure 2-7 presents a schematic of Church & Dwight's environmental communications system. It revolves around an environmental task force with representatives from key departments such as marketing, legal-regulatory, packaging, product design, and public affairs. It is the job of the director of the environmental task force to interface with the company's CEO and directors, the media, and stakeholders, such as regulators and environmental advocacy group leaders. The director of the environmental task force is often the chief environmental affairs officer, but that is not necessarily the best option. As discussed in greater detail below, corporate marketing executives are uniquely qualified for this role.

Church & Dwight's environmental communications guidelines cover three areas. The first incorporates quality management, while the second and third areas simply represent pragmatic, sensible business thinking:

Environmental Communication Management Flow Chart

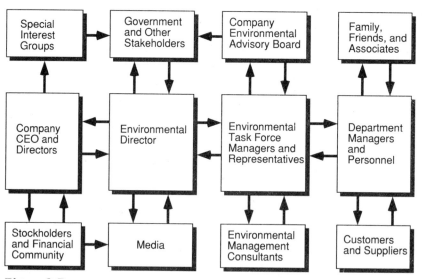

Figure 2-7.

■ *Internal—employee information and education.*   The role of the corporate environmental task force is central to internal environmental communications.

> [It] exists, in part, to serve the environmental information and education needs of all Church & Dwight employees. As each employee participates in the implementation of our Environmental Improvement Policy, questions will arise that should be addressed to (the) department's Environmental Task Force representative.... The Environmental Task Force will conduct seminars on conservation, waste reduction and pollution prevention as well as on specific corporate environmental management issues (as they arise). In addition, the Environmental Task Force has created a library of environmental books, magazines and articles for the use of all Church & Dwight employees.

■ *External—Stakeholder Communications (Public Relations).*   At Church & Dwight,

> As a rule, all communication by Church & Dwight employees with parties outside the Company [with the exception of suppliers] regarding environmental matters should be cleared by or channeled through the office of the Environmental Director.

■ *Marketing Communications (Advertising/Labeling).*   Here, the Church & Dwight environmental communications guidelines recommend that the "marketing department ... follow the FTC guidelines for the development and communication of product and packaging environmental claims."

It's Easy for Church & Dwight to Say

Church & Dwight's environmental credits far outweigh its debits. Its core product, baking soda, is about as environmentally benign as a product with multiple industrial and commercial uses can get. On top of that, the company has a long and incontrovertible record of environmental responsibility.

Most companies have much less favorable environmental bottom lines. Either their product lines are more problematic, or they have environmental skeletons in (or out of) their closets, or both. However, it isn't inherently more difficult for them to install a TQM-oriented environmental management system than it is for companies like Church & Dwight which have relatively clean records:

■ Senior management must make the necessary "deep-level" commitment to continuous improvement.

■ Rigorous standards must be established and insisted upon.

- Measurements—the price of conformance (POC) versus the price of nonconformance (PONC)—must be conducted on a regular basis.

- Employees must be empowered and de-hassled.

- Feedback communication systems must be developed which maximize efficiency and ensure a consistency of approach throughout the organization.

Once these steps have been taken, a company is on its way to having an environmental management process that anticipates rather than reacts to regulatory and "sustainability" environmental issues. How let's take a closer look at the role of the marketing executive in a quality-management-based environmental management program.

The Role of the Marketer

It is critically important for the marketer to be an active participant in the company's environmental management program. At Church & Dwight, for instance, the corporate director of public affairs (formerly a marketing director) is part of a triumvirate which is responsible for managing the company's environmental improvement process. (The other two members are the corporate director of quality control and the director of corporate engineering.)

The marketer's participation benefits both the environmental management process and his or her own marketing focus.

As noted earlier in this chapter, the environmental task force is the hub of a quality-management-oriented environmental management program. The marketer can and should play a central or leading role on that committee. Marketing executives bring two strengths to that activity: (1) strengths of perspective and (2) strengths of skillset.

Strengths of Perspective

Because they usually focus on marketplace issues, marketers contribute a special sensitivity to the external implications of environmental management decisions. This allows them to contribute to the environmental management process in three important ways:

- They can identify the marketing implications of corporate environmental exposures and initiatives. Marketers provide a much-needed voice from the marketing front, i.e., they can help management to understand the all-important marketing implications of a company's environmental strengths and weaknesses.

- Marketers can help to identify new business product and service opportunities that arise out of those same environmental exposures and initiatives. (More than one company has used its own hazardous-waste cleanup obligations as a springboard for entry into the hazardous-waste remediation business.)

- Marketers can work to ensure that when corporate environmental policies are developed, the marketing implications are given due consideration. It is much better to have input before the fact than to be left to gnash one's teeth after the damage has been done.

Strengths of Skillset

More often than not, the job of environmental management director has fallen to engineering or technical professionals. Vice president of environment, health and safety is a typical title.

Considering the nature of their training, it's not surprising that these people have tended to take a straightforward, linear approach to their work. What is the simplest way to get from Point A to Point B? That is often the technician's approach to problem solving, and it has been how environmental management has traditionally been handled.

But linear thinking is not what "total" environmental management is about. For one thing, environmental management places a premium on communication (including encouraging people to modify their behavior)—and communication is not an ability which technical specialists are renowned for possessing. Let me say, however, that I firmly believe it will be the conscientious and capable scientists and engineers who will mitigate the consequences of our excessive consumption.

Environmental management also requires enormous finesse at traversing the corporate bureaucracy. It is the environmental managers' unenviable task to coordinate activities across multiple divisions and departments—again, not a linear activity.

Finally, environmental management requires managers to work with information coming at them from a host of different disciplines—legal affairs, manufacturing, purchasing, marketing, and so on.

Few of these skills fit the profile of the typically trained or oriented engineer. The marketing executive, however, *is* often superbly qualified:

- As a matter of course, marketers must coordinate their activities across multiple departments (R&D, manufacturing, packaging, sales, public relations, etc.).

- In mapping their strategic directions, marketers take into consideration variables which come at them from a multitude of directions.

What is the competition up to? What is coming out of research and development? What are the demographics and psychographics of the marketplace, and how are they changing? What are the best advertising media? Both marketing and environmental management decisions are made in similar conceptual vortices.

■ Finally, marketers are professional communicators. This skill is enormously useful in virtually every aspect of environmental management—on the task force itself, and in such areas as environmental management training, emergency response training, community relations, and other domains which put a premium on communications.

The bottom line is that marketers contribute a unique and invaluable combination of experience, perspective, and communication and organizational skills to the environmental management function.

Benefits to the Marketer

In addition to benefiting the corporate environmental management process, marketers' participation in environmental management enhances their ability to do their jobs as marketers.

Forewarned Is Forearmed.   By being involved in environmental management activities, environmental marketers have a greater sense of the seriousness and depth of their company's environmental commitment, thus enabling them to gauge their environmental product-marketing positioning accordingly.

No Limits to Knowledge.   A popular phrase from the 1980s was, "You can never be too rich or too thin." Well, marketers can never be environmentally attuned enough, either.

By participating in environmental management, marketers become steeped in a wide range of environmental issues. Their expertise becomes, so to speak, organic. This can only benefit them as they devise they own environmental marketing plans.

Environmental Management and Marketing Synergy

There are close structural similarities between environmental marketing and environmental management.

As laid out in Figure 2-8, at least six forces drive the implementation of a corporationwide environmental management strategy: (1) regula-

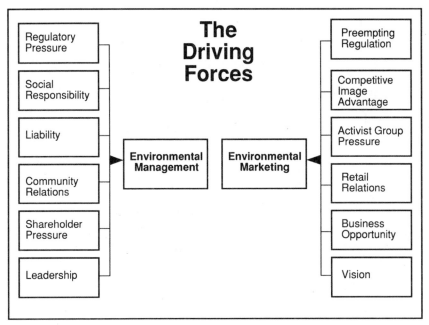

Figure 2-8.

tory pressure; (2) social responsibility; (3) concerns about actual or potential liability; (4) community relations; (5) shareholder pressure; and (6) leadership, i.e., the desire to set an example as an environmentally responsible company.

There is a close correlation between these six considerations and the drivers for environmental marketing (also listed in Figure 2-8):

- *Preempting regulation,* i.e., behaving in such ways as to avoid regulatory action, is also a response to *regulatory pressure* (actual or potential).

- *Competitive image advantage* is the direct consequence of behaving in a *socially and environmentally responsible* manner.

- *Activist group pressure* can create negative publicity. So does its parallel, *liability.*

- *Retail relations* and *community relations* are similar in that both involve stakeholder-relations issues.

- *Shareholder pressure* translates into demand to develop its corollary, *business opportunities.*

- Finally, *vision* and *leadership* are near cousins. No vision, no leadership.

Because environmental management involves many of the same issues as environmental marketing, the two activities are deeply synergistic.

Summary and Recommendations

The trend in environmental management is toward quality environmental management (QEM). As the name suggests, it is predicated on the principles of quality management, which posits a fundamental change in senior management's attitude toward a company's employees, customers, vendors, operations systems, and, of course, the environment.

At the heart of quality management is the notion that the best-operating organization is one that unleashes the latent creativity of its employees. Quality management consists of a set of management attitudes and practices that allow this to occur. Among them:

- Focus on process, not programs.

- De-hassle your employees.

- Establish rigorous environmental quality controls—and stick to them!

Quality management manifests itself as a dynamic, proactive approach to environmental problem solving (and problem anticipating!) which calls upon the collective resources of the entire organization.

Marketers are very well suited to play a central role on a company's environmental management team. Marketing executives contribute both strengths of perspective (e.g., sensitivity to the marketplace implications of environmental management decisions) and strengths of skillset (e.g., communication skills and finesse at traversing the corporate bureaucracy) to the enterprise.

In addition to providing invaluable assistance to the environmental management team, environmental marketers are themselves benefited. They gain expanded knowledge of the depth and seriousness of their company's environmental commitment, and they also substantially enhance their own knowledge of environmental issues—all of which enables them to do a better job of environmental marketing!

3

The Marketer and Environmental Intelligence

The Role of Environmental Intelligence

Information is the lifeblood of business. Without information, knowledgeable decisions can't be made. Sound strategies can't be developed.

Information is as crucial to environmental marketing as it is to every other facet of business. *Environmental intelligence* supplies product marketers with a critical competitive edge.

But how does one go about collecting environmental intelligence? It's often done haphazardly—a trade publication here, the occasional conference or seminar there, or too narrowly focused consumer research.

This approach reflects a failure to appreciate the critically important role which information plays as the foundation of every well thought-out marketing strategy. It makes about as much sense to gather intelligence randomly as it does to build a house on a couple of rocks thrown into a hole. A strategy for collecting environmental intelligence is required—and that's what we present in this chapter.

Collecting Environmental Intelligence

There are two basic ways for marketing executives to collect environmental information: (1) internally, i.e., using corporate resources to conduct primary and secondary research and establish a data management system to store and process the compiled information; and (2) via ongoing strategic alliances. I recommend using both ways.

Corporate Resources

There are at least four different ways to collect environmental intelligence internally through standard corporate channels: (1) primary research; (2) secondary materials; (3) conferences and seminars; and (4) informally, i.e., through networking.

Primary Research.   While *focus groups* do not provide statistical data, it has been our experience that their interpersonal format often provides more accurate information than a quantitative approach to market research. Quantitative research suffers from the so-called halo effect, i.e., many interviewees want to appear more virtuous than they actually are. Nowhere is this more true than in the case of environmental surveys, where consumers are notorious for exaggerating their proenvironmental activities. William Rathje, a highly regarded academic who specializes in analyzing the content of landfills, has even commented that the best way to find out if a given household recycles is to ask them if they think their neighbors do.[1]

The informal give-and-take of the focus group can elicit more truthful responses than people are willing to give in more formal and more distant research interviews. It has been our experience, for instance, that focus-group participants are much more truthful than survey respondents about their willingness (*non*willingness, actually) to pay a premium for green products.

Quantitative studies are available in a number of forms and at a wide range of price levels. Some studies are even made public at no cost. This was the case, for instance, with a landmark study on green consumerism which was conducted by The Roper Organization for S.C. Johnson & Co.

Syndicated quantitative research does not come cheaply. Here are brief descriptions, with pricing, of three of the leading tracking studies of consumers' environmental attitudes:

- *The Environmental Report*, from Environmental Research Associates (Princeton, New Jersey), is relatively inexpensive at $9500 for four quarterly reports, executive summaries, and data books.
- The Roper Organization has followed its S.C. Johnson study with a tracking study entitled *Green Gauge Global* based on the same methodology—and extended to western Europe and Japan. *Green Gauge*

Global carries a base price of $12,500 for the syndicated report and segmentation, with additional questions priced at $1000 to $3000 each.

- *Green Action Trends*, from Yankelovich Clancy Shulman (Westport, Connecticut), carries a base price of $15,000.

Proprietary market research, of course, tends to be that much more expensive. However, shortcuts are available. Opinion Research Corp. (Princeton, New Jersey), for instance, goes into the field weekly with its Caravan survey, and it is possible to tack questions on to this regular survey for under $1000 per question.

An extremely effective intelligence-gathering medium (for companies with the resources to afford it) is the *800-number consumer hot line*. The main purpose of such hot lines is to give consumers access to product information and to give them the opportunity to communicate their feelings about company products directly to the manufacturer. However, hot lines also give companies the opportunity to gather extensive information about consumer attitudes. Procter & Gamble, for instance, has found that its 800 number provides invaluable feedback on environmental labeling and other marketing initiatives. A unique benefit of 800-number information is that it is completely proprietary: only the sponsoring company has access to it.

Secondary Materials. Secondary materials include: (1) trade publications; (2) the general business press; (3) specialty consumer magazines; (4) trade- and professional-association materials; (5) specialty news services; (6) annual books; and (7) market studies.

1. *Trade publications.* The extent to which green-business issues are covered in the trade press varies from industry to industry and from publication to publication. It is also, to some extent, seasonal: with the coming of spring (more specifically, with the coming of Earth Day), the coverage of environmental issues seems miraculously to rise.

By reading a multitude of trade publications, marketing executives could probably cover most of the green-business bases. However, it makes no sense for them to do so. Most executives cannot afford the luxury of plowing through so much chaff to get at the environmental wheat.

It makes more sense to use the trade publications one reads as a matter of course as a starting point for collecting environmental information.

Of the trade magazines that cover environmental marketing issues relating to consumer packaging, I have found *Advertising Age, Food & Beverage Marketing, Food & Drug Packaging, Private Label, Supermarket News*, and *Progressive Grocer* to be particularly useful.

2. *The general business press.* Coverage of environmental marketing issues is much more sporadic in the general business press than in trade publications, but when a story hits a publication like *The Wall Street Journal, Forbes,* or *Business Week,* it tends to carry a great deal of weight. Most business executives read one or more of these publications. As is the case with trade publications, the general business press is a necessary but insufficient source of environmental intelligence.

3. *Specialty consumer magazines.* Over the last several years, three bimonthly consumer publications have come into being which are targeted directly at consumers' environmental concerns:

- *Buzzworm* magazine, published in Boulder, Colorado, is a sleek, glossy publication with beautiful photography and a regular column on green business.

- *Garbage* magazine (Gloucester, Massachusetts), which calls itself the "hands-on journal of the environment," has a funky, offbeat style with regular features like "In the Dumpster" which excoriate environmentally offensive products.

- *E Magazine,* based in Westport, Connecticut, is published on a nonprofit basis. While *Garbage* and *Buzzworm* are also clearly proenvironment, *E* has the heaviest activist flavor of the three.

While the coverage of business issues varies from publication to publication and from issue to issue, all three publications provide valuable insights into environmental subjects—and, more importantly, into the attitudes of today's environmentally aware consumers.

Another publication worth noting is *In Business.* Published by JG Press, Inc., of Emmaus, Pennsylvania, it carries the tagline, "The Magazine for Environmental Entrepreneuring," and is targeted at the growing group of "ecopreneurs" who are attempting to build green businesses.

4. *Trade- and professional-association materials.* Most trade and professional associations provide updates on environmental issues through occasional or regularly scheduled publications. For example:

- The Glass Packaging Institute assembles clips of relevant articles for its members.

- The Chemical Specialties Manufacturers Association publishes *Executive Newswatch,* which focuses on environmental issues.

- The Food Marketing Institute publishes the *Environmental Report,* a bimonthly update on environmental issues affecting the food-distribution industry.

Publications like these are valuable resources when read in full awareness of the publishers' industry biases. However, as is the case with trade and general business publications, they are only one piece of the information pie.

5. *Specialty news services.* Most business news services carry an annual price tag of $200 or more. When they're good, they're well worth the price.

The following newsletters are valuable for two reasons. First, they save time by aggregating all the information readers need on the subject in question into a single publication that can be read in 15 or 20 minutes. Second, some newsletters provide proprietary intelligence that is available nowhere else.

Green consumerism has produced a number of business newsletters, although fewer than one might expect, given the strength of the trend:

- *Green MarketAlert,* published out of Bethlehem, Connecticut, covers environmental marketing and related issues and provides insightful analyses of business trends. In addition, it supplies extensive proprietary information, including annual green-product market forecasts, annual analyses of the environmental coverage of annual reports, compilations of environmental groups' corporate-relations policies, comparison of green-consumer segmentations, and regular updates on green new-product introductions.

- The *Green Business Letter* from Tilden Press (Washington, D.C.), edited by Joel Makower, provides hands-on information on how businesses can get "clean and green" internally, e.g., by recycling, using recycled products, etc.

- *Business and the Environment,* published by Cutter Information Services (Arlington, Massachusetts), reports on environmental management strategies in the United States and abroad. Each issue covers corporate initiatives, emerging markets, and regulatory trends.

- *Environment, Health & Safety Management,* published by The Environment Group Inc. (Wainscott, New York), is an excellent environmental management tool, offering numerous case studies and, more generally, a broad perspective on environmental management issues.

Or, for $3000 per year, you can get your news on line:

- *Greenwire,* a news service of the American Political Network, Inc. (Falls Church, Virginia), is a daily electronic (i.e. via modem and PC) 12-page summary of the last 24 hours of news coverage of environmental issues.

6. *Annual books.* Several annual books are available on subjects of importance to the environmental marketer. The annual *Shopping for a Better World*, published by the New York–based Council on Economic Priorities, rates companies for their environmental and social responsibility. It provides a useful sense of which companies are perceived as being in leadership vis-à-vis the environment.

Another valuable resource is the annual *State of the World*, published by the Washington, D.C.–based Worldwatch Institute. This book addresses critical issues from a policy viewpoint, and is rich in useful analyses and data.

7. *Market studies.* Market studies aggregate the secondary information on a given subject, often add their own primary research, and provide market forecasts (usually 5-year, but with the occasional intrepid forecaster going out 10 years). Typically running to 150 pages or more, market studies are also known as off-the-shelf consulting studies because they attempt to provide the same sort of in-depth market analyses that a company would have to pay a consultant tens of thousands of dollars to develop on a proprietary basis.

FIND/SVP, a New York–based information publisher, publishes market studies on green consumerism and green-products markets. In addition, the staff of its publication *Green MarketAlert* is launching an annual *State of Green Business* report that provides detailed market forecasts and also analyzes the external and internal green-business environments.

Conferences and Seminars. Conferences and seminars are another useful vehicle for collecting environmental intelligence.

Most trade and professional associations sponsor conferences and seminars on environmental marketing–related topics as do some of the major financial and management consultancies.

Private organizations offering periodic conferences on environmental marketing-related topics include The Conference Board and the Institute for International Research, both based in New York. In addition, Eco Expo, based in Sherman Oaks, California, launched an annual green-business trade and business conference in Los Angeles in 1991.

Networking. Last but by no means least, marketing executives can collect enormous amounts of environmental intelligence simply by chatting informally and regularly with their counterparts in other companies, as well as with environmentally sophisticated and responsible suppliers, and with members of the press who as a matter of professional responsibility keep their fingers on the environmental marketing pulse. Many journalists are willing to chat, provided that the information flows in two directions. (And need I add that it never hurts to have the press on one's side?)

Strategic Alliances

An important, yet often overlooked, means of gathering information is the strategic alliance. By hooking up with other organizations, marketing executives get additional sets of eyes and ears which can only enrich their understanding of the "environmental environment":

- Environmental advocacy groups often read consumers' environmental temperature differently than do members of the corporate community.

- Scientific and technical groups can provide leading-edge insights into relevant technical developments.

- Government agencies can provide valuable information on regulatory directions.

- Educational institutions and think tanks often bring an in-depth, (relatively) unbiased approach to public-policy research which is simply not possible in the hurry-up, how-will-it-play-with-management, vested-interests-to-protect private sector.

- Although other corporations bring the same basic structural biases (profit orientation, vested interests, etc.) into their perspective on environmental issues, that does not mean that all companies have identical views. Corporate cultures vary enormously, and so do corporate attitudes. Affiliating with other private-sector companies also extends the eyes and ears of the organization.

In strategic alliances, environmental information is typically transmitted on two levels.

1. It occurs as part of a formal agreement, i.e., information exchange occurs as an integral aspect of a collaboration. For example, when McDonald's worked with the Environmental Defense Fund to develop a corporate waste-reduction strategy, it received an enormous amount of input on the relative merits of polystyrene and paper.

2. Access to information also occurs "beneath" a formal agreement. When people work together toward a common goal, they get to know each other better. This breaks down privacy shields and tends to produce disclosures that would not be forthcoming under more arms'-length conditions.

"Did you hear about the research project that's going on in Company X?"

"Did you know that the methodology for Research Project Alpha is fundamentally flawed?"

Behind-the-curtain confidences of this sort are a valuable by-product of the strategic alliance.

Strategic alliances are discussed in greater detail in Chapters 4 and 10.

Types of Environmental Information

Figure 3-1 is an environmental marketing–information-system planning blueprint prepared for one of our clients. The reader will note that there are three general categories of relevant environmental information: (1) stakeholder issues; (2) environmental-impact issues; and (3) technical issues such as best available technology (BAT) and regulatory agency mandates and guidelines. All three categories are indispensable to both environmental marketing and environmental management planning.

Stakeholder Issues

Your company operates because of and as part of a support system consisting of employees, customers, suppliers, host communities, stockholders, and watchdog or monitoring groups such as governments, advocacy groups, and the media. Each of these stakeholders brings an environmental perspective and often a specific agenda to its transactions with your company.

The environmental marketer needs to have a thorough understanding of these opinions and policies. Common agendas, like commonly held complaints, help marketers shape and prioritize their initiatives.

Corporate environmental policy, consumer research, environmental initiative reports, and regulators' and environmentalists' profiles become part of your stakeholder information database.

Environmental Impact Issues

At the company-specific level, marketing executives must know the impact of the company's operations on the environment in terms of resource consumption, emissions, and solid-waste production. More generally, marketing executives must also be versed in the full range of environmental problems that currently afflict the planet, even if their company is not contributing to them directly or significantly.

There are three basic reasons why this extensive background knowledge is so important.

1. *Ultimately, there is only one environment.* In the final analysis, all environmental issues are interconnected. Often, the connection is much

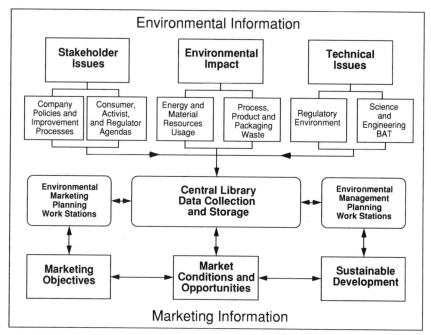

Figure 3-1. Environmental marketing information system.

closer than one might at first expect to be the case. Let's look at the three most popular global environmental issues; forest destruction, ozone depletion, and global warming. Forest fires and decomposing trees produce carbon dioxide, a greenhouse gas widely suspected of contributing to global warming and, along with chemicals such as CFCs, to the depletion of the stratospheric ozone layer. Public and private alarm over a projected rise in world temperatures and the health risks associated with ozone destruction is setting the stage for stronger air pollution regulations that will affect most manufacturing organizations.

For a company to understand its role and obligations with respect to air pollution, for instance, a broad understanding of global warming is required—and this at the very least requires a superficial understanding of the consequences of rain-forest destruction. In order to act locally, it is necessary to think globally.

2. *Consumers are concerned about background issues.* "Know your customer," conventional marketing wisdom recommends. In the context of the environment, that requires the marketer to understand (often, better than the customers themselves!) the issues that have aroused their concern.

3. *Every business is a citizen of the world.* Although this may sound corny, that doesn't make it any the less true. Despite appearances, there are no background environmental issues; it is only our ignorance that makes them seem that way. If we don't approach the problems of the world as citizens of the world, then we are doomed, both individually and collectively. Sooner or later, the big environmental picture will affect every company's bottom line. It is in every company's interest to address those issues before they get completely out of hand. And of course, to address those issues, you've got to understand them—and that requires environmental intelligence.

Technical Issues

Technical issues play a prominent role in virtually every phase of environmental management. Hazardous waste, air and groundwater emissions, overpackaging—these and a myriad of other despoilers of the environment will only be corrected by advances in the scientific and engineering state-of-the-art. What are state-of-the-art technologies that would minimize the environmental impacts of my production processes? What are their costs? Can I build those costs into my pricing? These are questions that responsible environmental marketers must ask.

And it is not enough for marketers to be familiar with the technical issues that a given environmental challenge presents. They must also understand the regulatory framework within which those technical issues occur. Take, for example, the so-called rates-and-dates packaging bills which are such a popular item in state legislatures these days. They require specific performance levels in terms of recycled-content or recyclability or reusability to be reached (rates) within certain time periods (dates).

Marketing involves planning and positioning for the future as well as for the present. For this reason, in addition to considering the current lay of the technical (and associated legal/regulatory) land, marketing executives must bring a trends orientation to their thinking, i.e., they must project current scientific, engineering, and legal issues into the future. Will Technology X make it feasible to recycle a given packaging material? If so, by when? Does the state-of-the-art currently allow credible comprehensive life-cycle analyses to be performed? If not, can we expect them and when? Without that all-important crystal ball, the marketer lives from moment to moment, without vision.

Figure 3-1 sets forth a framework for understanding the processing of environmental marketing information.

A Case Study

The following profile of the role of my company in arranging a typical environmental educational and promotional marketing partnership is provided in order to demonstrate the information-intensive nature of environmental marketing.

Company: A leading brewery.

Objective: To continue its successful practice of locally promoting its leading product in conjunction with local cause-related, nonprofit organizations.

Assignment: To identify an environmental advocacy group (or groups) to serve as the nonprofit promotional partner.

Methodology: (1) Identify an appropriate environmental cause or issue relative to the company, the product being promoted, product distributors and retailers, and the product consumer (Figure 3-2, Step A). (2) Identify the field of environmental groups that focused on the selected environmental cause or issue. In this case, we selected aluminum can and glass bottle recycling (Figure 3-2, Step B). (3) Generate a short list of advocacy groups that conformed to the partnership requirements (Figure 3-2, Step C). (4) Design a program that met the expectations and requirements of all partners (Figure 3-2, Step D).

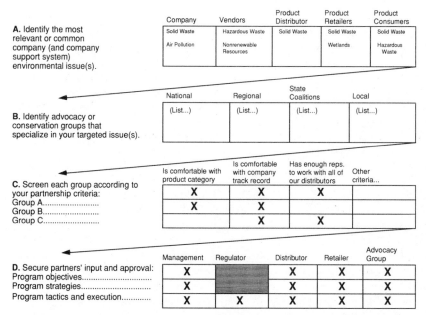

Figure 3-2. Environmental advocacy group partnership planning.

The process began with a procedure we call the corporate environmental positioning audit—a corporate environmental impact report card. The audit involved our soliciting environmental policy and impact information from every department manager in our client company:

- *Legal Affairs.* What was the company's environmental lobbying and litigation record? Was the company complying with SARA Title III, emergency planning, and community right-to-know requirements?
- *Manufacturing.* What kinds of solid and hazardous waste did the company's plants and processes produce? What if anything was being done to minimize pollution?
- *Purchasing/Production.* Was the company making a serious effort to buy used, recycled, or recyclable supplies?
- *Research and Development.* Did the company use animals to test product formulas and applications?
- *Sales and Customer Service.* What were customers requesting in the way of environmentally responsible activities and/or products?
- *Warehousing and Packaging.* What was being done to reduce packaging, reuse shipping and storage materials, and use recycled or recyclable materials for packaging?

In gathering this information, our primary objective was to be aware in advance of any issue that might compromise our client's environmental marketing positioning. We believe that without an in-depth understanding of our client's environmental profile, our strategic recommendations will lack the requisite foundation and protection against possible consumer and advocacy-group backlash.

Our next step was to look at our client's target market. It was predominantly young and male, so we focused on the environmental attitudes of that group. And because our program was regionally oriented, we focused on the environmental attitudes of young males in that specific area.

We surveyed distributors and retailers to determine what environmental issues concerned them most, what promotional activities they were currently involved with, and what environmental organizations they had had experience with.

We reviewed the most recent data on hundreds of environmental organizations (national, state, and local) that focused on or dealt with recycling. We then narrowed down the list of potential partners based on the criteria presented in Figure 3-2, step C.

Design of the marketing program had to meet the standards and objectives of all the marketing partners—a process we explore in detail in Chapter 10.

At one level, our assignment was about developing a promotional program. At another, deeper level, it was about information collection and analysis, pure and simple.

Summary and Recommendations

The environmental marketer must be on top of a wide array of information, including stakeholder, environmental-impact, and technical issues.

Several different avenues are available for acquiring this information. Traditional resources include primary research (e.g., focus groups, quantitative market research), secondary materials (e.g., trade and general business publications, newsletters), and conferences and seminars.

Strategic alliances are another—and frequently overlooked—channel for acquiring environmental intelligence. In part, intelligence is gathered through the information exchanges that are an intrinsic part of the formal relationship. In addition, however, strategic alliances breed trust; trust inspires confidences; and confidences can provide invaluable information.

Finally, as the above case study shows, most marketing assignments call for the collection and analysis of massive amounts of information. All of which goes to show that effective environmental marketing begins with an appreciation of the role of information.

4

Environmental Advocacy Groups

Environmental advocacy groups have come a long way. In the 1960s, many environmentalists were considered antibusiness, antiprogress extremists. This is no longer the case. Today, surveys find that 75 percent of Americans have a positive opinion of environmental groups. William Reilly, the current Environmental Protection Agency (EPA) chief, was formerly the chairman of the World Wildlife Fund. Environmentalism has entered the American mainstream.

During the 1980s, membership of environmental groups surged; increases of from two to ten times were not uncommon. As support for environmental advocacy group has grown, so have their influence and marketing sophistication. In 1988, the Natural Resources Defense Council (NRDC) engaged actress Meryl Streep to champion a ban on the pesticide Alar. She appealed to legislators and millions of Americans via television appearances and press coverage. Besieged by this publicity, Alar's manufacturer withdrew the product from the market.

"Dolphin wars" provide another example. As many as 10 million dolphins have died in the nets of tuna fishermen over the the last 30 years, even though the Humane Society had been promoting a national tuna boycott since 1978. It wasn't until the environmental group Earth Island Institute organized a national boycott (enhanced by secretly obtained, graphic videotape of dolphins dying in tuna nets) and a series

of classroom crusades that the three major packers (H.J.Heinz, Van Camp Seafood, and Bumble Bee Seafoods) announced in the spring of 1990 that they would henceforth use only "dolphin safe" tuna. As one Humane Society representative put it, "When young children approach boards of education to get tuna off the menu, companies have to listen."

Another example is the decision of McDonald's to abandon the polystyrene "clamshell" in favor of a quilted wrapping paper. Children across the country participated in "Operation Send It Back," mailing used polystyrene clamshells and Happy Meal toys to McDonald's corporate officers.

Today, hundreds of established local, state, and regional environmental organizations provide a strength and depth to the environmental movement that did not exist 20 years ago. Combined with the tremendous growth of the national groups, this presents many opportunities for corporations serious about developing green products and green-production processes.

Traditionally, what is bad for the environment has been good for fund raising and development at environmental groups. And environmental problems continue to grow: communities continue to run out of affordable landfill space; toxics materials and waste products are generated at an enormous rate with no consensus on how to manage their disposal; the ozone hole gets larger; global warming is accepted by nearly all the experts, leaving arguments only as to how fast the warming will occur; the continued cutting of remnant old-growth forests in the Pacific Northwest is causing unprecedented strife between workers and environmentalists; 150 million Americans routinely breathe air that the EPA considers unhealthy; and the list goes on.

The New Paradigm

Most environmentalists realize that while they can continue to win environmental battles, only business can win the war. In essence, the ecological fate of the world is in the hands of industry.

The basic rule of the new paradigm will be environmental innovation on the part of corporations. Corporate action ahead of or in excess of regulatory requirements will generally be the minimum standard for relations between advocacy groups and industry.

Three steps are needed to help accelerate meaningful environmental marketing partnership opportunities:

1. Corporations must move beyond being polluters and begin to truly build environmental protection into business operations. They must develop green-production processes and green products in an openly accountable fashion that includes public participation in the process of corporate greening.

2. Environmental advocates must recognize this potential in business and change their behavior to capitalize on it. Some groups have done this, particularly at the state level.

3. Corporations seeking to work seriously with environmental groups should look beyond charitable giving to substantive relationships that involve the production and promotion of green products—in short, to environmental marketing.

Before proceeding, it is important to make the distinction between environmental *advocacy* groups, and traditional *conservation* organizations. Advocacy groups are typified as more aggressive and more heavily involved in litigation, lobbying, and the media with the expressed goal of changing public policies to more fully protect the environment. Examples of national advocacy groups include a wide range of organizations from the Natural Resources Defense Council and the Citizens Clearinghouse for Hazardous Waste to organizations like the Audubon Society that blend a mix of advocacy, education, and ownership of sanctuaries to create an organization that straddles the line between pure advocacy and traditional conservation. Traditional conservation organizations are generally characterized by their less adversarial stance and their historic focus on habitat protection, land acquisition, and species conservation. Examples include The Nature Conservancy, Ducks Unlimited, and the Trust for Public Land, which focus almost exclusively on land preservation through purchases, easements, and similar strategies.

The Old Way

Traditionally, corporations have supported environmental *advocacy* groups through donations; this remains the dominant pattern today. Generally this involves relatively small donations ($500 to $10,000) either as core support or to programs that enhance the corporate image, serve corporate public relations objectives, fulfill the need for a tax write-off, and are low risk. For example the Natural Resources Defense

Council, perhaps the most respected environmental advocacy group in the nation, reported 55 corporate contributions in 1991.

In some cases, however, particularly for traditional *conservation* groups, contributions of this sort can be quite large. Miller Brewing recently contributed $1 million to The Nature Conservancy, which is widely respected and envied for its corporate fund-raising abilities. Examples of this type of giving abound, including beverage industry support for recycling programs, oil company support for land preservation, and timber industry tree-planting programs.

Corporate relationships with environmental groups (beyond charitable giving) have been generally focused on the less controversial albeit important issues, such as wildlife habitat preservation and, to a lesser extent, other soft issues such as recycling. These relationships often provide enormous public relations cover for major polluters. It is not uncommon for corporations that support recycling and habitat protection on the one hand to work against legislation on related issues such as waste reduction and restriction of mining and oil drilling on the other. Innovative corporate relations have in large measure been directed away from organizations that directly confront industry on environmental issues through Congress, the courts, the media, or at the community and state level.

With the notable exception of a few large national and regional land acquisition and conservation organizations, environmental groups receive a relatively insignificant portion of all their funds from corporate contributions. Based on a survey of 240 national, state, and local environmental organizations, Donald Snow reports in *Inside the Environmental Movement: Meeting the Leadership Challenge,* that, on average, environmental groups receive only 4 percent of their overall funding from corporations. This figure was fairly consistent across all organizations; 89 percent of all groups surveyed received less than 10 percent of total funds from corporations. Forty-nine percent (118) of the groups reported no corporate contributions at all. Groups with budgets of over $1 million received 7 percent of total funds from corporations, groups with budgets under $1 million received 2 percent. In a relevant observation Snow notes that conservation groups tend to be larger than advocacy groups (or to use Snow's terminology, environmental groups).

In order to accelerate substantive progress on environmental protection this old paradigm must be broken. We focus here on how to move beyond the current situation, toward serious green-product development and the resulting potential for collaboration between corporations and environmental advocacy groups.

The New Way

Sophisticated corporations will move beyond seeing environmental advocacy organizations as enemies or charities, and begin to view them as potential partners for constructive change. These same corporations will likely recognize and act on all the environmental opportunities in their manufacturing and business operations and products. Further, companies that are serious about increasing efficiencies and benefiting the environment will have little trouble working with environmental organizations. Many companies that have pursued environmental opportunities because they save money, increase efficiency, and build good relations within the community are reaping additional benefits because the serious environmental policies that they devised have created a basis for solid, ongoing, if not perfect, relations with environmental advocacy groups.

Obstacles to the New Paradigm

There are enormous obstacles to the new paradigm, particularly for environmental groups that want to work with corporations toward serious environmental change. The obstacles differ depending on the size of both the corporation and the environmental group. Large advocacy groups will have the most difficulty working with large corporations (i.e., those with the most polluting subsidiaries). Middle-sized groups, state and regional groups, and middle-sized and smaller corporations have fewer constraints on being creative.

The Biggest Obstacle: Conflict of Interest

The key obstacle for any environmental group seeking to work with corporations is any real or perceived conflict of interest. Any legitimate conflict of interest will normally rule out the possibility of collaboration.

Far more difficult to predict, but equally influential in the environmental psyche, are any *perceptions* of a conflict of interest. Relationships with certain corporations can evoke such strong negative emotions with certain sectors of the environmental movement, the public, the media, and the group's membership that they will be avoided at all costs. In other cases, it is the size of support that is seen as potentially influential and thus problematic. Some groups (Public Citizen, Citizens Clearinghouse for Hazardous Waste, Greenpeace) avoid any possibility of conflict by specifically refusing all contributions from corporations *and the government.* In general, any campaign, relationship, statement, or report that has a serious potential to tarnish a groups image, is considered a major gaff and will be avoided.

It is important to remember that traditionally there has been little reason for environmental advocacy groups to work with a corporate polluter when they could sue or generate a media campaign against them instead, or when green products offered comparatively limited prospects for environmental gain (a situation that exists even today).

A Second Obstacle: Compliance

Moving beyond charitable contributions to collaborative projects creates enormous compliance challenges. It is one thing to accept a charitable contribution from a major corporation and to compensate this gift with a listing in the annual report; it is quite another thing to endorse a particular product or to hold a joint press conference announcing a joint campaign. The image problems that this creates can only be addressed through strict enforceable standards on the part of the company involved. If the environmental benefit of the program or product is not easily monitored, or if its benefits are not clear and easily understood, then it will be difficult to sell.

The Third Obstacle: the More Closets, the More Skeletons

There can be enormous obstacles to working with *large* corporations, most of which have some significantly polluting operations that can complicate any proposed project that moves beyond the traditionally safe charitable giving described above. For an environmental group, association with such corporations—particularly in the chemical, oil, timber, mining, and other extractive or manufacturing industries—can mean an enormous image liability that will not be easy to overcome. Product-specific campaigns can work as a basis for collaboration, but they have been more successful with smaller national or state and regional groups. For large service industries, or for those perceived as service industries (AT&T or American Express, for example) there appear to be many more opportunities, although there is usually far less benefit to the environment.

Opportunities

The fewest obstacles to environmental marketing and joint ventures exist at the state and local level, where environmentalists view the local factory as not just another polluter, but as a major employer and player in the community. Established state and regional environmental organizations are more likely to seek out and present opportunities for serious relations with corporations. For these organizations, conflicts are clear and perceptions and image are less of a concern. Their constituency is primarily statewide or local, and the accomplishments of an organization can generally be evaluated firsthand by its supporters. If a relationship with a corporation bears environmental fruit, it is more likely to be accepted regardless of the nasty image of the parent company.

This does not mean that state and regional groups are pushovers. Hardly. They are likely to be your toughest adversaries, but they often present a much clearer target for collaboration, because they are motivated less by image concerns than by the environmental bottom line. If the deal can be enforced and meets their goals, they are more likely to go for it.

What to Watch for

As environmental groups have grown in size and proliferated in number, they have become more sophisticated. The large state and regional groups and the national groups are all skilled at direct mail and working the media, not to mention the hard-core skills of lobbying, litigation, and citizens action. Many of them have also become adept at working with corporations to achieve their objectives. This collaboration can take many forms; from accepting corporate contributions, to endorsing green products, to negotiations and joint environmental projects. There are as many possible ways to work with environmental groups as there are environmental organizations themselves.

Here are a few points to remember when you work with environmental advocacy groups:

1. Look at *the environmental bottom line.*   Few environmental groups are easily deterred from their mission. So, when looking for an organization to work with, identify with its goals. If the deal looks too good to be true, it probably is, and the group proposing it could cause you more problems than the project is worth. On the other hand, if the project is legitimate, you will find a group to support it.

2. *Different groups have different strategies and different styles.*   Some groups are litigators, some are educators; some have active members, some have passive members; some are centralized, some are decentralized; some have experience working with corporations,

some do not. Know the group you work with; it will help you to avoid surprises.

3. *Relationships can take many forms.* Some groups take money from corporations, others do not. Some endorse products, others do not. Some prefer negotiations to lawsuits, others prefer litigation to consensus building. Generally, it is difficult to absolutely categorize even the most strident of groups; some very progressive organizations have joined with corporations in support of certain initiatives on certain occasions.

4. *Work with groups in the community; be open; provide honest information.* The most promising and beneficial course of action for any corporation is to invite local environmental groups into direct talks with plant managers or other company representatives regarding the greening of operations and the development of green products. For real environmental results, however, much more than staged tours of facilities should be involved and higher-level management must provide its full support.

5. *There are no secret deals.* Expect the ultimate public and press scrutiny of any program you develop.

6. *There is never 100 percent predictability.* The politics and decision-making processes of environmental organizations can be quixotic, to say the least. If your corporation is trying to move beyond charitable giving to joint programs with environmental organizations, expect a process of learning on both sides.

7. *Take the initiative. Don't wait to get clobbered.* On rare occasions beneficial relationships develop out of lawsuits, citizens'-action campaigns, and the like. But it is best to begin looking toward environmental groups as potential partners, instead of just biding time until the next lawsuit.

Trends

Pollution Prevention. Prevention is now recognized as the superior strategy for reducing environmental pollution. The concept is simple: the fewer potential polluting substances that go into an operation, the less that will come out. Pollution prevention usually increases business efficiency and reduces the costs of pollution control. Pollution prevention represents a substantial opportunity for collaboration, and for the development of green products and green markets; when openly conducted it can be a centerpiece of the new relationships between environmentalists and corporations. But these concepts are new and run counter to traditional regulatory schemes that control pollution at the end of the proverbial pipe.

Pollution prevention as an effective form of public policy exists primarily in the states. Several state laws have created opportunities for citizen-environmentalist-business collaboration that have been extremely effective.

Massachusetts and California are generally recognized as having the two best pollution prevention policies in the nation. Both break new ground. Central to their effectiveness is public access to information on industrial operations, including facility inspections and analysis of processes. Both involve full disclosure of industrial operations, public participation, industry reporting of toxic-materials use, and toxic-use reduction goals. Public participation in pollution reduction is a fundamental trend in pollution prevention that should be fully capitalized on by industry.

Access to Information. An essential component to environmental marketing is access to information. More than regulations, lawsuits, or any other means, information can empower corporations and environmentalists to act rationally to reduce pollution, creating unprecedented opportunities. Time and again in the states where it is required, industries are discovering opportunities for the reduction of toxics simply through the process of taking inventories and making information available to the public.

Consumer Involvement in the Process through Product Labeling. Labeling has enormous power but will only work through a well informed process. Environmental impact labeling can be an effective environmental marketing tool, *if* you have a serious environmentally beneficial product, and when the label provides valuable information on the total environmental impact of the product (along the lines of federally required nutritional information on food products). Failing to provide consumers information on the environmental impact of producing, transporting, and disposing of green products undercuts each product's long-term market and environmental potential. Development of green labeling should be pursued by industry in a fully open process and in collaboration with environmental advocates.

Expectations Are Higher. "Green gimmick" marketing will not work over the long haul. Consumers are smarter, and environmental groups are on the lookout for bogus claims. Scientific Certification Systems and Green Seal are fighting for leadership in the products certification business, and are causing rapid development of product life-cycle analysis. This area offers big potential for cooperation, but again requires dramatic changes in the historical relationships between environmentalists and industry.

Profiles of National Environmental Advocacy Groups

What follows are descriptions of nine national environmental organizations. These particular organizations were chosen because they represent a diversity of organizational structures, memberships, strategies, missions, and relationships with corporations. Nine different organizations could have been chosen that would have been equally representative.

The point of these profiles is to give the reader a sense of the depth and diversity of national environmental advocacy groups. Three groups that accept no corporate contributions (Public Citizen, Greenpeace, and CCHW) have been profiled, because they are important and influential organizations, and because failure to present these profiles would leave the reader with an unbalanced understanding of the environmental movement at the national level.

The profiles are followed by a section that briefly characterizes the surging and increasingly sophisticated state and local environmental organizations.

Natural Resources Defense Council (NRDC)

Founded:	1970
1991 membership:	170,000
1991 revenue:	$17.5 million
Structure:	Members, no chapters, centralized
Accepts corporate contributions:	Yes, 55 corporate donors in 1991 (less than 1 percent of total received)
Staff size:	150 in three main offices
Contact:	John Murray Director of Development NRDC 40 West 20th St. New York, NY 10011

NRDC is a public-interest environmental law firm with major programs in air and energy, water and coasts, land, international and nuclear affairs, public health, and urban issues. Its mission is to defend the environment through the enforcement, amendment, and improvement of federal environment laws, international treaties and agreements, and (to a lesser extent) state environmental laws. These goals are achieved through active intervention in the rulemaking process; aggressive and strategic litigation on issues pertaining to nearly all federal environmental statutes; active involvement in international conventions; policy analysis and the development of policy options for legislative and regulatory reform; scientific reports; use of the media; and lobbying international institutions, the U.S. Congress, and selected state legislatures, primarily in California and New York.

NRDC has no chapters and operates as a centralized organization. Its headquarters are in New York City. Main regional offices are in Washington, D.C., and San Francisco, with smaller offices in Los Angeles and Honolulu. NRDC's headquarters are in an environmentally designed office building in New York City. NRDC's membership base grew from about 30,000 in 1980, to about 170,000 in 1990, helping to support substantial growth in the organization. In 1990, NRDC reported a staff of about 150 members. There are no member chapters, nor are members routinely called to action by NRDC. Members receive the bimonthly *Amicus Journal* as the basic membership benefit.

Beyond contributions, NRDC's traditional relationship with corporations has been adversarial—through the courts, the media, and in numerous legislative battles. NRDC is thoroughly expert in the trench warfare of the environmental movement. Opportunities occasionally emerge for cooperation and collaboration with industry on certain issues, but it is safe to say that these cases are rare.

The two most high-profile NRDC campaigns involving corporations are the Alar situation and an aborted deal with Conoco in Ecuador. The Alar situation has been well reported and was described earlier in this chapter. With Conoco, NRDC attempted to facilitate a settlement among the oil giant, Ecuadoran environmental groups, and the Ecuadoran government to place tight controls on oil drilling in the Ecuadoran rain forest. A collection of local environmental groups, led by several international networks including Rainforest Action Network, embarked on a vicious frontal assault against NRDC claiming that it was sanctioning and encouraging oil drilling in the Ecuadoran Amazon over the objections of the local people. Needless to say, the deal fell apart.

The organization is an excellent model for its integration of science, law, and the media, and for its ability to take on the largest industrial forces as well as the federal government through the legislative and legal process, and win.

The Nature Conservancy (TNC)

Founded:	1951
1991 membership:	600,000
1991 revenue:	$254 million in support, revenue, and capital additions
Structure:	National group with strong state chapters and international programs in the Americas and the Pacific
Accepts corporate contributions:	Yes, 650 corporate contributors in 1991, 12 percent of total funds and contributions
Staff size:	1,400
Contact:	Bradford C. Willis Assistant Director, Annual Support The Nature Conservancy 1815 North Lynn St. Arlington, VA 22209

The mission of The Nature Conservancy is the preservation of bio-logical diversity and the protection of endangered species through purchase of strategic habitat. Their well-focused mission capitalizes on strong scientific expertise and savvy legal understanding of land-purchase and land-preservation options. TNC does not lobby or litigate and should not be considered an environmental advocacy group. This makes them an extraordinarily safe contribution for many corporations and is the principal reason that they are by far the largest recipient of corporate dollars of all U.S. environmental organizations.

TNC operates very active chapters in 50 states. Chapters operate relatively independently of the national organization, devising strategic habitat preservation plans and targeting specific tracts and the means to protect them on a state-by-state basis. At the same time, chapters work with the national organization to purchase and secure large tracts of land. State chapters have directors and boards independent of the national organization. Upon joining the national group, all members are assigned to a state chapter.

TNC also operates an international program with projects in 14 Latin America countries, Canada, and the Pacific. The organization Conservation International was spun off and created by the TNC international staff. TNC international operates worldwide with a primary objective of cataloging species through its conservation database program. TNC's Parks in Peril program works to establish priority ecological areas and to use rapid assessment techniques to collect data for the planning of future parks. TNC has also participated in several debt for nature swaps.

To date, TNC has protected over 6 million acres in North America, most of which is purchased by or donated to TNC and then sold to federal or state land-management agencies. Land acquisition and sale is a major source of income for TNC, accounting for $83 million of revenue in 1991.

TNC is the wealthiest conservation group in the United States with annual revenue of over $250 million. In 1991, $172 million of this was in the form of contributions from individuals, members, and corporations ($51 million); investment income ($14 million); land sales ($83 million); and other income ($23 million). Capital acquisitions involving land sales and revolving funds generated an additional $81 million in income. TNC has a well-established corporate funding program and receives contributions of $1000 to $15,000 from over 650 corporations. Numerous wealthy individuals, estate giving, and other mechanisms generate substantial cashflow for the organization. Members receive the national magazine and the state chapter newsletter.

Citizens Clearinghouse on Hazardous Waste (CCHW)

Founded:	1981
1991 membership:	7500 grassroots groups nationwide
1991 revenue:	$680,000
Structure:	Information and technical training primarily serving independent local activists
	Field organizers in six regions
Accepts corporate contributions:	No
Staff size:	15
Contact:	Lois Gibbs
	Executive Director
	CCHW
	P.O. Box 6806
	Falls Church, VA 22040

CCHW's mission is to block hazardous and solid-waste incinerators and landfills in communities across the nation and to achieve a comprehensive nationwide reduction and recycling of hazardous and solid waste. CCHW does not lobby or litigate at the federal level, but is extremely active at the local level organizing and training community leaders and working against local incinerators and landfills.

CCHW is a leader in the fight for environmental justice and the struggle to build a broad based, racially-diverse grassroots environmental movement. The group is notoriously effective at converting mainstream working people into passionate, knowledgeable, and effective environmental advocates, by educating them about the lack of certainty and potential health threats connected with the safety of burning or burying hazardous and solid waste. The basic services CCHW provides are organizing training; disseminating information on the health effects, costs, and harmful consequences of incineration and leaky landfills; media training; and lending support to a large network of activists working for the same goal.

All of CCHW's program funds are devoted to helping communities organize. CCHW operates a clearinghouse and a network of hundreds of activists who fight incinerators and landfills nationwide. Regional coordinators train activists in communities; technical support is provided both in the field and through the national office. CCHW produces a widely read newsletter, *Everyone's Backyard*, and publishes numerous guides and pamphlets on organizing strategies and updates on scores of local landfill and waste-incinerator fights across the nation. The organization was founded and is directed by Lois Gibbs, who became a leader in the grassroots antitoxics movement after toxic waste bubbled up in her front yard in Love Canal, New York.

CCHW also monitors the activities of 200 corporations and keeps an especially close eye on major waste industry corporations such as Waste Management Inc. and Browning Ferris.

CCHW operates a community leadership development grants program under which small grants ($5000) are made to local organizations for fighting toxics and waste battles.

Sierra Club

Founded:	1892
1991 membership:	650,000
1991 revenue:	$41 million
Structure:	National organization, active state chapters, local groups, and national field offices
Accepts corporate contributions:	Yes, 20 contributions in 1990
Contact:	Rosemary Carroll Director of Development Sierra Club 730 Polk St. San Francisco, CA 94109

The Sierra Club, founded by John Muir in 1892, is the oldest environmental group in the nation. Its mission is to preserve and protect the environment, a goal it achieves in a wide variety of ways. The club has perhaps the greatest number of tools and the broadest presence on the widest range of issues of any environmental organization in the United States. Its headquarters are in San Francisco, with other national offices in Washington, D.C. The club has 14 regional offices, chapters in every state, and hundreds of clubs in different communities. Although the club is not the largest environmental group, it is the best organized and the organization most able to rally its members to action on national issues.

The Sierra Club is also uniquely structured to be able to conduct lobbying and education and to make campaign contributions. The Sierra Club itself is a nonprofit public benefit corporation classified as a 501 (c)(4) by the IRS. Contributions that are *not* tax deductible support the club's active lobbying of the U.S. Congress and of state legislatures. The Sierra Club Foundation is the club's sole source of tax-deductible support. Individual, corporate, and foundation gifts provide income to the Sierra Club Foundation which supports nearly all club activities other than direct lobbying. The Sierra Club Political Committee is the club's political-action committee through which campaign contributions are made to candidates in federal elections.

The club is organized into 14 regional offices (plus 3 in Canada) that represent the national club in the field, 57 chapters, and 382 local groups. The chapters and groups received about 12 percent of the total program expenses of the national organization, or about $2.7 million out of $24 million, in 1990. The state chapters operate relatively independently of the national organization, although lobbying-support services from the national club to state chapters have improved as of late. Most state chapters have designated lobbyists; some states have paid professional lobbyists. The effectiveness of club chapters varies from state to state, but some, such as the ones in Texas, constitute an extremely strong presence in the state capital fighting for strong state environmental policies and the strict implementation and enforcement of federal environmental laws. Activist chapters and members make the Sierra Club the national environmental group with the greatest ability to mobilize thousands of citizens and activists on national environmental issues.

Greenpeace

Founded: 1971
1990 membership: 5 million supporters in 26 countries
1990 revenue: Greenpeace USA: $47 million

Structure:	46 offices in 26 countries. Main USA offices: Washington, D.C., San Francisco, Calif. No state chapters, only individual members
Accepts corporate contributions:	No
Staff size:	1000 full time globally in 1990
Contact:	Peter Beyhouth Executive Director Greenpeace USA 1436 U St. NW Washington, DC 20009

Greenpeace was founded in 1971 by a group of Canadian peace activists opposed to nuclear testing on Amchitka Island in Alaska. Since that time the group has become world renowned for its nonviolent direct action to protect the environment. Its members confront huge whaling ships in motorized rubber rafts, hang off smoke stacks, and lie down in front of bulldozers. The organization is unmatched at staging high profile media-grabbing events designed to "bear witness" in the Quaker tradition to a host of environmental problems.

More recently Greenpeace has been actively involved in direct action against toxics and the nuclear power and weapons industry and for the protection of Antarctica, marine mammals, and the oceans. They are fighting to stop the ozone hole and prevent global warming. In the 1980s the organization grew enormously. And as Greenpeace grew, so did its tactics, which now include community organizing; research into the finances, policies, and activities of major corporations; the production of scientific reports and analyses; legislative lobbying in the U.S. Congress; and campaigns to influence major international institutions such as the World Bank and the United Nations.

Greenpeace has experienced severe growing pains as it has tried to remain true to its grassroots, direct-action style of advocacy while ballooning almost overnight into what is arguably the largest, most recognized environmental organization in the world. Yet in most ways Greenpeace has remained true to its origins. The organization continues to define the environmental debate in moral terms, eschewing the details of compromise and clinging to the moral high ground. It does not see itself as an arbiter of compromise or the solver of difficult problems; it sees itself as no less than our collective environmental conscience. It is hardly surprising that Greenpeace accepts neither corporate nor government contributions.

Typical Greenpeace victories include a ban on driftnets for tuna harvesting; the 1991 26-nation Antarctic Treaty banning mining and oil development for 50 years; and delaying the test launch of a Trident 2 missile by occupying the exclusionary zone with motorized rafts.

The Wilderness Society

Founded:	1935
1991 membership:	354,000
1991 revenue:	$18 million
Structure:	National organization, no chapters, 14 regional offices
Accepts corporate contributions:	Yes, 31 corporate contributions in 1991, strict guidelines
Staff size:	130
Contact:	Rebecca Wodder Vice President, Membership and Development Wilderness Society 900 17th St. NW Washington, DC 20006-2596

The Wilderness Society is dedicated to the protection of wilderness areas and the expansion of protected wild lands and ecosystems in the United States. Current priority areas include the old-growth forests of the Pacific Northwest, the north woods of New England and New York, the northern Rockies and greater Yellowstone ecosystems, the California desert and Yosemite valley, the canyonlands of Utah, the Everglades, and the southern Appalachian forests.

Like other major advocacy groups oriented toward natural resources (as opposed to pollution control), the society has evolved dramatically over the past 20 years. It now employs economists, attorneys, journalists, and planners in addition to foresters, ecologists, and wildlife biologists. Its Washington, D.C., headquarters and its 14 regional offices give it a strong presence both at the national level and in the field, where, like most national organizations, it increasingly seeks to coordinate strategies with state and grassroots advocates. The diverse talents of its staff enables it to bring a passionate yet highly professional voice to the task of protecting wilderness.

Recently the society has effectively employed economic analyses to make the case for wilderness protection. These analyses have focused on federal subsidies of timber sales, and have revealed the relatively small contributions that extractive industries (mining, timber, cattle) actually make to the economies of the Pacific Northwest and the greater

Yellowstone region. This type of work is indicative of a trend in environmental advocacy; increasingly, advocacy groups are bringing more sophisticated economic arguments to bear on a wide range of environmental issues. By documenting the potential and current economic benefits of less destructive, more sustainable development and the use of the ecosystems surrounding major wilderness and park areas, organizations like the Wilderness Society attract a broader base of political and business support to the task of wilderness protection.

The society also runs a major education program and produces a quarterly magazine, *Wilderness,* which is the standard membership benefit of the organization.

The society actively solicits and accepts corporate contributions within strict guidelines that prohibit any conflict of interest or potential compromise of the society's reputation. Contributions without any direct conflict of interest are generally assumed not to compromise the reputation of the organization if they are less than one-tenth of 1 percent of the society's annual budget (about $18,000). Any contribution greater than this amount or that raises any questions relative to the guidelines is referred to the president and the chair.

National Audubon Society

Founded:	1905
1991 membership:	550,000 plus
1991 revenue:	$41.9 million
Structure:	516 chapters in 50 states, 80 sanctuaries
Accepts corporate contributions:	Yes, with strict guidelines. Corporate contributions are the fastest growing sector of Audubon contributions.
Staff size:	370
Contact:	Susan Parker Martin Senior Vice President, Development and Marketing National Audubon Society 950 Third Avenue New York, NY 10022

The Audubon Society blends a unique mix which includes advocacy; public education through the schools and through a corporate-sponsored nature series on Turner Network Television; growing direct action by a membership traditionally known as bird watchers; and the ownership and management of a system of 80 wildlife sanctuaries.

The society was founded by "forward thinking people" concerned about the use of bird feathers and plumage in the production of hats. At the time of the formation of the National Audubon Society, numerous state Audubon Societies already existed. Thus, there are currently many state-level Audubon Societies—such as Connecticut Audubon—that are completely independent and not affiliated in any way with the National Audubon Society.

The society is heavily involved in wetlands and endangered-species protection and in the fight to preserve the forests of the Pacific Northwest and the Arctic wildlife refuge. The Audubon Society advocates primarily through its national office but has recently embarked on a campaign to get its local activists more involved in environmental-protection and habitat-preservation issues in their communities. It now produces excellent educational and organizing materials for its chapters, conducts leadership-training workshops, and teaches lobbying at the Washington, D.C., headquarters. Subscriptions to the *Audubon Activist* newsletter jumped from 20,000 to 100,000 in 1991 alone. Such efforts, if successful, will greatly increase the overall effectiveness and power of the organization.

Through its sanctuary system and its *Audubon Adventures* program, the society is also actively involved in environmental education. A recent program reaching out to inner-city children got to 110,000 urban kids in 1991.

Corporate contributions are the fastest growing component of the organization's funding base. This has led to some tension with state Audubon chapters (most dramatically in Florida) concerning advocacy strategies on specific issues.

Audubon is the only national environmental advocacy group with its own television show, a show which has both attracted and confounded corporate sponsors. Sponsors walked away from and industry interests attacked several shows, most notably a 1991 special documenting the poor conditions of much of America's western rangelands. Nevertheless, Audubon continues to hold its ground on content.

Public Citizen

Founded:	1971
1991 membership:	150,000
1991 revenue:	$7.2 million
Structure:	Centralized, Washington-based organization

Accepts corporate contributions: No, accepts neither government nor corporate support

Staff size: 85

Contact: Joan Claybrook
President
Public Citizen
2000 P St. NW
Washington, DC 20036

Public Citizen is a nonprofit citizen-research, lobbying, and litigation organization founded by Ralph Nader in 1971. The organization works on fundamental citizens'-advocacy issues through programs focusing on government and corporate accountability, consumer protection, clean and safe energy sources, and a healthy environment and workplace. Public Citizen has been very involved in a broad range of high profile issues including its leadership role in the fight for campaign finance reform, the struggle to remove silicon breast implants from the market, the campaign against the nuclear power industry, and the battle for energy efficiency and renewable energy as the cornerstones of U.S. energy policy.

Recently the organization launched a campaign to reform or block the General Agreement on Tariff and Trade (GATT) on environmental grounds. This effort brings together major farm, labor, and environmental organizations (including the Sierra Club, Friends of the Earth, Rainforest Action Network, and the National Toxics Campaign) concerned about the potential of GATT to undermine decades of hard-won environmental and health statutes.

Public Citizen's environmental programs have historically revolved around energy and health-related issues such as pesticides. Although not an environmental organization per se, Public Citizen embodies the essence of public-interest advocacy. It accepts no government or corporate grants and generates income strictly from small individual contributions and publication sales. The group is skilled at gathering grassroots support for its position and maintains perhaps the best list of grassroots antinuclear, energy-conservation, and renewable-energy advocates. Its litigation team is extremely experienced; in 20 years it has argued 29 cases before the Supreme Court. The record: 19-9-1.

Public Citizen is also directly involved in the marketplace through Buyers Up, a consumer-controlled, fuel-oil purchasing cooperative. Buyers Up purchases home heating oil at prices 10 to 20 percent below the rate charged by major suppliers, and then delivers it to members through commercial home heating oil companies. Buyers Up presents testimony before the Congress and federal agencies for home energy efficiency programs and incentives and for consumer protection from wild swings in the price of oil.

National Wildlife Federation (NWF)

Founded:	1936
1991 membership:	5.3 million members and supporters
1991 revenue:	$87 million, $16 million for affiliates
Structure:	National organization, 51 state and territorial affiliates, organized and run as a true federation
Accepts corporate contributions:	Yes, maintains a Corporate Conservation Council, 45 corporate donors in 1991
Staff size:	650
Contact:	National Wildlife Federation 1400 16th St. NW Washington, DC 20036

NWF is generally recognized as the nation's largest environmental advocacy organization, with 5.3 million members and supporters and 51 state and territorial affiliate organizations. The organization operates as a true federation, with policies and priorities set at an annual meeting of affiliates. The board is comprised primarily of regional directors elected by the affiliates in the regions. The advocacy programs of the national office are limited to priorities set by the state affiliate organizations. This decentralized structure gives the federation a strong presence in many states; the state and territorial affiliates had a combined budget of $16 million in 1991, more than most national environmental groups.

State organizations run the full range of philosophies from hard-core advocacy and litigation groups like the Natural Resources Council of Maine (the NWF Maine affiliate), which works on issues such as air pollution and transportation, to more traditional hook and bullet groups like the Montana Wildlife Federation, which focus on maintaining in-stream flows for fisherman and access to public lands for hunters. The federation also operates eight natural resource centers around the nation.

The national office lobbies, litigates, and intervenes in the rule-making process, runs a large educational and public outreach program, produces numerous videos and several television shows each year, and operates an international program. Important issues in 1991 included wetlands, Pacific ancient forests, the Arctic wildlife refuge, reform of the federal grazing-fee structure, and elevating the EPA to cabinet status.

NWF is well known among the general public for its Christmas cards, and its children's magazine, *Ranger Rick,* which generates millions of dollars of revenue each year. The federation owns a building in Washington, D.C., which has offices for several hundred NWF employees and where space is leased to a number of other conservation organizations. It also owns an educational and publication production facility in Vienna, Virginia, where about 500 employees produce educational materials.

In 1982, under the then new leadership of Jay Hair, NWF established the Corporate Conservation Council to enable corporate leaders to have candid discussions with the federation. The council is limited to 20 members and primarily comprises large multinational chemical and manufacturing corporations. The creation of the council raised the eyebrows of more than a few environmental organizations, especially grass-roots groups, who continue to see it as evidence of corporate infiltration within the movement as orchestrated by the large Washington-based organizations. NWF poured fuel on this fire when it added Dean L. Buntrock of Waste Management Inc. to its board of directors. The council, meanwhile, is a totally separate organization from the federation, with funds reserved for council activities only. There is little evidence that the council has had any influence on NWF policies; it is equally unclear whether the council has had any major beneficial effect on the environment or on the environmental policies of council members.

The New Foundation of the Environmental Movement

On issues from air toxics to safe drinking water, wetlands, and pesticides, community and state laws and regulations often exceed even newly enacted federal laws. And on issues where federal standards are virtually nonexistent, such as waste reduction, recycling, toxics, growth management, and transportation, strategies and policies emerge and evolve almost exclusively at the local and state level.

These policies are by and large the product of the fastest growing, most powerful sector of the environmental movement: independent local, state, and regional organizations.

In the past decade hundreds of regional, state, and even local environmental organizations have become institutionalized. These organizations come in all shapes and sizes, from large regional powerhouses, like the Chesapeake Bay Foundation, to local organizations fighting toxic substances and suburban sprawl or working to implement recycling programs. Some are staffed by volunteers, others have large professional staffs; some have large memberships, while other established groups have neither members nor staff and are supported by a core group of volunteers who donate time and resources. Nearly all of the larger local, state, and regional groups have the full range of skills and capacities of the large national groups, the difference primarily being one of scale. Common to all of these organizations is a hands-on presence in the politics, economy, and environment of a precise geographic region, a presence that is far more more difficult for national organizations based in Washington to achieve.

The surge in local, state, and regional environmental groups has three basic causes:

1. The failure of the federal government and of national environmental policies to protect local environments, resources, and ecosystems.
2. The fact that many national environmental laws are designed to be implemented at the state and regional level, thus creating a system that requires state and local presence to ensure its effectiveness.
3. The natural evolution of a movement that is sinking roots all across the nation to meet the more immediate needs of its followers.

Regional Organizations

Regional groups tend to focus on a resource, a park, or some natural wonder that they are organized to protect. Examples include the Greater Yellowstone Coalition, The Chesapeake Bay Foundation, The Southern Utah Wilderness Alliance, Save the Bay (Rhode Island), The Grand Canyon Trust, and Friends of the Boundarywaters Wilderness. These groups tend to have appeal and power at the national as well as the state and regional level. They are less strictly focused, however, on state legislatures than are those state coalition groups or national coalitions of state organizations that are discussed below. Of all the nonnational groups discussed here, these groups have the strongest funding bases. They tend to have national fundraising abilities due to their mission and focus, and they can usually attract national foundations because of the national treasures they try to protect. All strong regional organizations have a cadre of individual, business, and community supporters.

Because these organizations are concerned with a natural resource, their interests and influence typically transcend state lines. This geographic and ecological focus often parallels the economy of the region where the organization works. For example, much of the economy of

Maryland, Virginia, and Pennsylvania revolves around Chesapeake Bay. The economies of Wyoming, Montana, and Idaho—states that surround Yellowstone Park—are critically linked to the greater Yellowstone ecosystem. Regional organizations are thus typically at the forefront of conservation policies that address the issues of jobs and economic development in relation to the protection of the natural wonders of a given area.

Increasingly, these organizations are looking to broaden their base of support within their regional communities. To achieve this, they embark on community-level consensus building, education, field programs involving community groups, and programs designed to clarify everybody's personal stake in the protection of the regional environment.

State Coalition Groups

Perhaps the most powerful and least known of all environmental organizations are the state environmental councils that represent coalitions of local organizations at state capitals. These groups are independent from national organizations. Examples include the Michigan Environmental Council, the Tennessee Environmental Council, the Washington Environmental Council, the New York Environmental Planning Lobby, and the California Planning and Conservation League.

State councils and coalitions constitute the principal environmental advocacy force at state legislatures, typically working on a number of issues and representing or coordinating a broad coalition of organizations from around the state. State coalitions are very effective at influencing state legislation, referenda, and state implementation of federal environmental laws. They are conceptually different from the regional groups because they are strictly limited to in-state activities, and thus appeal generally only to a statewide audience.

Effective state lobbying coalitions or councils currently operate in about 40 states, and usually represent from 20 to 80 local organizations through a range of organizational structures that varies widely in formality. Some state councils require dues for membership, others are very loose coalitions with no dues that tend to come together to deal with specific crises. Funding for the state councils comes from a mix of foundation support, individual members, and local groups. State councils generally (but not always) tend to be have a somewhat smaller financial base than regional organizations, due in part to their less high-profile cause (state-level policy can hardly compete with "Saving the Grand Canyon"). Many states have several organizations that could be described as a state council or coalition. Most states also have several independent state groups that are neither councils nor coalitions.

National and Regional Groups that Operate Primarily at the State Level

National or multistate groups that operate at the state level include Citizens for a Better Environment, Clean Water Action, and the network of public interest research groups (the PIRGs). Many of these groups use canvassing as a fundraising tactic and usually have a decidedly grassroots focus.

Such groups have many of the skills and objectives of state coalitions, but are different primarily because they are supported by a national coalition of affiliated organizations and are often more effective at national coalition-building because of this network. Unlike the national groups described at length above, however, their work is aimed toward influencing policies at the local, state, and regional level.

Established Local Organizations

These groups are the fastest growing sector of the movement. They are often powerful in communities or metropolitan regions and work well with national coalitions and regional and state groups.

The strongest local groups typically exist in large metropolitan regions. Groups serving populations smaller than 50,000 people have a hard time maintaining secure funding and paid staff, although organizations with a volunteer structure and few paid staff members are notoriously effective in more sparsely populated areas. In some cases large local organizations can take on the characteristics of smaller regional groups when the metropolitan region cuts across state lines (New York City, Washington, D.C., Philadelphia). A good example of a strong regional local group is the Delaware Valley Coalition for Clean Air, which operates in Pennsylvania, Delaware, and New Jersey, using Philadelphia as its hub.

The most established local groups tend to have their roots in one particular issue with strong and broad appeal to the community. A good example is the Coalition for Clean Air in Los Angeles, a very strong local group with obvious allure. Others include the Silicon Valley Toxics Coalition, Transportation Alternatives in New York City, and the North Carolina Waste Awareness Reduction Network (NCWARN). Without question, local groups routinely employ the widest range of tactics and strategies. They are by far the most likely players to be involved in direct citizen action—marches, protests, and civil disobedience—but they are equally likely to lobby the city or county council, file a lawsuit, or work with the media to achieve objectives.

At the facility, factory, or timber-sale level, these are the groups that corporations must learn to respect and talk to. More than any other sector of the environmental movement, local organizations confront the issue of jobs and the environment, and more than any other sector of the movement, local organizations are willing to get involved in direct negotiations with corporate management if the negotiations are serious. Many of these groups set direct negotiations as an objective, which can create significant opportunities for corporations determined to clean up their production processes. Sham negotiations and bogus processes for public participation, however, have taken their toll on this promising avenue. As a result, there is growing disagreement within the movement about the viability and usefulness of direct talks with industry, particularly in light of the limited time and resources of such groups.

Most of these organizations rely on events, members, promotional sales, local foundations, and individuals for funding. Some function very effectively, however, using a dedicated cadre of volunteers. Many local groups have active board members who are involved in the issues and volunteer time, resources, in-kind services (printing, publicity), or cash. The financial status of these groups is as varied as the organizations themselves: some are well endowed; some are organized to be very effective with little long-term need for cash; most could use more money; and all are passionate about what they do.

Conclusions

Business is at the environmental crossroads. The green path beckons, yet for most corporations the temptation to continue business as usual remains too powerful to resist. Three-quarters of all Americans claim to be environmentalists, yet the potential power of this block has not been captured in the marketplace or in electoral politics.

Numerous obstacles stand in the way of a green society, not the least of which is the awesome political and economic power of *business as usual* with American business. Compounding this force of stagnation is the failure of environmentalists and business to move beyond their traditional adversarial relationship.

Industry fears the environmental movement, yet business remains an infinitely more powerful force in our society. Environmentalists are now an influential voice for social change, but they will never reach their goals (particularly in time to avoid devastating environmental losses) if these goals remain opposed by business and industry. Business controls our productive capacity, the products that are produced, and the means used to produce them. Ultimately, business will decide whether or not our economy—including its goods, services, and manufacturing systems—is in harmony with nature and sustainable over the long haul. Without business leadership and participation in reversing current environmental trends, progress will be too slow to save many valuable resources. The world will survive, but it will be hugely diminished.

For every environmental rule and regulation undone in Washington, D.C., there are community activists and plant managers who prove that more can be done to increase efficiencies, reduce pollution, provide secure skilled jobs, and produce green products. The future of the environment will be held together by the mortar of these hard-fought achievers; it is up to leaders in the business community to accelerate this process of change.

5
The Consumer Market

Introduction

Today's consumer is much more environmentally aware than the typical consumer of two decades ago. This has not happened out of the blue. Landmark event after landmark event have driven the environment ever deeper into consumers' awareness. Figure 5-1 identifies the most important of these occurrences.

But today's consumers are confused as well as concerned. For one thing, scientists often disagree about what is best for the environment. Is paper or plastic environmentally superior? How about cloth versus disposable diapers? Allegedly scientific studies generally seem to come out supporting the position of whoever is footing the bill. This fact doesn't escape consumers and they are left scratching their heads about what to do and who to trust.

Consumers' uncertainty has been compounded by some highly publicized cases in which companies have been charged with making false and deceptive advertising claims. The negative fallout from this so-called green marketing has turned many consumers off to green products generally.

But green consumerism is by no means a lost cause for marketers. In this chapter, I provide an overview of the current state of green consumerism and conclude with general recommendations about strategies for releasing green consumerism's substantial latent potential.

Figure 5-1.

A Chronology
of Environmental Events

- **1950s.** Reconstruction and economic growth—pollution and waste grow unabated.
- **1962.** Rachel Carson's *Silent Spring* is published.
- **1964.** The Wilderness Act is passed.
- **1966.** The Federal Water Pollution Control Act is enacted.
- **1969.** The National Environmental Policy Act is enacted.
- **1970.** The first Earth Day is celebrated in the United States.
- **1971.** The Environmental Protection Agency is established.
- **1972.** The U.N. Conference on the Human Environment leads to the formation of the U.N. Environment Program in 1973.
- **1973.** The Endangered Species Act is enacted.
- **1973.** The Organization for Economic Cooperation and Development adopts "polluter pays" principle.
- **1973.** Oil price hike prompts a massive effort to conserve energy.
- **1973.** EC Environmental Action Plan is established.
- **1973.** IBM (U.S.) and Philips (Europe) draw up first corporate environmental policies.
- **1974.** International Chamber of Commerce environmental guidelines are introduced.
- **1975.** 3M's ground breaking "Pollution Prevention Pays" program is launched.
- **1976.** The Resource Conservation and Recovery Act is enacted and the Toxic Substances Control Act is passed.
- **1978.** The phase-out of CFCs in aerosol products is mandated.
- **1980.** International Union for Conservation of Nature publishes World Conservation Report which launched concept of "sustainable development."
- **1983.** Election of 28 Green Party representatives to the Bundestag sends strong signals worldwide.
- **1984.** Union Carbide leak in Bhopal kills several thousand people.

- **1985.** Hole located in the stratospheric ozone above the Antarctic confirms fears of CFCs.

- **1986.** Fire breaks out at Sandoz's warehouse in Schweizerhalle, Switzerland.

- **1986.** Explosion at the Chernobyl nuclear plant ends nuclear power programs in Italy and Sweden.

- **1987.** World Commission on Environment and Development, Brundtland Report, popularizes "sustainable development" with many governments and corporations.

- **1987.** Montreal Protocol to the Vienna Convention—first global agreement on environmental protection—leads to 1989 consensus that CFCs be phased out by end of the century.

- **1989.** The Exxon oil tanker Valdez spills 11 million gallons of oil into Prince William Sound, less than 15 percent of which is cleaned up.

- **1990.** The second Earth Day is celebrated by 43 million people in 120 countries worldwide.

- **1992.** The United Nations Conference on Environment and Development is held in Rio de Janeiro.

(More detailed marketing recommendations will be provided in later chapters, especially Chapters 9 through 12, and a detailed discussion of the regulatory environment appears in Chapter 6.)

Just for the why-do-people-care perspective, a 1992 Roper study cosponsored by *The Atlantic Monthly* cites the following reasons average Americans give for protecting the environment: (1) to protect human health from pollution (63 percent); (2) to protect natural resources for the use of future generations (42 percent); (3) to ensure that natural places and wildlife will always exist (32 percent); (4) to protect natural resources that our economy relies on, such as timber and fisheries (21 percent); and (5) to preserve recreational areas, such as national parks (17 percent).[1]

Who Are the Green Consumers?

General Levels of Concern

Although American consumers' attitudes about the environment run the gamut from empassioned concern to complete indifference, an extremely high percentage of consumers express strong concern about the environment. A typical survey finding, this one from a 1991 *Wall Street Journal*/NBC News survey, found that more than 80 percent of consumers find it more important to protect the environment than to keep prices down.[2]

Just as importantly, consumer concern about the environment is remaining high, despite the Gulf War and the recession.

The Roper/S.C. Johnson Segmentation

The best-known segmentation of consumers' environmental attitudes was developed in 1990 by The Roper Organization for the consumer goods company S.C. Johnson & Son, Inc. The Roper/S.C. Johnson segmentation identified five categories of consumer:

- *True-Blue Greens* are the most actively green consumers. In the words of The Roper Organization, their "actual behavior is consistent with very strong concerns about the environment. They are far more environmentally oriented than other Americans and could be considered, in fact, the leaders of the green movement among the general population." They comprise 11 percent of the population.

- *Greenback Greens* (11 percent) are characterized by the fact that "their commitment to the environment is mainly manifested by their willingness to pay substantially higher prices for green products."

- *Sprouts* (26 percent) "show middling levels of concern about the environment and equally middling levels of behavioral response. The Sprouts certainly seem to have green tendencies, but they have yet to exhibit a clearly established pattern of proenvironmental behavior."

- *Grousers* (24 percent) "consistently rationalize their lack of proenvironmental behavior by offering all kinds of excuses and criticizing the poor performance of others."

- *Basic Browns* (28 percent) "simply do not believe individuals can make a difference in solving environmental problems; indeed, they do not *want* to make an effort."[3]

Other Segmentations

The Roper/S.C. Johnson survey is only one among many surveys of consumers' environmental attitudes which have been made public in the last few years. Table 5-1 provides an overview of the most important

Table 5-1. Definitions of Green Consumer Segments

Company	Segment	Definition
Cambridge Reports	Green Consumer (12%)	Strongly identify with term *environmentalist* and support environmental organizations.
FIND/SVP	Dedicated (1.4%)	Bring environmental concerns to bear on most or all purchase decisions.
	Selective (12%)	Engage in environmentally aware shopping on a selective basis, isolating specific products and companies for scrutiny.
	Impulsive (20%)	Engage in green shopping on a stimulus-response basis.
J. Walter Thompson	Greener-than-Green (23%)	Make many sacrifices for the environment.
	Green (59%)	Concerned about environment but make only some sacrifices.
	Light Green (15%)	Concerned but not willing to make any personal sacrifices.
	Un-Green (3%)	Plain don't care about the environment.
Roper/S.C. Johnson	True-Blue Greens (11%)	Actual behavior is consistent with very strong concerns about the environment.
	Greenback Greens (11%)	Commitment to the environment mainly manifested by willingness to pay substantially higher prices for green products.
	Sprouts (26%)	Show middling levels of concern about the environment and equally middling levels of behavioral response.
	Grousers (24%)	Consistently rationalize their lack of proenvironmentl behavior by offering all kinds of excuses and criticizing the poor performance of others.
	Basic Browns (28%)	Do not believe individuals can make a difference in solving environmental problems, and do not want to make a difference.
Green MarketAlert	Visionary greens (5–15%)	Have embraced the "paradigm shift." Green is a way of life for this group, not a shopping style. Passionately committed to environmental change.
	Maybe-Greens (55–80%)	Express high degrees of environmental concern but act on those concerns only irregularly.
	Hard-core Browns (15–30%)	Indifferent or implacably antienvironmentalist. Tend to have lower incomes and educational levels.

Table 5-1. Definitions of Green Consumer Segments (*Continued*)

Company	Segment	Definition
Simmons Market Research Bureau	Premium Green (22%)	Sophisticates, totally committed, in word and deed, to protecting planet Earth. Willing to spend more, do more, vote more.
	Red, White & "Green" (20%)	Traditionalists, equally committed to the environment, but think more in terms of their own turf and their beloved outdoors.
	No-Costs Ecologists (28%)	Sound like dedicated ecologists, but less likely to commit actions and money, unless it's the government's.
	Convenient Greens (11%)	Environmental attitudes strong, but actions are motivated by convenience in lifestyle.
	Unconcerned (19%)	The name says it all.
Angus Reid	Activists (15%)	Very green. Young vanguard of environmental movement.
	Community Enthusiasts (8%)	Very green. Leaders in environmentally correct behavior but fundamentally conservative.
	Ambitious Optimists (21%)	Somewhat green, this segment, which is comprised largely of yuppies, is not overly worried about imminent environmental Armageddon, but is willing to take certain steps.
	Mainstream Followers (21%)	Moderate in terms of environmental involvement. Less interested than most in purchasing green products.
	Hostile Conservatives (13%)	Very skeptical about the severity of environmental problems. Very resistant to the environmental movement.
	Disillusioned Survivors (14%)	Cynical and with a fairly pessimistic environmental outlook, this group sees environmental problems as serious and support a tougher legislative climate, especially where industry is concerned.
	Privileged bystanders (8%)	Do not care enough about the problem of the environment to make any changes in their lifestyle.

SOURCE: Green MarketAlert

of these segmentations. Note that two of these segmentations—the ones from FIND/SVP and Green MarketAlert—were qualitative rather than quantitative.

An Overview

An analysis of Table 5-1 produces several generalizations, all of which basically are in line with the Roper/S.C. Johnson findings.

First, the number of deeply committed green consumers appears to be in the 10 to 15 percent range. Roper/S.C. Johnson's True-Blue Greens comprise 11 percent of the populace, Cambridge Reports puts the percentage of Greens at 12 percent, Angus Reid's Activists are 15 percent strong, FIND/SVP's Dedicated and Selective Greens total 13.4 percent of consumers, and Green MarketAlert's Visionary Greens are in the 5 to 15 percent range.

A second tier of reasonably active and dedicated greens comprises roughly another 10 percent of the population. Roper/S.C. Johnson's Greenback Greens make up 11 percent of the population, Simmons Market Research Bureau's Premium Greens are 22 percent-strong (this group would seem to cover both the first and second tiers), and Angus-Reid calls 8 percent of consumers Community Enthusiasts, bringing their total of active greens to 23 percent.

These two tiers of genuinely green consumers are followed by a large middle group of light greens which the pollsters cut and slice in different ways. Although this fact does not show up in Table 5-1, one general truth about this group is that it is "softly" proenvironment, i.e., this middle group expresses high degrees of concern about the environment but only inconsistently translates that concern into actual buying behavior. In most studies, over 70 percent report a high degree of concern about the environment. However, 40 to 55 percent of consumers report boycotting products or companies with environmentally unfavorable reputations, or selecting products based on the product's or manufacturer's positive environmental reputation.

This large swing group is a critical one for marketers. If this group's buying behavior ever begins to match its concern about the environment, green consumerism will become not *a*, but *the*, dominant force in the U.S. marketplace.

Bringing up the rear in the green segmentation are the Browns who are often too poor to be able to focus on anything other than their own survival. Roper/S.C. Johnson's Basic Browns have a 28 percent share, Green MarketAlert puts this group at as high as 30 percent, and Simmons Market Research Bureau's Unconcerned make up 19 percent of the population.

About one-quarter of Americans would appear to qualify as genuinely green, although only about one-half of that group appears to be deep-green. The next 50 percent of the population is green-ish, i.e., they talk green but only sometimes put their wallets where their mouths are. The final one-quarter of the population is not green now and is unlikely to become green in the near future.

Shortly after the first draft of this manuscript was finished, S.C. Johnson & Son and The Roper Organization released the findings of their 1992 study of green consumerism:

- The percentage of the True-Blue Greens almost doubled, from 11 percent to 20 percent.

- The Greenback-Greens segment shrank from 11 percent to 5 percent.

- The Sprouts segment grew from 26 percent to 31 percent of the population.

- Grousers decreased in number from 24 percent to 9 percent.

- The Basic Browns increased from 28 percent to 35 percent.

Roper concludes that America is, indeed, greening, and attributes opposite shifts in population largely to the recession. I believe, however, that another factor is partly responsible for the formation of more distinctly grouped or positioned green and nongreen consumers, and that is an increase in environmental education and awareness. As consumers become more educated they are better able to form distinct opinions and take sides instead of just wavering in the middle.

Other Demographics

A few additional generalizations may be useful:

- First, people tend to be more green in direct proportion to their income and educational levels, i.e., the more they earn and the more schooling they have had, the greener they tend to be.

- Women tend to be greener than men.

- Most surveys show the east and west coasts to be the strongest bastions of green consumerism.

It's logical to assume that the greener a consumer, the better that person's behavior will be for the environment. However, that is not necessarily the case. It is *consumption* that is environmentally unfriendly, after all, and greener people tend to consume more because they are richer. Even if they bring heightened environmental consciousness to that consumption, it is entirely possible that many do more harm to the environment than their poorer, less green, less consumption-oriented counterparts. Which raises a curious possibility—that in their impact if not in their attitude, the Roper/S.C. Johnson Basic Browns are actually greener than the True-Blue Greens!

Children

Another important factor to keep in mind about green consumerism is the immensely important role that children play in shaping their parents' environmental behavior. Nor is it only their parents' behavior they affect. Consider this 1992 press release from Archie Comic Publications Inc. (most of whose readers are children):

> Archie Comic Publications Inc. has announced that all comics in its line will be printed using 100% recycled paper. Archie is the first comic book to do so and joins only a handful of other nationally distributed newsstand magazines to "go green." *A number of letters from Archie readers motivated the decision* [italics added].[4]

Quantitative research confirms how profoundly children affect their parents' environmental buying behavior. A national survey conducted by INFOCUS Environmental (Princeton, New Jersey) on the impact of children on their parents' environmental behavior produced the following findings:

■ That more than one in three parents (34 percent) have changed their shopping behaviors because of what they learned about the environment from children in their home

■ That 17 percent of all households with children have avoided a product they ordinarily would have purchased because they learned from their children that the product or package was bad for the environment

■ That 20 percent purchased a product specifically because they learned from their children that it was better for the environment[5]

Since about 71 percent of U.S. households have children, these data tell us that about 24 percent of U.S. households have changed their buying behavior because of the influence of children. And since most studies indicate that 30 to 40 percent of all consumers report buying or avoiding a product for environmental reasons, it also suggests that 60 to 80 percent of green buying behavior has been driven at least in part by the lobbying of children. Even if we take these data with a grain or two of salt, they still tell us that children have a significant impact on household buying decisions.

The Maslow Hierarchy

To give us more insight into the psyche of the various Roper/S.C. Johnson green-consumer segments, let us turn to the Maslow hierarchy of human needs and behavior.

Abraham Maslow, the father of humanistic psychology, posited that people have a set of higher needs which, in the words of the psychiatrist Stanislav Grof, "represent an important and authentic aspect of the human personality structure and cannot be reduced to, or seen as, derivatives of the base instincts."[6] This approach, which represented a significant departure from Freud's gloomy view of the human psyche, posited a pyramid-like structure consisting of five levels of human need:

- At the base of the pyramid are *physiological needs,* i.e., the need for basics such as food, drink, and shelter.

- Once these needs are met, the individual can climb to the next level of the pyramid, which involves *safety needs,* e.g., security, protection, and order.

- Once these still-basic needs are satisfied, the next set of needs can be attended to. These involve *social needs* such as the need for affection and acceptance.

- This is followed by *esteem needs* such as the desire for self-esteem, recognition, and status.

- At the top of the pyramid of needs is *self-actualization.* This involves the desire for self-development and personal fulfillment.[7]

Where the majority of people reside in this hierarchy of needs depends in large measure on the culture that they inhabit. In underdeveloped cultures, people tend of necessity to remain in one of the lower levels of the pyramid, struggling merely to survive. In more developed societies, people have the security and leisure to attempt to gratify higher-level needs. But it is still the relatively rare individual who pursues the set of needs at the top of the pyramid. In our culture, the buck tends to stop with the satisfaction of social or esteem needs. Indeed, much of our consumer society is built upon peoples' attempt to enhance their social needs for affection and acceptance through the acquisition of material objects.

If we put Maslow's five-part hierarchy alongside the Roper/S.C. Johnson five-part segmentation (see Table 5-2), we are, I believe, afforded a further glimpse into the character and needs of the various green and nongreen consumer segments:

- True-Blue Greens are self-actualizers.

- Greenback Greens build their lives around the gratification of esteem needs.

Table 5-2. Hierarchies of Needs and Behavior

Maslow, 1954	Roper, 1990
Self-actualization (Self-development and fulfillment	*True-Blue Greens* Opinion leaders Trend setters Executives, professionals Proregulation
Esteem Needs (Self-esteem, recognition, status)	*Greenback Greens* Intellectually concerned Not activists Busy lifestyle Up-and-coming

Social Needs
(Affection, belonging,
   acceptance)
	Sprouts
	Key swing group
	Not certain whether to vote
	   environment or economy

Safety Needs (Security, protection, order)	*Grousers* Object to higher prices Blame others for mess Lots of excuses for noninvolvement Consider themselves mainstream
Physiological Needs (Food, drink, shelter)	*Basic Browns* Least enviro-active group Most socially and economically disadvantaged group

- Grousers and Basic Browns tend to be poorer and focused more extensively than the three wealthier segments on issues of basic survival and the gratification of physiological and safety needs.

It has been suggested that our culture is in the process of a profound transition in values, and that one element of this transition is increasing openness to the possibility that there is something higher on the hierarchy of human needs than the gratification of the need for self-esteem needs through public recognition and social status. If there is any merit in the parallels we have drawn between (a) self-actualizers and True-Blue Greens and between (b) the esteem-need satisfiers and the Greenback Greens, it may also be possible that, as more and more people progress from esteem needs to self-actualization, they will simultaneously graduate from Greenback-Green to True-Blue-Green status. In short, it is at least conceivable that there is an underlying correlation between consumers' levels of environmental activism and their climb up the pyramid of needs.

Purchase Considerations

Green products operate in a free-market environment. They must compete on equal footing with established product lines which enjoy the advantages of extensive name recognition, economies of scale, and established footholds in mainstream retail channels. If the government ever puts its weight behind green products, their competitive position will be improved tremendously. Pending this occurrence, most consumers base their decision whether or not to buy green products on the following purchase considerations.

Price

Quality and performance being equal, consumers will usually choose the cheaper brand. This is especially true when consumers are strapped for funds, as during a recessionary period.

It is difficult to move premium-priced products off the shelves when those products are unknown. Many consumers need the inducement of a price break to try out a new product.

These facts operate to the disadvantage of green products, which historically have tended to be more expensive than their less-green counterparts—and also new and unknown. The overwhelming majority of consumers will not pay more for a product or package simply because it is environmentally benign. These consumers do not understand why they should pay *more* for a product that states that it has *less* (i.e., fewer harmful ingredients and less packaging) in it. They also tend to believe that manufacturers are responsible for our environmental problems and should therefore absorb the costs of fixing them.

But green-product pricing, if not consumer attitude, is changing. Price parity is now common—and as the supply of recycled materials increases, the prices of green products are expected to grow still more competitive. Over time, price should be less and less of a problem for green products. Indeed, as the cost of recycled-content feedstocks drops below that of virgin materials and as suppliers' economies of scale improve, price could eventually become a selling point.

Which raises another point. Green product suppliers are trapped in a Catch-22. Historically, consumers have tended to assume that products made of "used" materials would not perform as well as products made from virgin materials. Indeed, some companies hid the fact that their products contained recycled materials, for fear of alienating consumers. One indirect advantage of pricing green products at a premium has been that it has played into consumers' assumption that "if it's more expensive, it must be better." By dropping their prices below their competitors', green-product suppliers risk playing into consumers' concerns about green-product quality.

Consumers' price sensitivity varies from product category to product category. Paper products are particularly price sensitive. Ashdun Industries, a marketer and distributor of recycled-content paper products, based in Englewood Cliffs, New Jersey, found that although it had to pay more for recycled-content supplies, it could not tack that cost onto the price. Consumers' price sensitivity required them to charge no more than competitive products.

Other product categories are somewhat less price sensitive. Laundry detergents are at a midpoint on this continuum. Brand loyalty is a significant factor here, and this reduces price sensitivity. But brand loyalty isn't so extensive that it will keep consumers from buying a different brand of detergent if it is priced at a significant discount to their usual brand.

The fact that there are differing levels of price sensitivity from product category to product category does not change the basic rule that green products which are priced at a premium operate at a severe competitive disadvantage. It means only that the extent of the impact varies in different product categories.

Performance

Many early green paper products such as paper towels and toilet paper were rough in texture. Some nontoxic cleaning formulations do not clean as well or as effortlessly as their more toxic counterparts. Yet product performance is essential. Only the most ardent environmentalists will purchase a low-performing green product more than once.

The uneven performance of some early green products has caused some consumers to become turned off to green products generally. This extract from a 1992 press release from Seventh Generation, a green-product supplier and the nation's leading green-product catalog house, shows one company's strategy for addressing this problem:

> There has been a lot of confusion about green products. Many people cling to one, or both, of the following misconceptions:
> - Environmental products are too expensive
> - Green products don't work
>
> *Independent laboratory report dispels both myths.* Recent tests conducted by Schuster Labs in Massachusetts, an independent laboratory, show conclusively that Seventh Generation's vegetable-based laundry detergent is the first environmentally responsible brand to work as effectively as Procter & Gamble's laundry liquid, Tide. These tests also found that on a per-use basis the cost is virtually the same.

Green-product performance is improving. However, suppliers must continue to address problems of perception as well as problems of actual performance.

Convenience

A sizable proportion of our solid-waste problem can be attributed to the desire of Americans for packaged convenience products such as fast-food, frozen-food, and single-serving packaged goods. Working mothers and fathers across all economic brackets seem to have convinced themselves that they have less time to be cook, housekeeper, and home manager—and two of the consequences of this have been an increase in energy consumption and an increase in solid waste.

Many green products are less convenient than their nongreen counterparts. For instance, it takes more time to mix up a concentrated cleaner than it does simply to point and spray. And it is much easier to use and discard a disposable diaper than it is to store, wash, and fold cotton diapers.

Even consumers who do shop green tend not to do so in a vacuum. They factor environmental considerations into a matrix in which price, performance, and convenience have at least equal status. When these other considerations are added together, the environment often winds up taking a backseat.

Health and Safety

Generally, products that are environmentally sensible are safe as well. But some Americans who have grown up on preservatives, pasteurized milk, sanitized surfaces, and artificially air-freshened rooms perceive green products as lacking in precisely those ingredients which ensure the demise of the ubiquitous, invisibly perceived menaces to their health and safety.

Interestingly, a countermovement is simultaneously taking form. More and more people are claiming that excessive exposure to chemicals of the sort described above can wear down peoples' immune systems and damage their health. There is even a new name for people who claim to have been completely debilitated by exposure to chemicals—the "chemically sensitive." Many of these people have regained their health only by completely eliminating chemical "contaminants" from their lives.

This group is still a tiny minority, and chemical sensitivity continues to be a small voice in the medical wilderness. The great majority of

Americans continue to view a life built upon chemical-based consumer products as pro- rather than antihealth. As long as that perception endures, this will mitigate against the wide acceptance of green products.

Availability

Another critically important issue for green-product suppliers is availability. If consumers can't find green products to buy, they will not be able to determine for themselves if the popular perceptions about issues such as performance and safety have any merit.

Green products have suffered from a general lack of availability in mainstream distribution channels. There are four main reasons why this is so.

1. Retailers are basically risk-averse. With profit margins sometimes as low as about 2 percent, that comes as no surprise—but it does operate to the disadvantage of green-product suppliers who need retailers who are willing to take a flyer on their success.

2. Many green-product manufacturers have only one product in their product arsenal. Retail stores don't generally buy single-product offerings in volume. They prefer to do business with companies that can offer multiple SKUs (stock-keeping units).

3. Green-product suppliers are often blocked by daunting slotting allowances—up-front fees charged by retailers in return for allowing new products to be stocked on the supermarket's shelves. While well-heeled suppliers can absorb these fees, that is not the case for many small green-product suppliers.

4. With so much uncertainty about what actually constitutes a green product, some retailers are loath to market products as "green," even when they carry the products on their shelves in order to make sure that green consumers don't take their business elsewhere.

Purchase Behavior

The 1992 Roper/S.C. Johnson study reported the following specific purchase behavior:

- That 14 percent of consumers regularly buy products in refillable packaging
- That 19 percent buy products made from or packaged in recycled materials

- That 28 percent avoid buying products in aerosol containers
- That 29 percent use biodegradable, low-phosphate detergents

All of the above indicated percentages represent an increase of 4 to 5 percent over 1990 figures.

Consumers and Green Claims

Awareness

The 1990 Roper/S.C. Johnson Organization poll discussed above found that since 1987, public concern about the environment has grown faster than concern about any other national problem. In a typical survey, over 70 percent of Americans describe themselves as very concerned about the environment. Polls also find that, even against the double whammy of war and recession, levels of concern have stayed high.

However, awareness of environmental marketing, including the use of environmental claims on product packaging and in product advertising, is much lower. In a late 1990 survey by Environmental Research Associates, a Princeton, New Jersey–based survey house, 1000 adults were asked if they looked for green labeling when they shopped. The answers were as follows:

- "Always"—9 percent
- "Usually"—23 percent
- "Rarely"—15 percent
- "Once in a while"—32 percent
- "Never"—20 percent
- "Don't Know"—1 percent[8]

Thus, only 32 percent of consumers reported seeking out green labeling on anything other than an extremely infrequent basis.

Other surveys confirm Environmental Research Associates' basic finding that consumers awareness of green labeling is substantially lower than their concern about the environment:

- A J. Walter Thompson tracking study found only 14 percent of Americans to be aware of advertised environmental claims.[9]
- A 1990 study sponsored by the Food Marketing Institute and the magazine *Better Homes and Gardens* found that only 24 percent of all shoppers surveyed were aware of products in the supermarket which are packaged with recycled materials.[10]

- The Roper/S.C. Johnson study discussed above found that 26 percent of the total public report that they "read the labels on products to see if the contents are environmentally safe on a regular basis." Another 36 percent reported that they read labels for environmental reasons "from time to time."

- The 1992 *Advertising Age* consumer survey conducted by Yankelovich Clancy Shulman found that 22 percent of consumers are often influenced by environmental claims and 51 percent are sometimes influenced.[11]

Whether these findings are positive or negative signs for green consumerism is a matter of opinion. Although the media tends to turn the gap between consumers' expressions of concern and their actual behavior into a putdown of consumers ("They don't practice what they preach"), the data lend themselves to a different yet equally plausible construction. When close to 80 percent of consumers seek out environmental information on product labels, even if the majority of them do it only rarely, that can be seen as evidence of how deeply environmental awareness has penetrated consumers' psyches.

Comprehension

Generally, consumers' comprehension of environmental labeling is low. For instance, telephone surveys conducted by American Opinion Research (Princeton, New Jersey) have found that (1) 60 percent of Americans aren't aware that environmental symbols are being used to identify recycled and recyclable products and packaging, and (2) only 10 percent of respondents could identify even one symbol.[12]

Our own research confirms that consumers are not familiar with the meanings of the familiar chasing-arrows symbols. Virtually none of the participants in our focus groups are aware that when the logo is not identified by accompanying text copy, there are modifications in logo design that designate different stages in the recycling process (i.e., recyclable or recycled).

A 1991 study by the University of Illinois at Urbana-Champaign confirms this. The study found consumers to be also extremely confused about the meaning of the recycled and recyclable chasing arrows, as well as about the Society of the Plastics Industry (SPI) code for differentiating among different types of plastic. Only 18.5 percent of respondents in the University of Illinois study could correctly identify the recycled chasing arrows, and for the SPI code the figure was 17.7 percent. Consumers were more knowledgeable about the recyclable symbol, with 39.1 percent of respondents correctly identifying it.[13] (In early

1992, the EPA recommended that one symbol be used for both terms—recycled and recyclable—when accompanied by the actual word.)

Our focus groups have also found widespread confusion about whether the symbols and environmental claims refer to the product or to the packaging, unless the copy specifically tells them. Again, the University of Illinois study confirms this finding. When asked "What does the word recycled mean when you see it on a product label?" 15.5 percent of the respondents to the University of Illinois survey defined the word in relation to the product, 16.6 percent in relation to the package, and 3.4 percent in relation to the product or the packaging (the remaining 64.5 percent did not identify the referent).

Other labeling terms meet with just as much confusion. The American Opinion Research poll described above found that about one-third of U.S. consumers do not know the meaning of the term *biodegradable*. And a J. Walter Thompson report has found that 64 percent of Americans are not confident that they understand the term.[14]

The University of Illinois study found further evidence of confusion about environmental labeling language. Consumers' ignorance regarding the terms *preconsumer* and *postconsumer* approaches the universal. In testimony before the EPA, the study's author, Brenda Cude, reported that two-thirds of the respondents did not know what preconsumer waste meant and 75 percent were unable to define postconsumer waste.

One reason for consumers' extensive ignorance appears to be resistance to language that sounds overly technical or legal. A focus group on environmental labeling language organized by the Chicago-based American Marketing Association found "dislike for technical or legal sounding terms [to be] common with the group."

The message is clear. Many current and proposed environmental labeling terms simply go whizzing by consumers. Conventional environmental labeling language is clearly doing a poor job of delivering its intended messages.

But that does not mean that terms like *recycled* and *recycled content* do not have a substantial impact on consumers' buying decisions. The University of Illinois found that, assuming price parity, 64.3 percent of respondents would choose paper towels labeled recycled paper over paper towels without the label. For a plastic shampoo bottle marked recycled, the figure was virtually identical—63.1 percent. Similarly, 59.3 percent of respondents indicated they would choose a glass peanut butter jar labeled recyclable over one without the label, and 64.7 percent of respondents said they'd opt for a plastic shampoo bottle marked recyclable. To the extent that environmental messages are clearly communicated, they become a significant factor in consumer buying decisions.

Attitude

Most consumers are basically dubious about all manufacturer advertising and product claims, environmental or otherwise. This general skepticism, coupled with conflicting information about environmental issues and a few highly publicized instances of green-gimmick marketing, has given rise to an attitude that all green products and green-marketing claims are guilty until proven innocent.

Market research confirms this point. According to the Good Housekeeping Institute, among those American women who have seen or heard advertising claims about products being environmentally safe, only 43 percent believe that most of them are accurate. About the same percentage feel that only some or almost none of these claims are valid.[15]

When asked about the general trustworthiness of companies' environmental claims, consumers express even more skepticism. For instance, in a 1991 survey by the Newport Beach, California-based Hartman Group, only 13 percent of respondents expressed the belief that corporations are "trustworthy sources of information about environmental matters."[16]

Marketers must fight against the tide to persuade consumers of the legitimacy of their environmental claims. This requires labeling and advertising language to be drafted with scrupulous attention to any possible misimpressions that might be created. But if proper care is taken, environmental claims can work to a company's benefit. As we have said above, consumers have a strong (if only irregularly expressed) desire to do something positive for the environment.

Dealing with Backlash

As we have seen, environmental marketing has received a number of harsh blows over the past several years. The credibility of green-product claims has been tarnished. Generally, we can say that there are three levels or degrees of consumer backlash:

- *First degree—general skepticism.* The company or product is subjected to doubts about the motives behind its sudden environmental responsibility, but business doesn't suffer and little, if any, corrective action is taken by either party.

- *Second degree—claims or other issue controversy.* Serious questions are raised about a product's environmental performance based on its claims. However, these are not so severe that they cannot be addressed by consumer education campaigns. Disposable diapers provide an excellent example of this kind of backlash. Many consumers hesitated to use them because of concerns about the space they took up in landfills. But Procter & Gamble, the leading provider of disposable diapers, launched an aggressive campaign which included a life-cycle analysis of disposable diapers that concluded their environmental impacts were roughly equivalent to those of cloth diapers. Coupled with disposable diapers' appeal to consumers' desire for convenience, the P&G initiative seems to have effectively quelled the incipient consumer backlash.

■ *Third degree—boycott.*   On occasion, the backlash becomes so intense that companies have no choice but to change how they do business. This was the case for the tuna industry, which found itself under a boycott for the use of fishing practices which trapped dolphins. Now the U.S. tuna industry has gone "dolphin-safe." Similarly, many companies are finding it necessary to switch out of aerosols because of consumer concerns about the environmental impacts of the technology.

Consumer backlash usually is triggered by one of the three following sources: (1) environmental or other special interest advocacy groups who organize consumer protests and/or bring a given issue to the attention of the media or regulators; (2) politicians with strong environmental leaning or constituencies; and (3) competitors who challenge rival marketing claims or manufacturing processes.

In one sense, this entire book is about how to avoid consumer backlash via responsible environmental management and marketing practices. The following, however, introduces the major strategies:

1. *Get your company on the right track.*   Even if your record is poor and progress is coming slowly, it's serious *commitment* that consumers are looking for.

2. *Anticipate rather than react to environmental issues, regulations, and consumer concerns and needs.*

3. *Get closer to your potential detractors.*   Not only is communication a great reconciler, but environmentalists have valuable insights and information (relative to point number 2) to share.

4. *Be consistent and even-handed in your communications.*

The Role of Consumer Education

Consumer education can also play an important role in preventing or minimizing consumer backlash. To the extent that consumers understand environmental issues, they are that much less likely to engage in emotional and environmentally counterproductive behavior.

Research indicates that consumers most often want to know where manufacturers stand on the following issues:

- Source reduction
- Use of recycled materials
- Recyclability of packaging
- Solid-waste management
- Toxic-materials use
- Toxic-waste management
- Long-term commitment to environment
- Local recycling support

The following principles of environmental education (and keys to an effective consumer environmental education) come from the International Strategy for Action in the field of Environmental Education and Training for the 1990s, prepared by the United Nations Educational, Scientific and Cultural Organization in collaboration with the United Nations Environment Programme:

1. *Continuity.* Environmental education should be ongoing, not short term.

2. *Comprehensiveness.* An environmental education program should be comprehensive. It should take into account all relevant economic, social, and ecological realities.

3. *Motivational and Inspirational Core.* An environmental education program should encourage *right attitudes* that in turn encourage *right behavior*. Among the right attitudes are: (1) an appreciation of the concept of sustainable development; and (2) an awareness of the role of the individual, i.e., of the importance of action at the individual level.

4. *Even-Handedness.* A consumer environmental education program must treat all constituencies equally. Care must be taken not to neglect or give short shrift to any single group. This applies not only to ethnic consumer segments (e.g., Blacks, Hispanics), but also to the channels through which consumers are reached (media, retailers, etc.).

We will address consumer education again in Chapters 10 and 11.

Summary and
Recommendations

For green-product marketers, consumers are a good-news/bad-news story. The good news is that they are increasingly concerned environmentally and eager to take action. The bad news is that they don't know what actions to take and they think twice before listening to corporations.

Green consumerism has enormous potential, but businesses must fight through a miasma of distrust and confusion to realize it. We have found that three basic strategies will help companies reach that goal.

1. *Achieve price and performance parity (or better)* with competitive products.   We know that it is the rare green consumer who will buy an environmentally benign product that is more expensive than its more traditional counterpart. Performance is equally important. The product that does not perform up to snuff will be bought only once.

The environment is the tiebreaker. If all other factors are equal, then consumers will buy the environmentally friendlier product.

A corollary of this principle is that it is generally more advisable to target consumers' primary purchase criteria (i.e., price, performance, and convenience) rather than their underlying psychographics.

2. *Woo retailers aggressively.*   Green products that don't get stocked are green products that don't get bought. It is critically important to solicit the support of retailers to help make green products a success. Specific retailer-support strategies are discussed in Chapters 7, 9, and 10.

3. *Be environmental educators.*   Consumer education serves two purposes. First, it encourages consumers to seek out environmental information on product labels. Second, it helps them to understand the labels once they read them.

A variety of strategies can be deployed to guide consumers to environmental product information. In-store campaigns can make a big difference. So can media advertising. And, of course, as the environmental-education water table continues to rise among Americans, that in and of itself will induce a higher percentage of consumers to shop in a more environmental state of mind.

The labeling language that is used also plays a critically important role. Testifying before the EPA on behalf of the American Marketing Association, Jane Barnett of Jergens Inc. spoke of the need for a "consumer-friendly vocabulary." Her warning: "We are leaving the public behind.[17]

6

Regulation and Product Certification

A Brief History of Environmental Marketing Regulation

The Urgency (and Confusion) of Earth Day

Environmental marketing arose out of the crescendo in consumers' environmental concerns that accompanied Earth Day 1990. During that period and for the year or so immediately following, consumers felt a desperate urgency to do something about the environment—now! One side effect of this laudable and indeed well-founded sentiment was a wealth of well-intended but often ineffectual or counterproductive legislation, almost all of it at the state and local levels. Plastics-bashing was endemic, with numerous bills to prohibit plastics introduced at the state and local levels. Disposable diapers were banned in several jurisdictions, and laws in several states required plastic bags to be degradable.

In retrospect, Earth Day 1990 represented a surge at the beginning of consumers' environmental learning curve. For instance, at that time the concept of degradability seemed like an environmental cure-all. The logic went something like this: We have piles of garbage, and more keeps piling up all the time. If that garbage is designed to degrade, the piles will start getting smaller instead of bigger. Our problem will be solved!

It has taken only a few years for people to realize that modern sanitation requirements require trash in landfills to be constantly covered over. As a result, neither air nor light penetrates landfills, and nothing whatsoever degrades. The most that "degradable" plastics have to offer is the occasional specialty application (e.g., agricultural mulch film) along with the dubious distinction of decomposing into plastic "sand" when exposed to direct sunlight.

Disposable diapers provide another case in point. For years, they were a central target of environmental-group and consumer ire—reasonably enough, given that they constitute an impressive 2 percent of the solid waste in the nation's landfills. But then an independent consulting firm conducted an analysis that concluded that disposable diapers are no more environmentally harmful than cloth-diaper services once the energy costs of picking up, delivering, and washing diapers and the environmental damage associated with growing cotton have been factored in.

This study must be taken with a grain of salt because it was commissioned by disposable-diaper manufacturer Procter & Gamble. Still, it does serve as a reminder that the environmental impact of any product involves many factors, many obvious and many not-so-obvious.

Our ability to assess environmental impact is imperfect at best. As a result, we must live in uncertainty, with no clear answers about the relative environmental impacts of competing products. Fueled by the energy of Earth Day 1990, regulators and consumers were so eager to find solutions to the nation's many environmental problems that they tended to focus a great deal of attention on the seemingly "obvious" environmental villains while ignoring the essential fuzziness of environmental-impact analysis. The times were marked by a clear tendency to rush to judgment.

Marketers Rush In

Marketers couldn't miss the fact that the rush of environmental energy that accompanied Earth Day presented a powerful marketing opportunity. Simply tout the environmental performance of a product and presto! Increased sales.

The problems that followed were not due to the basic concept, which is innocuous enough, but with its execution. Environmental claims began to appear on product packaging which either had not been substantiated or were incapable of substantiation because their formulations were so vague as to be virtually meaningless.

"Ozone-friendly"

"Environmentally friendly"

"Degradable"

"Biodegradable"

"Recyclable"

"Recycled"

These were some of the terms that consumer-goods companies used to tout their products, and they shared one common characteristic: no one was quite sure what they meant.

At this point, we would be remiss if we failed to mention our personal favorite: "Nuclear-free."

Nuclear-free! As best we can interpret the term, it is intended to tell us one of two things about the product: Either it was not manufactured inside a nuclear power plant, or it is not an atom bomb.

The fact that both of these statements are true does not make the claim any more appropriate. Many environmental claims are problematic not because they are false, but because they are either trivial or irrelevant. It may be nice to know that a product wasn't bred in a nuclear reactor, but that doesn't make the information particularly relevant to the buy decision.

Absurd as it is, the nuclear-free claim tells us something important about the nature of many early environmental claims. They were not intended to give hard information so much as to convey warm, fuzzy, feel-good messages that would in effect coddle consumers into buying the product in question. Words like *recycled, degradable,* and, yes, *nuclear-free* were intended to create a simple link in consumers' minds: The environment ...the product ...we care ...it's good ...buy. These claims urged consumers not to think, but to react. They appealed to emotion, not to knowledge—a logical if not particularly ethical strategy, during a time when emotions were running high.

Enter the Law

Although the majority of marketers were conscientious in their environmental claims, there were enough attempts to manipulate consumers' environmental concerns through vague, unsubstantiated, trivial, or false claims to draw the attention of regulators. An early leader in the attempt to control environmental claims was Hubert H. Humphrey III, the attorney general of Minnesota (and the son of the late senator and vice president). As head of the Task Force of State Attorneys General, Humphrey spearheaded a landmark action against Mobil Chemical Company for labeling language claiming that its Hefty Trash Bags were degradable. Mobil based its claim on a chemical added to the plastic that decomposed in the presence of sunlight, allegedly making the bags photodegradable. Mobil acknowledged, however, that the majority of discarded trash bags ended up in incinerators and in landfills where the sun did not reach them. In regulators' minds, this fact made the degradable claim irrelevant. Mobil eventually settled with the states, paid a total of $150,000 in fines, and agreed to remove the word from its packaging.

From the earliest days of environmental marketing, Attorney General Humphrey and his task force have attempted to forge a middle ground between, on the one hand, allowing environmental claims to run amok, and on the other, having them disappear completely. Humphrey's position from the outset has been that environmental claims are desirable because they educate consumers and encourage manufacturers to compete on an environmental basis—but that false or deceptive environmental claims must be strictly controlled.

In attempting to control environmental claims, Humphrey's task force has followed two paths. It has brought legal actions such as the one against Mobil Chemical, and it has also produced two reports (commonly known as *Green Report I* and *Green Report II*) which attempt to lay out guidelines for environmental marketing. While these reports don't have the force of law, they do carry the power of persuasion. The company whose labeling practices fly in the face of the task force's recommendations either does so out of ignorance or is willfully inviting regulatory scrutiny.

The Task Force of State Attorneys General has not been alone in attempting to control environmental claims. California, Indiana, New York, Rhode Island, and other states have environmental labeling laws along with the necessary regulations in place.

In late 1991, the EPA issued preliminary recommendations for the terms *recyclable* and *recycled content*.

There has also been legislative activity. Senator Lautenberg of New Jersey and Congressman Sikorski of Minnesota have jointly introduced environmental labeling legislation that would require the EPA to develop regulations governing environmental marketing claims. These regulations would preempt FTC guidelines. As currently drafted, they would override weaker state laws but would not affect stronger state regulations. The likeliest outcome for this legislation is that it will become incorporated into the reauthorization of the landmark Resource Conservation and Recovery Act (RCRA), which is expected to be reenacted in either 1992 or 1993.

In lobbying for FTC environmental marketing guidelines, national marketers argued that it would either be too unwieldy or plain impossible for them to conform to the differing requirements of each state. If state environmental labeling regulations continued to proliferate, they said, they would simply stop making environmental claims about their products. This may or may not have been an idle threat. What *was* sure was that marketers *preferred* a single set of national guidelines.

These warnings may have served the political purpose of helping to achieve that end. In July 1992, the Federal Trade Commission issued voluntary environmental marketing guidelines.

As the completed manuscript of this book goes to press, it's too early to tell how national marketers will generally manage their environmental marketing claims against a backdrop of voluntary federal guidelines and differing state regulations.

Tables 6-1, 6-2, and 6-3 give a sense of the current state of environmental labeling regulation. The tables lay out differing definitions of key environmental labeling terms, as put forward by state regulations and various other "authorities." *Industry working group* refers to an informal business alliance which developed a set of voluntary environmental labeling guidelines.

Three Categories of Environmental Marketing Claim

Degradability. During the early period of environmental marketing, before "the law," headed up by Hubert H. Humphrey III, entered into the fray, many environmental marketing claims involved degradability. But as regulators started to come down on these claims, and as the media started treating degradability as a scam rather than a cure-all, degradability claims all but disappeared from the scene.

Environmentally Friendly/Ozone-Safe. Another popular claim in the early days of environmental marketing was of the environmentally-friendly, ozone-safe, or ozone-friendly variety. These claims have now become basically extinct, as is the case with degradability. Vague and unsubstantiated claims of this sort continue to surface from time to time, which only goes to show the extent to which some marketers have their heads in the sand. Even the most cursory familiarity with the current regulatory environment will make it clear that vague, unsubstantiated claims of this sort are virtually guaranteed to attract the attention of regulators.

Recyclability/Compostability. More recently, attention has focused on the term *recyclable* and the companion concept *compostability*. Here, uncertainties revolve around the terms' vagueness. Used without amplification, recyclable and compostable

Table 6-1. Definitions of *Recyclable*

State or organization	Recyclable standard
California	The article can be conveniently recycled in every county with a population exceeding 300,000.
CONEG	The material has achieved a statewide recycling rate established by the regulations (20% by 1/1/90, 35% by 1/1/95, 50% by 1/1/2000).
Industry Working Group	Urges caution in using the term *recyclable*. Provides nine examples of cases in which the use of the term would be appropriate or inappropriate.
New York	Material must meet one of the following criteria: (1) 75% of population has access to recycling programs for the material; (2) statewide 50% recycling programs for the material; (3) recycling rate of 50% for a particular product or package, achieved by the manufacturer, distributor, or retailer; (4) the product or package is recyclable within a particular jurisdiction.
Northeast Recycling Coalition	Package-product standards as described in (1), (2), and (3) for New York, above.
Procter & Gamble	A product or package is recyclable if it can be collected or otherwise placed into currently available state-of-the-art recycling facilities, and from those facilities can be practically processed into a commodity or product for which a market exists. The qualifying phrase "where facilities exist" should always be used, because recycling capacity is not available everywhere.
Rhode Island	For most materials, material must achieve a 50% recycling rate. Products also can be labeled "recyclable" if they are labeled as such in at least five northeast states representing at least 75% of the population, even if the material is not recyclable in Rhode Island.
State Attorneys General *Green Report*	Products should not be promoted as recyclable unless the particular items is currently recycled in a significant amount in the state in which the advertisement is made. (*Editor's Note:* The revised *Green Report*, due out in April, may define recyclable differently.)

SOURCES: *Green MarketAlert*, Wisconsin Department of Agriculture, Trade & Consumer Protection.

Table 6-2. Definitions of *Recycled Content*

A brief review of the chart reveals how sharply the approaches to defining "recycled content" differ. New York establishes minimum standards, including postconsumer content levels; Rhode Island merely calls for specificity; Scientific Certification Systems, the product certification program, adds a "state-of-the-art" requirement.

Amidst this maelstrom of definitions, marketers have little choice but to conform their use of "recycled content" to the definition of the state with the most rigorous requirements in which they plan to distribute product.

State, bill, or organization	Recycled content standard
California	The article contains at least 10% postconsumer material by weight.
Scientific Certification Systems	To be certified as having recycled content, a product or package must contain a minimum of 10% recycled content. The percentage of recycled material used in a product must equal or exceed at least 80% of the level verified to be state-of-the-art for a given product. Consumer and industrial waste qualifies as recycled material, but industrial scrap does not.
Industry Working Group	Urges caution in use of term *recycled* by itself. Encourages statements of the percentage of recycled material in a package or product. Suggests claims be clear as to which part of a package contains recycled material except where average recycled content of a multicomponent package is being stated. Considers material to be recycled if it would otherwise have ended up in the solid waste stream.
New York State	Package or product must contain a minimum percentage by weight of secondary material and a minimum percentage by weight of postconsumer material, with specific requirements differing by product category, e.g., plastic packaging (30% recycled material of which 15% must be postconsumer), high-grade printing and writing papers (50% recycled material of which 10% must be postconsumer beginning in 1994).
Northeast Recycling Coalition	The product or package must identify the pre- and postconsumer composition (by weight) of the product or package.
Procter & Gamble	For a product to contain recycled materials, the formulation must consist of secondary materials which include postconsumer materials. For a package, the type of recycled material should be specified and, if the amount of recycled content is less than 25%, the claim should specify the actual percentage content.

Table 6-2. Definitions of *Recycled Content (Continued)*

State, bill, or organization	Recycled content standard
Rhode Island	The recycled emblem can be used if the product or package states the percentage by weight of preconsumer and postconsumer material it contains.
S.615—Environmental Marketing Claims Act	Postconsumer materials must equal 25% by weight prior to 2000, and 50% by weight after 2000. If this standard is not met, the term recycled can still be used if, in lettering no smaller than the lettering of the claim, the package clearly states the actual percentage of recycled material in the product.
State Attorneys General *Green Report*	The percentage of recycled material used in the product should be disclosed on any product labeled recycled. A distinction should be made between preconsumer and postconsumer recycled material.

SOURCES: *Green Market Alert*, Wisconsin Department of Agriculture, Trade & Consumer Protection.

seem to suggest that the product or package in question is universally recyclable or compostable, when that is often not the case.

A turning point in this controversy came when legal actions were brought against the makers of aseptic packaging (and eventually also against their advertising agency) for advertisements in newspapers claiming that aseptic packages (also known as drink boxes) were "as easy to recycle as this page." The text went on to state that "It may be surprising to know that drink boxes are as easy to recycle as your daily newspaper. That's because separating the components of a drink box is no more difficult than separating newsprint paper from a coating of ink."

Although aseptic packages are technically recyclable, that doesn't help the consumer from Somewhere, U.S.A. who wants to recycle a drink box—not unless that person happens to have the good fortune to live in one of the handful of regions where pilot aseptic packaging programs are under way. The "as easy to recycle as this page" ads blurred the important distinction between *feasibility* and *availability*.

Another important environmental marketing case involved a print ad by Procter & Gamble. A photograph showed a handful of soil, and large-print text read: "Ninety days ago this was a disposable diaper." Then, in smaller text, came text lauding accelerated composting technology. One sentence read: "While (accelerated) composting isn't available everywhere, ten U.S. communities already have programs in place." Despite

Table 6-3. Definitions of *Degradable* and *Compostable*

State, bill, or organization	Definition
California	*Biodegradable:* A material has the proven capability to decompose in the most common environment where the material is disposed, within one year, through natural biological processes into nontoxic carbonaceous soil, water, or carbon dioxide.
	Photodegradable: A material has the proven capability to decompose in the most common environment where the material is disposed, within one year, through physical processes such as exposure to heat and light, into nontoxic carbonaceous soil, water, or carbon dioxide.
	A proposed bill would amend the definitions of biodegradable and photodegradable and also add a definition of compostable. As finally adopted, compostable may be brought under the revised definition of "biodegradable."
Florida	Plastic shopping bags must be tested by an independent service, under ASTM standards, to show degradability and limits for toxicity.
Industry Working Group	Encourages use of *compostability* in appropriate contexts such as "compostable where facilities exist." Does not address degradable.
Rhode Island	Retail packaging cannot be imprinted with the terms degradable, biodegradable, or photodegradable.
S.615 Environmental Marketing Claims Act	A product/package is compostable if the manufacturer, retailer or distributor can show it will be composted at a 25% rate before 2000 and 50% after 2000, and will not release toxic or harmful materials.
State Attorneys General *Green Report II*	Products that are primarily disposed of in landfills or through incineration—whether paper or plastic—should not be promoted as degradable, biodegradable, or photodegradable. Unqualified compostability claims are not to be made unless a significant amount of the product is currently being composted everywhere the product is sold. In all other cases, compostability claims should be accompanied by a clear disclosure about the limited availability of this disposal option.

SOURCES: *Green MarketAlert*, Wisconsin Department of Agriculture, Trade & Consumer Protection.

the smaller-print text describing the limited nature of current accelerated composting operations, the Task Force of State Attorneys General deemed this advertisement misleading enough to bring suit.

When is availability sufficient to justify the use of the term recyclable? What sort of qualifying language is appropriate for notifying consumers that recyclability may differ from area to area? The debate about the term has revolved around these two questions. The California environmental labeling law currently requires an article to be "conveniently recycled ... i n every county in California with a population of over 300,000 persons." This piece of legislation requires marketers to perform a double miracle: first, by tracking on an ongoing basis which of the qualifying counties is up to recycling speed; and second, by controlling distribution so as to ensure that the right labels go to the right counties.

The Task Force of State Attorneys General's *Green Report II* is much more reasonable. The report states;

> Unqualified recyclability claims should not be made for products sold nationally unless a significant amount of the product is being recycled everywhere the product is sold. Where a product is being recycled in many areas of the country, a qualified recyclability claim can be made. If consumers have little or no opportunity to recycle a product, recyclability claims should not be made.[1]

Summary of FTC Environmental Marketing Guidelines

Now let's turn to the Federal Trade Commission for further environmental claims guidance. The following is a summary of the FTC Environmental Marketing Guidelines as issued by the FTC:

Background:

> The Federal Trade Commission's Guides for the use of Environmental Marketing Claims are based on a review of data obtained during FTC law-enforcement investigations, from two days of hearings the FTC held in July 1991, and from more than 100 written comments received from the public. Like all FTC guides, they are administrative interpretations of laws administered by the FTC. Thus, while they are not themselves legally enforceable, they provide guidance to marketers in conforming with legal requirements. The guides apply to advertising, labeling and other forms of marketing to consumers. They do not preempt state or local laws or regulations.
>
> The Commission will seek public comment on whether to modify the guides after three years. In the meantime, interested parties may petition the Commission to amend the guides.

Basically, the guides describe various claims, note those that should be avoided because they are likely to be misleading, and illustrate the kinds of qualifying statements that may have to be added to other claims to avoid consumer deception. The claims are followed by examples that illustrate the points. The guides outline principles that apply to all environmental claims, and address the use of eight commonly used environmental marketing claims.

General Concerns:

As for any advertising claim, the FTC guides specify that any time marketers make objective environmental claims—whether explicit or implied—they must be substantiated by competent and reliable evidence. In the case of environmental claims, that evidence often will have to be competent and reliable scientific evidence.

The guides outline four other general concerns that apply to all environmental claims. These are:

1. Qualifications and disclosures should be sufficiently clear and prominent to prevent deception.
2. Environmental claims should make clear whether they apply to the product, the package, or a component of either. Claims need not be qualified with regard to minor, incidental components of the product or package.
3. Environmental claims should not overstate the environmental attribute or benefit. Marketers should avoid implying a significant environmental benefit where the benefit is, in fact, negligible.
4. A claim comparing the environmental attributes of one product with those of another product should make the basis for the comparison sufficiently clear and should be substantiated.

The guides then discuss particular environmental marketing claims. In most cases, each discussion is followed in the guides by a series of examples to illustrate how the principles apply to specific claims.

General environmental benefit claims. In general, unqualified general environmental claims are difficult to interpret, and may have a wide range of meanings to consumers. Every express and material implied claim conveyed to consumers about an objective quality should be substantiated. Unless they can be substantiated, broad environmental claims should be avoided or qualified.

Degradable, Biodegradable, and Photodegradable. In general, unqualified degradability claims should be substantiated by evidence that the product will completely break down and return to nature, that is, decompose into elements found in nature within a reasonable short period of time after consumers dispose of it in the customary way. Such claims should be qualified to the extent necessary to avoid consumer deceptions about: (a) the product or package's ability to degrade in the environment where it is customarily disposed and (b) the extent and rate of degradation.

Compostable. In general, unqualified compostable claims should be substantiated by evidence that all the materials in the product or package will break down into, or otherwise become part of, usable compost (e.g., soil-conditioning material, mulch) in a safe and timely manner in an appropriate composting program or facility, or in a home compost pile or device. Compostable claims should be qualified to the extent necessary to avoid consumer deception: (1) if municipal composting facilities are not available to a substantial majority of consumers or communities where the product is sold; (2) if the claim misleads consumers about the environmental benefit provided when the product is disposed of in a landfill; or (3) if consumers misunderstand the claim to mean that the package can be safely composted in their home compost pile or device, when in fact it cannot.

Recyclable. In general, a product or package should not be marketed as recyclable unless it can be collected, separated, or otherwise recovered from the solid waste stream for use in the form of raw materials in the manufacture or assembly of a new product or package. Unqualified recyclable claims may be made if the entire product or package, excluding incidental components, is recyclable.

Claims about products with both recyclable and non-recyclable components should be adequately qualified. If incidental components significantly limit the ability to recycle product, the claim would be deceptive. If, because of its size or shape, a product is not accepted in recycling programs, it should not be marketed as recyclable. Qualification may be necessary to avoid consumer deception about the limited availability of recycling programs and collection sites if recycling collection sites are not available to a substantial majority of consumers or communities.

Recycled Content. In general, claims of recycled content should only be made for materials that have been recovered or diverted from the solid waste stream, either during the manufacturing process (pre-consumer) or after consumer waste (post-consumer). An advertiser should be able to substantiate that pre-consumer content would otherwise have entered the solid waste stream. Distinctions made between pre- and post-consumer content should be substantiated. Unqualified claims may be made if the entire product or package, excluding minor, incidental components, is made from recycled material. Products or packages only partially made of recycled material should be qualified to indicate the amount, by weight, in the finished product or package.

Source Reduction. In general, claims that a product or package has been reduced or is lower in weight, volume, or toxicity should be qualified to the extent necessary to avoid consumer deception about the amount of reduction and the basis for any comparison asserted.

Refillable. In general, an unqualified refillable claim should not be asserted unless a system is provided for: (1) the collection and return of the package for refill; or (2) the later refill of the package by consumers with product subsequently sold in another package. The claim should not be made if it is up to the consumers to find ways to refill the package.

Ozone Safe and Ozone Friendly. In general, a product should not be advertised as "ozone safe," "ozone friendly," or as not containing CFCs if the product contains any ozone-depleting chemical. Claims about the reduction of a product's ozone-depletion potential may be made if adequately substantiated.[2]

The Impact on Business

It's not regulatory action per se that is so damaging to a corporation—actual penalties are usually modest—but the attendant publicity. A number of environmental marketing actions, especially the ones against Mobil Chemical, the aseptic packaging manufacturers, and American Enviro Products (the latter for a degradability claim), have been accompanied by extensive media coverage.

Many companies have opted to proceed cautiously rather than risk this sort of negative exposure. However, the issuance of guidelines by the FTC is widely expected to give environmental labeling a boost.

It is nevertheless important to distinguish treading water in environmental labeling from inactivity on the green product or environmental-management fronts. Regulation is producing caution in companies' strategic approaches to labeling (more caution than necessary, perhaps), but it is not preventing U.S. corporations from moving forward aggressively in other areas. Companies are constantly improving the environmental performance of their products, if not touting that fact on their packages. They are also taking a multitude of steps in other areas to improve their overall environmental performance. However, evidence of these activities is not appearing on supermarket shelves.

Table 6-4 presents a comprehensive list of the environmental marketing actions that were brought in 1990 and 1991.

Self-Regulation

As I mentioned earlier, the FTC guidelines are just that—guidelines. They may not preempt existing (or future) state regulations. So who do you trust?

The *Advertising Age* Environmental Marketing and Advertising Council is advocating that business turn to the Council of Better Business Bureaus' National Advertising Division (NAD) for claims guidance and industry self regulation. According to Robert M. Viney, vice president of international marketing at Church & Dwight Co., Inc.

Table 6-4. Green Marketing Oversight Index (through December 1991)

First announced	Company	Product type	Type of claim	Language	Regulatory body	Action taken
October 17, 1990	American Enviro Products	Disposable diapers	Degradability	"Biodegradable" "Will biodegrade before your child grows up"	State Task Force of AGs	Consent Agreement
December 9, 1990	Combibloc, Tetra-Pak	Drink boxes	Recyclability	"As easy to recycle as this page"	Consumer Affairs Department, City of New York	Consent Agreement
March 21, 1991	Webster Industries	Plastic waste bags	Degradability	"Degrade into harmless organic powder" "Contain photodegradable additive"	Consumer Affairs Department, City of New York	Consent Agreement
March 21, 1991	Key Food	Plastic shopping bags	Degradability	"Degrades in sunlight"	Consumer Affairs Department, City of New York	Consent Agreement
March 21, 1991	RKO Warner Video	Plastic shopping bags	Degradability	"This bag is photodegradable"	Consumer Affairs Department, City of New York	Consent Agreement
March 21, 1991	Daffy's Stores	Plastic shopping bags	Degradability	"This bag is recycled plastic and is degradable"	Consumer Affairs Department, City of New York	Consent Agreement
March 21, 1991	Procter & Gamble	Disposable diapers	Compostability	"Ninety days ago this was a disposable diaper"	Consumer Affairs Department, City of New York	Consent Agreement
March 21, 1991	Icelandic Spring Water	Drink boxes	Degradability	"Biodegradable packaging"	Consumer Affairs Department, City of New York	Consent Agreement

Date	Company	Product	Claim	Quoted Claim	Agency	Status
April 22, 1991	Zipatone, Inc.	Spray cement	Environmentally friendly	"Ecologically-Safe Propellant" "...you get the job done quickly without damaging the environment"	Federal Trade Commission	Consent Agreement
May 9, 1991	Sloan's Supermarkets	Plastic shopping bags	Degradability	"Degradable bag" "Will begin degrading within three days of exposure to ultraviolet light"	Consumer Affairs Department, City of New York	Consent Agreement
May 9, 1991	Pathmark Supermarkets	Plastic shopping bags	Degradability	"Degradable," "Non-toxic when incinerated"	Consumer Affairs Department, City of New York	Consent Agreement
May 9, 1991	Love Pharmacy	Plastic shopping bags	Degradability	"Degradable bag," "Will begin degrading within three days of exposure to ultraviolet light"	Consumer Affairs Department, City of New York	Consent Agreement
May 9, 1991	Down to Earth stores	Plastic shopping bags	Degradability Recyclability	"This bag is biodegradable and recyclable"	Consumer Affairs Department, City of New York	Pending
June 5, 1991	Jerome Russell Cosmetics	Hair care and other beauty aid products	Ozone-safe	"Ozone-safe" "Ozone-friendly"	Federal Trade Commission	Consent Agreement
June 27, 1991	Mobil Chemical Company	Plastic waste bags	Degradability	"Degradable"	State Task Force of AGs	Consent Agreement
July 2, 1991	Webster Industries	Plastic waste bags	Environmentally friendly Degradability	"Environmentally safe" "Photodegradable"	State Task Force of AGs	Consent Agreement

SOURCE: Green MarketAlert.

Table 6-4. Green Marketing Oversight Index (through December 1991) (*Continued*)

First Announced	Company	Product type	Type of claim	Language	Regulatory body	Action taken
August 5, 1991	Alberto-Culver Company	Hair spray products	Environmentally friendly Ozone safe	"Environmentally safe" "Ozone friendly"	State Task Force of AGs	Consent Agreement
August 28, 1991	Tetra Pak Combibloc Lintas, Inc.	Drink boxes	Recyclability	"As easy to recycle as your daily newspaper	State Task Force of AGs	Consent Agreement
August 30, 1991	American Enviro Products	Disposable diapers	Biodegradability	"Will dispose in landfill "within 3–5 years" or "before your child grows up"	Federal Trade Commission	Consent Agreement
October 9, 1991	First Brands	Plastic waste bags	Environmentally friendly Degradability	"Safe for the environ-ment" "Offers a significant en-vironmental benefit when consumers dis-pose of them as trash."	Federal Trade Commission	Consent Agreement
October 10, 1991	Clairol, Inc.	Hair sprays	Environmentally friendly	"Environmentall safe"	State Task Force of AGs	Consent Agreement
October 10, 1991	The Drackett Co.	Household cleaners	Ozone safe	"Use with confidence... contains no fluorocar-bons alleged to damage ozone"	State Task Force of AGs	Consent Agreement
October 10, 1991	Westwood Pharmaceu-ticals, Inc.	Sunscreen	Ozone safe	"Ozone safe"	State Task Force of AGs	Consent Agreement

Date	Company	Product	Claim	Quote	Agency	Status
October 15, 1991	Rockline, Inc.	Coffee filters	CEnvironmentally friendly	"Environmentally friendly product and packaging"	National Advertising Division/Council for Better Business Bureaus	Advertising modified or discontinued
October 16, 1991	Colgate-Palmolive	Dishwashing liquid	Vague use of "new" Unsubstantiated exclusivity claims	"New Bottlel With 20% recycled plastic" "...the only dishwashing liquid made with 20% previously used plastic..."	National Advertising Division /Council for Better Business Bureaus	Advertising modified or discontinued
November 14, 1991	Procter & Gamble	Disposable diapers	Compostability	"Ninety days ago this was a disposable diaper," "Environmental Information... This product is compostable in municipal composing units."	State Task Force of AGs	Consent Agreement
July 17, 1991	Revlon, Inc.	Hair sprays	Environmentally friendly	"Environmentally safe"	Consumer Affairs Department, City of New York	Consent Agreement
July 17, 1991	Procter & Gamble	Anti-perspirants	Ozone safe	"Contain no CFCs which harm the ozone layer"	Consumer Affairs Department, City of New York	Pending
July 17, 1991	S.C. Johnson & Son	Furniture polish, air fresheners, shaving gel	Ozone safe	"Contain no propellant alleged to damage ozone"	Consumer Affairs Department, City of New York	Consent Agreement
July 17, 1991	Gillette	Shave cream, hair sprays, anti-perspirants	Ozone safe	"Ozone Friendly No CFCs"	Consumer Affairs Department, City of New York	Pending

Source: Green MarketAlert.

and a member of the Environmental Marketing and Advertising Council:

> The NAD [review] process is quick—it is completed in 60 days—it is open, objective and effective in getting claims revised or dropped when appropriate. National guidelines from the FTC, endorsed by the EPA, supported by an effective and easily accessible NAD review process to help ensure compliance, might be preferable to an overly proscriptive legislative approach on either a state-by-state or federal basis.[3]

Product Certification

We have seen in Chapter 5 how environmental labeling claims in the United States have been met with suspicion from consumers and regulators alike. That is precisely the reason why product certification programs exist—to allow credible, third-party organizations to pass judgment on the environmental performance of products and packages, rather than leave the assertions to the product manufacturers themselves, who are of course biased.

U.S. consumers strongly support the idea of a product certification authority. In a survey conducted by the Good Housekeeping Institute, 82 percent of consumers indicated that a product certification program would affect their buy decisions (Figure 6-1).[4]

The United States is lagging behind other countries in the development and deployment of a product certification system. The main reason for this is the failure of the federal government to put its weight behind the concept. Lacking formal authorization from either the White House or Congress, the EPA has supported projects to further the state of the art of scientific life-cycle analysis (LCA), but otherwise has been inactive. It has been left to two competing private organizations, Green Seal and Scientific Certification Systems (formerly known as Green Cross), to try to bootstrap a product certification system into being in the United States.

An International and Historical Perspective

Germany. The first environmental labeling program was launched in (then) West Germany in 1978. Called the Blue Angel program, the program got off to a slow start but now has certified over 3500

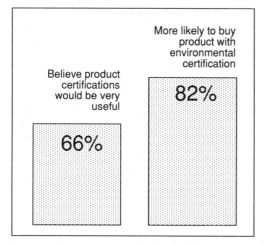

Figure 6-1. Green-product certification programs: consumer opinion (*Good Housekeeping Institute*)

products. The Blue Angel symbol comes from the United Nations Environment Programme.

The program explicitly sets out to increase the market share of green products. Applications to certify products that already have a substantial share of market will not be entertained, on the principle that approval would not tilt the overall balance of the market toward more environmentally-friendly products.

Given the track record of the leading product certification program in the world for intentionally tinkering with market dynamics, it comes as no surprise that the major consumer goods companies in the United States have been ardently resisting product certification programs. Their logic is as impeccable as it is unfortunate for the green-products marketplace: "We're winning without this extra referee—why ask for trouble?"

Another interesting point about the Blue Angel program is that early versions of the logo included the term *Umweltfreundlich* (environmentally-friendly). It's likely that many consumer goods companies took this as a seal of approval of sorts and promptly began sticking environmentally-friendly claims on their own packages. By now, environmentally-friendly has evolved into one of a handful of Class-A-felony environmental marketing phrases (others being ozone friendly, ozone safe, and the several variants of degradable). *Umweltfreundlich* no longer appears on the Blue Angel logo.

West Germany was the first country with a product certification program, but it is by no means the only one. Over 10 countries currently have product certification programs, and the number is growing rapidly.

Canada.   Canada's Environmental Choice program was launched in 1988, with labeled products first appearing on store shelves in March 1990. According to a 1991 study entitled *Environmental Labeling in OECD Countries*, written by James Salzman of the OECD, four principles guide the Environmental Choice program's product-approval process:

> First, favor is given to addressing significant long-term environmental issues rather than short-term issues that are likely to be addressed through regulations.
>
> Second, the entire life cycle of a product should be considered before establishing criteria, even though the guidelines can only cover a few of the product's aspects.
>
> Third, the program should serve to educate the consumer of environmental trade-offs, that even a labeled product may not be *absolutely* safe for the environment and that the label certifies the product, not the company.
>
> Finally, the label should promote industry leadership through identifying the environmentally superior goods. In fact, in setting high criteria, the program has set a rough target of 10%-20% of the eligible market which can qualify for the label. Over time this percentage should increase as the product category as a whole improves its environmental norms. At a certain point, the criteria will be raised to new standards to once again identify a small number of environmentally superior goods.[5]

To date, some 650 products in 34 product categories have received the Environmental Choice label.

Environmental Choice is serving as the model for product certification programs in New Zealand and Australia.

Japan.   Japan's Eco-Mark program was launched in February 1989. The Eco-Mark symbol consists of two arms embracing the world. The arms form the letter *e*, standing for environment, earth, or ecology— take your choice.

The Japanese program differs somewhat from other programs by working within a simplified structure which facilitates product certification. This allowed the Eco-Mark program to certify 850 labels in 31 different product categories in its first year and a half in existence. Now Japanese authorities are reportedly rethinking this bring-everyone-on-board approach.

European Community. Most international marketers are paying close attention to the eco-label program unfolding in the European Community. Baker & McKenzie, the world's largest international law firm, provides us with this current overview of the EC eco-label program:

> In an attempt to promote the production and purchase of products with as low an environmental cost as possible, the Council adopted in principle on December 12, 1991 a regulation to establish a "European Ecological Label" which would be affixed only to products meeting certain environmental standards. The proposal is concerned with the total "cradle to grave" impact of the product, from its production through its distribution, use or consumption and disposal. A product will only be permitted to bear the label if, on the basis of such an assessment, it is substantially less damaging to the environment than other products of the same category. The label will be awarded on the basis of detailed specifications for each product category by a jury established at Community level and including representatives of industry, commerce, consumer and environmental protection groups, trade unions and the media. The award of the label itself will be by national bodies, but the Commission may be entitled to object.[6]

At a conference on EC environmental policies and practices that was held in the summer of 1992, a senior representative of the IBM Corporation was asked if his company would consider applying for an EC eco-label if one of his competitors did. His reply was "Yes."

Back in the U.S.A

In the United States, two private, nonprofit organizations are vying to become the product certification organization of choice and, in the process, to institutionalize product certification. Unfortunately, the road to product certification has to date been rocky.

The Contenders. The two competitors for the title of product certification champion, Green Seal and SCS, have similar objectives but strikingly different identities.

Green Seal until recently was headed by Denis Hayes, an ex-lawyer with impeccable environmentalist credentials: he is widely recognized as the principal organizer of Earth Day. The roots of SCS, by contrast, are more scientific than environmentalist. The President of SCS is Stanley Rhodes, a toxicologist by training.

This has caused the two organizations to approach product certification issues from somewhat different standpoints. SCS has tended to stress its scientific expertise, implying more than once that it takes a squadron of Ph.D.s to deliver the sort of know-how that can make a success of product certification. Green Seal has tended to be somewhat more market- and consumer-oriented, speaking in less technical language and directing its public comments less to issues of feasibility and more to questions of marketplace impact.

This disparity in approaches can be illustrated by differing strategic approaches which the two companies had in the 1990–1991 time frame. During this period, SCS was only certifying specific aspects of a product's or package's environmental performance—for instance, the recycled-paper content of a package. Thus, a typical SCS label would state something like, "Certified to contain 70 percent recycled material, of which 20 percent is postconsumer."

During this period, SCS argued that this was the only reasonable approach to product certification because more comprehensive life-cycle analyses (LCAs) were not feasible. Green Seal countered that slicing the product pie in this manner would do more harm than good because consumers would mistakenly assume that the logo constituted a general product endorsement. What about the case, Green Seal argued, when a product's package did contain recycled materials but was otherwise an environmental disaster?

Given SCS's heavy emphasis on its scientific know-how, it would be reasonable to expect them to have a much more methodical *modus operandi* than Green Seal, but this has not been the case. After arguing against life-cycle analysis on the grounds that accurate LCAs were not feasible, the organization did an abrupt flip-flop in 1991 and came out for life-cycle analysis, arguing that breakthroughs by the British specialist Ian Boustead had caused them to change their tune.

The SCS/Boustead model examines life-cycle performance in six distinct areas of what it calls environmental burden:

1. Raw materials consumption

2. Energy consumption

3. Emissions into air

4. Emissions into water

5. Solid-waste generation

6. Collateral resource consumption (e.g., destruction of wildlife habitat, species preservation)

Some life-cycle experts believe that SCS is promising the impossible—that life-cycle analysis is not yet sufficiently advanced to deliver what

SCS claims it can. Other experts believe that SCS has gone beyond the leading edge on life-cycle assessment.

Green Seal has proceeded with no reversals of direction and much less fanfare than SCS, enduring substantial criticism along the way for moving too slowly in an area that seems to demand prompt action. But by early 1992 proposed certification criteria had begun to flow from Green Seal, with re-refined motor oil, water-efficient fixtures, and toilet and facial tissue among the organization's early proposed standards.

Recently, Green Seal partnered with the well-established and highly regarded Underwriters Laboratories, Inc. (UL). UL conducts most of Green Seal's product evaluations and factory inspections.

Green Seal's approach to product certification is patterned after Canada's Environmental Choice program. Its so-called environmental impact evaluations do not make any claims to comprehensiveness, as the SCS/Boustead model does. Instead, only selected aspects of a product's life-cycle performance (e.g., manufacturing, recycled content, toxic contaminants) are scrutinized. Whereas SCS proposes to examine every letter of the environmental alphabet, Green Seal is taking what it believes to be the more realistic approach of limiting itself to evaluations of specific letters.

Unlike Green Seal, SCS is offering manufacturers a menu of options. In addition to opting for a full-scale Boustead LCA, companies can have specific aspects (e.g., recycled content) of the product-packaging combination certified. Or, they can opt for the middle ground of certification in one or more of SCS's six areas of environmental burden.

The Price of Competition.   By and large, the major U.S. consumer goods companies are not favorably disposed toward product certification. For them, third-party certification represents an unwelcome and unnecessary intrusion into a laissez-faire market environment which has allowed them to thrive. They are leery about supporting the creation of any independent authority that could take decision-making authority away from them—and when the authorities they are being asked to raise into being are as small and as untested as SCS and Green Seal, they are doubly leery.

Many smaller manufacturers feel quite differently about product certification. For them, product certification is a way to create a more level playing field.

But the future of product certification is not in the hands of these small suppliers. Product certification requires the support of the major consumer goods companies.

The ongoing competition between SCS and Green Seal has added a host of additional uncertainties to what for many manufacturers is the already problematic nature of product certification. *Even if product certification is a good idea, how do I know which program to sign up with? If there are two active product certification programs, will the public-policy benefits of product certification be undone?* These are the sorts of questions that consumer goods companies are asking, and they are not making product certification any easier to sell.

The Prospects.   Based on the above discussion, it is clear that it will not be easy for SCS and Green Seal to establish product certification in the United States. These small, modestly funded organizations have taken on a task which by all rights should belong to the federal government. Around the world, it has taken the enormous monetary and jawboning power of central governments to give birth to effective product certification programs.

Still, things are not as bleak as they might appear. As I write, Green Seal has indicated that they are evaluating the products of two national brand marketers and SCS just recently certified—as containing no smog-producing ingredients (VOCs)—two paint lines of The Glidden Company (an ICI Americas company).

There are a number of countervailing forces which, taken cumulatively, suggest that despite the many challenges which lie ahead for SCS and Green Seal, product certification may eventually establish itself in the United States.

For one thing, SCS's and Green Seal's efforts are not occurring in a vacuum. Internationally, the momentum for product certification is strong. The various roadblocks notwithstanding, it is not at all clear that the United States will be able to resist this momentum.

In addition, although manufacturers resist third-party product certification, consumers support the idea. It is one of capitalism's most fundamental tenets that the company that listens to its customers gains a competitive edge. Eventually, one of the consumer goods companies may hark to this fact in the context of product certification—and this in turn could open the floodgates.

There are three scenarios for how this could occur:

- *Scenario 1.*   A major consumer goods company decides to steal a march on the competition by taking a flyer on product certification.
- *Scenario 2.*   Although none of the leading consumer goods companies throw their weight behind product certification, many small companies sign on and measurable cumulative shifts in market share begin to occur, drawing the attention of the majors and making their conversion to product certification a foregone conclusion.

- *Scenario 3.* The federal government gets more actively involved in product certification, raising the confidence level of the consumer goods majors.

In short, in order to succeed, product certification needs one big break, or lots of little ones. Despite the many challenges facing SCS and Green Seal, both of these outcomes remain distinct possibilities.

The Business Impacts of Product Certification

Will product certification help boost a company's market share? The answer to that question depends in part on the state of advancement of a product certification program. In the early stages, i.e., when only a few companies have received it, product certification is likely to supply a greater competitive advantage than when the program is more advanced, at which point product certification will do less to differentiate a product from the pack.

The OECD report mentioned above directly addressed the question of the impact of product certification on market share:

> The twelve years of operation of the German program provide the best data base for assessing the effect of environmental labels. The program apparently does affect consumer purchasing patterns, because manufacturers are increasingly proposing new product categories for labels (about 200 proposals per year) and applying for labels in already selected product categories. This, in itself, suggests that manufacturers believe environmental labels will increase product sales....

The fact that manufacturers believe that product certification increases market share, although significant in its own right, does not prove that it does. However, the OECD report goes on to cite another study (*Eco-Labels: Product Management in a Greener Europe*, from the U.K.-based Environmental Data Services), which found, according to the OECD study, that "environmental labels could influence *consumer* and manufacturer behavior [italics added]."

The Environmental Data Services report went on to hedge its bets, stating that the impact of product certification varies from market to market. In the worst cases, according to the OECD's discussion of the Environmental Data Services report, demand increased only slightly.

The salient point to us is not that the benefits of product certification were only slight but that, even in the worst cases, they exist at all. We conclude from the OECD report that product certification has a positive effect on sales, regardless of the market.

In the United States, anecdotal evidence suggests that product certification to date has had little if any measurable impact on sales. Still, product certification in our estimation remains a viable business strategy. At this point, there are five main reasons for pursuing product certification:

1. Product certification allows companies to establish a product's environmental merits while sheltering them from the storm that is currently blowing around much of today's "private" (usually retailer) environmental labeling.

2. Certification can facilitate a company's entry into retail channels. A number of major retailers have strongly encouraged their suppliers to seek product certification.

3. As we noted earlier, consumers want environmentally certified products—overwhelmingly. From this perspective, environmental seals are straightforward exercises in customer satisfaction.

4. More generally, certification helps companies establish their environmental *bona fides*. This aids in the recruiting process, and it also improves their long-term marketing positioning.

5. More abstractly, but no less significantly, third-party product certification is a way for a company to stand up and be counted, to publicly come out in favor of the need for a quantum leap in the importance assigned by consumers and the business community alike to the environment. Once product certification becomes widespread in the United States, it will be more of a competitive necessity than a mechanism for differentiation. In the meantime, however, it offers a way for companies to establish the depth of their environmental commitment. Product certification amounts to a shifting of priorities, to a declaration that the environment is so important that a modest reduction in a corporation's "strategic freedom of choice" is an acceptable price to pay.

Summary and Recommendations

Both the regulatory and product-certification environments are in flux. The regulatory situation is currently characterized by a multiplicity of authorities and by the concern of product marketers about possible regulatory balkanization. Product certification proponents SCS and Green Seal are in the early stages of trying to bootstrap a product certification system into existence. Here, marketers are concerned not about possible balkanization so much as about the possibility that by helping to bring into being a quasi-regulatory product certification authority, their own strategic independence might be undermined.

Caution is warranted with regard to environmental labeling. However, it would be premature to abandon the area entirely. Judiciously worded environmental labeling provides a competitive advantage, and it is also important for public-policy reasons to attempt to educate consumers through environmental labeling.

Product certification must also be approached circumspectly. The current environment is complex and confusing. Here, too, however, a stand-aside strategy also has its risks. Product certification warrants serious examination.

7
The Environmental Marketing Infrastructure

Introduction

In previous chapters, we have discussed three players who go a long way toward establishing the rules of the game in environmental marketing—consumers, environmental advocacy groups, and regulators. In this chapter, we examine the role of five additional key sets of players in the environmental marketing mix: (1) retailers; (2) industry and trade associations; (3) regulatory bodies; (4) policy and educational institutions; and (5) scientific and technical institutions.

Retailers

Reason for Concern

Supermarkets are the battleground where the forces of supply and demand meet. Although many national marketers have 800 numbers, it is still the retailers who must respond daily to consumers' complaints, worries, and desires. It is retailers who must pick up the packaging which customers bent on making a political statement strip off and leave on their floors. It is retailers who are expected to supply paper bags instead of plastic—and if they *do* offer plastic, either as an alternative or exclusively, they'd better have a plastic-bag recycling program in place or risk incurring the immediate and strident wrath of local green consumers. It is retailers who are expected to be at the center of local solid-waste management efforts—the not-all-that-rational rationale being that by carrying all those products they're responsible for much of the waste. It is retailers who are expected to serve as de facto centers for community environmental organizing efforts.

It is retailers, in short, who are the lightning rods for consumers' environmental concerns. If a consumer is unhappy with a manufacturer's environmental performance, as likely as not it will be the retailer, not the manufacturer, who receives the outrage.

In the unlikely event that retailers need another reason to be environmentally active, there is the specter of prospective packaging "take-back" legislation. Germany now requires retailers to take back certain packaging from consumers. This has led to the establishment of a complex, industry-managed infrastructure for package recycling—and it is the sort of development that has retailers and manufacturers on tenterhooks in other countries. It reminds U.S. retailers that the company that doesn't take matters into its own hands today faces the prospect that someone will take the matter *out* of their hands tomorrow.

The Track Record

To date, leading retailers (especially supermarkets and first-tier mass merchandisers) have embraced the environmental cause quite actively. The great majority of supermarkets either give rebates to customers who bring in their own shopping bags, sell canvas shopping bags, or both.

Many retailers also offer private-label lines of green products. This is largely a defensive maneuver. Consumers tend to do all their shopping in a single supermarket. The retailer who fails to stock green products risks losing a small but significant number of shoppers to the supermarket down the road that does offer them—and because consumers tend to buy everything at one supermarket, they will likely lose that customer not just for green products, but for good.

You may recall that in Chapter 5 we cited retailer hesitancy as a key reason for the relatively uninspired performance of green products to date. Which raises a question. Doesn't what we're saying here contradict those earlier statements? The answer is no. For all the reasons we mentioned earlier—regulatory concerns, dubiousness about green claims, low profit margins, etc.—retailers have been hesitant to stock non-private-label green products. But in other environmental areas, especially those directly involving community-relations issues such as supporting recycling programs, they have on the whole been extremely proactive. There has been a clear dichotomy in their behavior—on the one hand caution towards green products, and on the other a leadership role in terms of making a visible public commitment to the environmental cause in general and recycling in particular.

Supermarkets. An early example of environmental commitment came from a brace of four west coast–based supermarkets. Ralph's Grocery Co.(Compton, California), ABCO Markets Inc. (Phoenix, Arizona), Raley's (Sacramento, California), and Fred Meyer (Portland, Oregon) actively supported Scientific Certification Systems in an effort to get product certification off the ground. The companies used Green Cross shelf talkers and also strongly encouraged suppliers to seek Green Cross certification.

As noted above, most supermarkets have a number of ongoing environmental initiatives. In addition to shopping-bag rebates and recycling programs, there are many back-room programs involving such activities as recycling wooden shipping pallets. At the same time, there are areas where more work needs to be done, such as food wrappers in deli sections, where consumers continue to be most worried about health and appearance issues.

Sometimes, supermarkets' environmental efforts backfire. That was the case for Giant Foods of Landover, Maryland, when it decided to do its part for community recycling by placing recycling bins in its parking lots. To its dismay, it found that the materials it received were so hopelessly commingled that they couldn't be recycled efficiently. Not only that, but so many materials were returned that they spilled over the bins and turned the adjacent parking areas into a garbage dump. The Giant Foods program succeeded so well that it failed. Eventually, the retailer abandoned the program.

Safeway Stores based in Oakland, California, also encountered problems when it tried to cater to consumers' environmental concerns. The company's Environmental Options program, which was intended to flag environmentally superior products for consumers, came under fire from environmental groups for alleged inaccuracies, trivialities, and general shoddiness.

Experiences like these have caused supermarket retailers to be very selective in their choice of environmental programs. On balance, however, they continue to be proactive in their efforts to demonstrate environmental leadership.

Mass Merchandisers. Wal-Mart Stores, Inc. (Bentonville, Arizona) was one of the first retailers to climb aboard the environmental bandwagon, and it has been extremely active in educating shoppers about environmental issues and in encouraging suppliers to be more environmentally conscientious. The company's Green Aisles program flags over 1000 environmentally friendly products. In addition, the company is offering green products in its Sam's American Choice line of private-label products.

Recently, Wal-Mart announced plans for a prototype green store in Lawrence, Kansas, that will be a model of environmental state-of-the-art efficiency and responsibility and will serve as a laboratory for practices that could be implemented in other stores' locations. The Lawrence store will highlight green products, allow consumers to drop off recyclables, use natural light and heat, and accommodate group visits from schools and businesses.

Other leading mass merchandisers have also been active:

- Target Stores based in Minneapolis, Minnesota, sponsors a children's environmental club called "Kids for Saving Earth" which has been an enormous success—enormous enough, in fact, to inspire Wal-Mart to introduce a similar program.

- Atlanta-based Home Depot has announced that it will stop selling lead solder in its plumbing departments. The company has also teamed up with SCS to identify and evaluate environmental marketing claims on suppliers' labels.

- K mart of Troy, Michigan, has teamed up with Exide Corporation (Reading, Pennsylvania) to collect and recycle used batteries. The program offers consumers a $2 refund for any used car or marine battery they return to a K mart store. Another K mart initiative involves a used-tire recycling test. The company hopes to convert the used tires into products such as rubber mats, parking-lot asphalt, and plastic shelving.

- While Sears has lagged a bit behind the other leading mass merchandisers, in late 1991 the company launched a packaging reduction initiative designed to bring about a 25 percent reduction in the volume of packaging in the company's stores by 1994.

Despite this list of achievements, mass merchandisers have been somewhat less aggressive than supermarkets in the environmental arena, particularly at the second- and third-tier levels. One reason for this is that mass merchandisers tend not to be community centers in the same way many supermarkets are. In addition, many of the products that mass merchandisers carry (e.g., clothes, durables) are less packaging-intensive than the products stocked by supermarkets.

Product Promotions

Because supermarket retailers are under such heavy pressure to establish their environmental *bona fides*, they are very receptive to the notion of collaborating with product suppliers on environmentally oriented product promotions. The fact that environmental promotions allow retailers to make an environmental statement without actually footing the bill makes them particularly appealing. Thus, the needs of retailers and suppliers dovetail perfectly. Retailers get a healthy dose of no-cost image enhancement and suppliers get the enthusiastic support of their trade partners, leading to such sales boosters as prominent displays for their products.

Church & Dwight's Enviro-Centers.   In 1991, Church & Dwight Co. Inc. set up freestanding Enviro-Centers in over 7500 supermarkets nationwide. The units displayed Church & Dwight's ARM & HAMMER baking soda offerings; an EPA brochure entitled *Be An Environmentally Alert Consumer*; and a built-in–baking-soda-use wheel entitled "Thirty-seven Environmentally Safe Household Cleaning and Personal Care Alternatives." Information about how to obtain the use wheel at no charge was also provided. The Enviro-Centers were custom made and featured the retailer's name.

Reports from the field suggest that mass merchandisers seem to need a little more persuading than supermarket chains to engage in environmental promotions. Some product suppliers have even suggested that mass merchandisers require as much wooing as consumers themselves, especially in parts of the country where environmental awareness is relatively less advanced. But mass merchandisers will be receptive to the right promotion.

Target Stores' Earth Day Promotion.   During the week surrounding Earth Day 1992, Target Stores had a special section featuring a range of environmentally safe products, including environmental books and games for children, food products from the rain forests, and canvas bags. The program had a double purpose: to increase consumer awareness, and also to provide feedback on how consumers would respond to permanent environmental-product sections.

Solid-Waste Management

As mentioned above, retailers often find themselves at the center of a local community's concerns about solid waste. This offers manufacturers a second way to work with retailers, namely, by developing programs that address solid-waste management issues.

Closing the Loop.   In 1991, Procter & Gamble joined with Giant Food, a plastics reprocessor, an environmental group, local government agencies, and television stations to form a major recycling education program entitled *Closing the Loop* (see Figure 7-1).

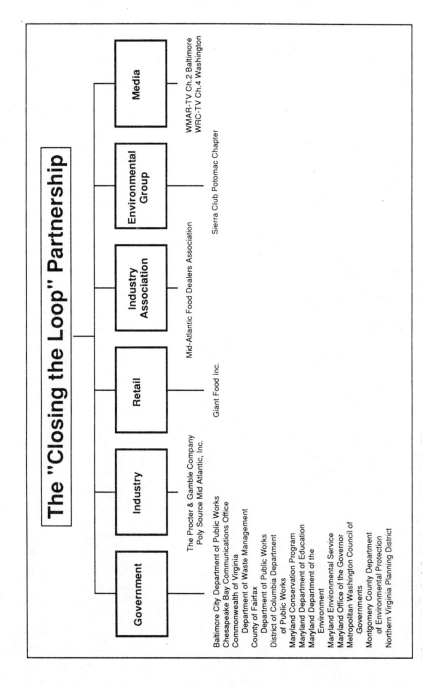

Figure 7-1. Solid-waste management alliance.

Based in the greater Baltimore and Washington, D.C., region, the program's objectives were as follows:

- To educate the community about the need to recycle and about how to participate in a local recycling program
- To encourage the rapid expansion of comprehensive recycling programs
- To give positive recognition to program sponsors
- To gather information for replicating the program in other parts of the country

The public education elements consisted of sixteen 30-second program promotional messages (including sponsor identification), a half-hour documentary on recycling in the region, a curriculum on recycling for middle-school students, brochures for consumers (distributed at Giant Food retail outlets), and a toll-free recycling hot-line number.

Cosponsor Procter & Gamble benefited in two ways—through enhancement of its image as a good corporate citizen, and by gaining access to a greater supply of recycled *polyethylene terephthalate (PET) and mixed-color high-density polyethylene (HDPE) plastics.*

Lobbying and Litigation

The interests of retailers and suppliers often coincide in the related areas of lobbying and litigation. Under the German packaging take-back law, to take just one example, retailers are only a stopping-off point for the packaging. It is the manufacturers who are ultimately responsible for making sure that used packaging gets routed back into the production process.

In the United States, too, retailers and suppliers often find themselves looking up the barrel of the same gun. If an environmental claim backfires, it may be the supplier who gets sued, but the retailers who stock the product are sure to catch flak, too.

This communality of interests makes an excellent case for collaboration on the lobbying front, and in fact retailers and suppliers have a reasonably good track record for doing so.

At the 1991 FTC hearings on whether or not to have national voluntary guidelines on environmental claims, for instance, retailers and suppliers presented a united front through testimony by the National Retail Federation, the Grocery Manufacturers of America, and other trade associations from both camps.

On the other hand, coordination between the two groups has on occasion been conspicuously lacking. In 1990, a California initiative was launched which if passed would have had profound implications for the future of environmentalism and green business. Popularly called Big Green, the proposition called for aggressive measures to combat global warming, protect marine resources, and address food-safety issues. Retailers opposed the measure—but did not get much direct support from suppliers, who were their natural allies. (Suppliers were represented through their trade associations, but many individual suppliers were reluctant to get directly involved.) Although Big Green went down to defeat, retailers and suppliers would have benefited from a more aggressive coalition that worked to further their common interests.

Industry and Trade Associations

Inside a given industry or trade, companies are often in direct competition with each other. For this reason, although they often have common interests, it is rare for one organization to speak out on behalf of any company but itself.

Industry and trade associations are umbrella organizations that allow otherwise competing entities to speak with a common voice and to gain the power of numbers. They serve a particularly valuable function for the chemical, oil, plastics, and other industries that are under tremendous pressure from consumer activists and environmental advocacy groups. Collective pressures of this sort are best responded to in a collective voice. The role played by the National Food Processors Association and other associations in the 1991 FTC hearings on voluntary labeling guidelines exemplifies the positive role that trade associations can play in giving voice to an industry position.

But a good thing can be overdone. It has been my experience that too many companies hide behind the skirts of industry associations, especially when it comes to environmental initiatives. As a marketing consultant in touch with many company representatives, I often hear the comment, "Our industry association is handling the issue for us." The existence of an industry association too frequently gives companies an excuse to do nothing at all. Although industry associations have a useful role, companies must take care not to become so reliant on them that they slip into passivity.

The names, addresses, and telephone numbers of leading industry, trade, and professional associations with a particularly active involvement in environmental issues are presented in Appendix A.

Responsible Care

Perhaps the foremost example of an association-driven environmental position is the Responsible Care program, developed by the Chemical Manufacturers Association. Born in response to the devastating chemical explosion in Bhopal, India, Responsible Care has two basic goals: (1) to shore up the public's shaky confidence in the chemical industry; and (2) to actually improve individual companies' environmental performance.

Although the chemical industry has an uphill battle when it comes to convincing consumers of its trustworthiness, the Responsible Care initiative has on the whole done a good job of persuading the public that the chemical industry is taking its environmental responsibilities with new seriousness.

With respect to the impact that the Responsible Care charter has had on the industry's environmental track record, some environmentalist are skeptical—as skeptical perhaps as industry at large is of the environmentalists' CERES Principles (formerly known as the Valdez Principles, a set of 10 environmental operating principles developed in 1989 by a coalition of pension funds, environmental groups, and religious organizations).

In Figure 7-2, we present the basic principles of the Responsible Care program and the CERES Principles. Although Responsible Care's 10 general principles are backed up by "Codes of Management Practice," these codes are not mandatory. They (in the words of a Responsible Care brochure) "identify expected management practices as objectives rather than prescribing absolute or quantitative standards."

I believe both initiatives, the Responsible Care Principles and the CERES principles, deserve serious consideration. Every company may not be able to manage its business according to these principles (and, therefore, may not formally subscribe to the principles), but they should establish these principles as goals or benchmarks much as many companies do the Baldridge pillars of management or Deming's 14 (quality management) points.

Regulatory Bodies

We addressed the issue of regulation in Chapter 6. However, the roles of key regulatory bodies relative to each other and to the emerging green-products marketplace is another variable with which environmental marketers should be familiar.

Figure 7-2. The Ceres Principles and Responsible Care Guidelines

The Ceres Principles

1. *Protection of the Biosphere.* We will reduce and make continual progress toward eliminating the release of any substance that may cause environmental damage to the air, water, or the earth or its inhabitants. We will safeguard all habitats affected by our operations and will protect open spaces and wilderness, while preserving biodiversity.

2. *Sustainable Use of Natural Resources.* We will make sustainable use of renewable natural resources, such as water, soils and forests. We will conserve nonrenewable natural resources through efficient use and careful planning.

3. *Reduction and Disposal of Wastes.* We will reduce and where possible eliminate waste through source reduction and recycling. All waste will be handled and disposed of through safe and responsible methods.

4. *Energy Conservation.* We will conserve energy and improve the energy efficiency of our internal operations and of the goods and services we sell. We will make every effort to use environmentally safe and sustainable energy sources.

5. *Risk Reduction.* We will strive to minimize the environmental, health and safety risks to our employees and the communities in which we operate through safe technologies, facilities and operating procedures, and by being prepared for emergencies.

6. *Safe Products and Services.* We will reduce and where possible eliminate the use, manufacture or sale of products and services that cause environmental damage or health or safety hazards. We will inform our customers of the environmental impacts of our products or services and try to correct unsafe use.

7. *Environmental Restoration.* We will promptly and responsibly correct conditions we have caused that endanger health, safety or the environment. To the extent feasible, we will redress injuries we have caused to persons or damage we have caused to the environment and will restore the environment.

8. *Informing the Public.* We will inform in a timely manner everyone who may be affected by conditions caused by our company that might endanger health, safety or the environment.

(Continued)

We will regularly seek advice and counsel through dialogue with persons in communities near our facilities. We will not take any action against employees for reporting dangerous incidents or conditions to management or to appropriate authorities.

9. *Management Commitment.*   We will implement these Principles and sustain a process that ensures that the Board of Directors and Chief Executive Officer are fully informed about pertinent environmental issues and are fully responsible for environmental policy. In selecting our Board of Directors, we will consider demonstrated environmental commitment as a factor.

10. *Audits and Reports.*   We will conduct an annual self-evaluation or our progress in implementing these Principles. We will support the timely creation of generally accepted environmental audit procedures. We will annually complete the CERES Report, which will be made available to the public.

Guiding Principles for Responsible Care

Member companies of the Chemical Manufacturers Association are committed to support a continuing effort to improve the industry's responsible management of chemicals. They pledge to manage their business according to the following principles:

1. To recognize and respond to community concerns about chemicals and our operations.

2. To develop and produce chemicals that can be manufactured, transported, used and disposed of safely.

3. To make health, safety and environmental considerations a priority in our planning for all existing and new products and processes.

4. To report promptly to officials, employees, customers and the public, information on chemical-related health or environmental hazards and to recommend protective measures.

5. To counsel customers on the safe use, transportation and disposal of chemical products.

6. To operate our plants and facilities in a manner that protects the environment and the health and safety of our employees and the public.

Figure 7-2. *(Continued)*

---

8. To work with others to resolve problems created by past handling and disposal of hazardous substances.

9. To participate with government and others in creating responsible laws, regulations and standards to safeguard the community, workplace and environment.

10. To promote the principles and practices of Responsible Care by sharing experiences and offering assistance to others who produce, handle, use, transport or dispose of chemicals.

Figure 7-2. (*Continued*)

Environmental Protection Agency (EPA)

As the federal government's chief environmental oversight agency, the EPA has a critically important role to play.

In areas related to environmental labeling and environmental marketing, the EPA has kept a rather low profile. This is not to suggest that the agency has been completely invisible. Indeed, a list of some of its initiatives is not unimpressive:

- Sponsorship of a conference on environmental labeling
- Publication of reports on the green-products marketplace
- Publication of a brochure counseling consumers on how to shop green
- Support of infrastructure development
- Support of life-cycle analysis research
- Issuance of a set of proposed guidelines for the terms recyclable and recycled content.

Despite the EPA's low public profile in environmental marketing, it remains an important institutional presence whose actual and potential roles environmental marketers should keep in mind in developing and implementing their business strategies.

An EPA organizational chart is presented as Figure 7-3.

U.S. ENVIRONMENTAL PROTECTION AGENCY

Office of the Administrator/Deputy Administrator

Associate Administrators for:
Regional Operations and State/Local Relations
Congressional and Legislative Affairs
Communications and Public Affairs

Staff Office:
Administrative Law Judges
Civil Rights
Executive Support
Executive Secretariat
Science Advisory Board
Small and Disadvantaged Business Utilization
Cooperative Environmental Management

Assistant Administrator for International Activities
International Cooperation Division
International Issues Division
Program Operations Division

Assistant Administrator for Administration and Resource Management
Office of Administration
Office of Administration and Resources Management, Research Triangle Park, NC
Office of Administration and Resources Management, Cincinnati, OH
Office of the Comptroller
Office of Human Resources Management
Office of Information Resources Management

Assistant Administrator for Enforcement
Office of Compliance Analysis and Program Operations
Office of Criminal Enforcement
Office of Civil Enforcement
Office of Federal Activities
National Enforcement Investigations Center (NEC)
Office of Federal Facilities Enforcement

General Counsel
Air and Radiation Division
Grants, Contract, and General Law Division
Inspector General Division
International Activities Division
Pesticides and Toxic Substances Division
Solid Waste and Emergency Response Division
Water Division

Assistant Administrator for Policy, Planning and Evaluation
Office of Pollution Prevention
Office of Policy Analysis
Office of Regulatory Management and Evaluation

Inspector General
Office of Audits
Office of Investigations
Office of Management and Technical Assessment

Assistant Administrator for Water

Policy and Resources Management Office

Office of Ground Water and Drinking Water

Office of Science and Technology

Office of Waste Water Enforcement and Compliance

Office of Wetlands Oceans and Watersheds

Assistant Administrator for Solid Waste and Emergency Response

Chemical Emergency Preparedness and Prevention Office

Technology Innovation Office

Office of Emergency and Remedial Response (Superfund)

Office of Solid Waste

Office of Underground Storage Tanks

Office of Waste Programs Enforcement

Assistant Administrator for Air and Radiation

Office of Program Management Operations

Office of Policy Analysis and Review

Office of Atmospheric and Indoor Air Programs

Office of Air Quality Planning and Standards (Research Triangle Park, NC)

Office of Mobile Sources

Office of Radiation Programs

Assistant Administrator for Pesticides and Toxic Substances

Office of Program Management Operations

Office of Compliance Monitoring

Office of Pesticide Programs

Office of Toxic Substances

Assistant Administrator for Research and Development

Office of Research Program Management

Office of Technology Transfer and Regulatory Support

Office of Exploratory Research

Office of Health Research

Office of Environmental Processes and Effects Research

Office of Environmental Engineering and Technology Demonstration

Office of Health and Environmental Assessment

Office of Modeling, Monitoring Systems, and Quality Assurance

| Region 1 Boston | Region 2 New York | Region 3 Philadelphia | Region 4 Atlanta | Region 5 Chicago | Region 6 Dallas | Region 7 Kansas City | Region 8 Denver | Region 9 San Francisco | Region 10 Seattle |

Figure 7-3. U.S. EPA organization.

Federal Trade Commission (FTC)

In 1991, the FTC found itself under siege by an unlikely coalition of businesses, trade associations, and environmental advocacy groups to issue a set of voluntary environmental labeling guidelines. This, and subsequent FTC Guidelines (see Appendix B), has made the FTC the regulatory cornerstone of environmental marketing—but it is a cornerstone with rounded edges. Guidelines, once again, are only that—guidelines; regulations have more teeth. However, not even the most anti-industry environmental groups have petitioned the FTC for regulations. It takes years for regulations to be enacted, and the universal perception is that environmental marketing is in too much of a crisis situation to be left lingering that long in regulatory limbo. The consensus was that it is better to have soft guidelines now than toothier regulations much later.

Other Federal Agencies

A host of other federal agencies are involved in the oversight of environmental issues, a fact that has led some critics to charge that one of the main reasons for the federal government's history of ineffectual environmental management has been excessive bureaucratic fragmentation. Among the other agencies with direct or indirect responsibility for environmental matters are:

- The Department of Energy (nuclear cleanup)
- The Nuclear Regulatory Commission (nuclear plants)
- The Interstate Commerce Commission (interstate transportation of hazardous waste)
- Department of Defense (hazardous waste on military sites)

The White House

The White House's Office of Consumer Affairs was part of the team that worked on developing the EPA's proposed guidelines for recycled-content and recyclable claims. It is also active in a variety of other environmental arenas, including sponsorship of the President's Environment and Conservation Challenge awards, which are presented annually to individuals and organizations whose activities best exemplify, in the words of the White House, "the cooperative, innovative spirit of the new environmental era." The White House is also the home of the

Council on Environmental Quality, an organization whose mission is to formulate and recommend national policies to promote environmental improvement.

But as the primary institution for defining national political agendas, the White House has been conspicuous mostly by its absence from environmental labeling, thereby leaving it to the Task Force of State Attorneys General and the various other forces of the marketplace to formulate policy in this critically important area.

Task Force of State Attorneys General

As discussed in Chapter 6, a State Task Force of Attorneys General headed by Minnesota Attorney General Hubert H. Humphrey III has played a leading role in raising the alarm about misleading environmental claims and in working to develop guidelines that are acceptable to both business and environmental and consumer groups. As of this writing, the Task Force has brought nine legal actions and has also published a second report—*Green Report II*—which lays out guidelines for environmental labeling. The organization played a crucial role in the interim period pending the issuance of FTC guidelines.

With the issuance of those guidelines, the role of the Task Force is expected to diminish somewhat—but only somewhat. Attorney General Humphrey made it clear that, whether it was guidelines or, for that matter, regulations that were forthcoming from the federal government, states should continue to have the right to bring actions for false and deceptive environmental advertising. Even after the federal government begins to swing its weight in the environmental labeling arena, Humphrey's Task Force can be expected to continue in its dual role as regulatory stick-waver and as energetic "spokesgroup" for reasonableness in environmental labeling.

State and Local Regulators

Currently, 10 states have enacted environmental labeling laws, and more states are expected to come aboard soon.

It is not, strictly speaking, only the states that are active on the sub-federal front. In terms of bringing environmental labeling actions, the most active regulatory body has been New York City's Department of Consumer Affairs, headed by the aptly named Mark Green. And in the area of solid-waste legislation generally, local governments have been in the forefront in terms of enacting restrictive—and sometimes impractical—legislation. Minneapolis, for instance, has banned the use of food packaging that is not degradable, returnable, or collectible for recycling, while Suffolk County, New York, introduced a highly publicized law banning the use of polystyrene, PVC food packaging, and plastic grocery bags by local retailers. (After going through a long series of legal hoops, the Suffolk County legislature eventually abandoned the law.)

Table 7-1 presents selected local laws enacted in 1990 and earlier.

Policy and Educational Institutions

Policy and educational institutions both play an important role in the environmental marketing arena. *Public policy institutions* help to provide the roadsigns that define the directions of environmental management and marketing strategies. The Los Angeles, California–based Reason Foundation, for instance, has sparked controversy in the recycling arena by questioning the desirability of the current national approach to recycling. According to the Reason Foundation, some forms of recycling may be undesirable because they are too costly in terms of the human, financial, and environmental capital they require. Instead of so-called rates-and-dates legislation that requires packaging materials to contain a certain percentage of recycled materials by a given date, the Reason Foundation favors a consumer-driven approach to solid-waste management whereby consumers would be charged for each bag of trash they contributed to the solid-waste flow. Although somewhat heretical, this is perhaps not a bad idea.

On the other coast, the Tellus Institute (Boston, Massachusetts) created a furor in a 1992 study whose preliminary findings suggested that paper might be environmentally superior to plastic as a packaging material.[1] The think tank's methodology was roundly criticized, but the very vigor of the objections underscores the impact that studies of this sort can have.

The Pacific Research Institute (San Francisco, California) and the Political Economy Research Center (Bozeman, Montana) won an international award for their study entitled Free Market Environmentalism. The book suggests how market processes can be applied to forest, pollution, energy, water, wildlife, and even global warming.[2]

Think tanks like these and many others help to shape the dialogue on environmental issues generally and, by extension, on environmental marketing. The information they provide can help corporations to prioritize their strategies and to better understand long-term market trends.

Educational institutions from kindergartens to universities play a variety of roles. Primary and secondary schools are obvious targets for mar-

Table 7-1. Selected Local Ordinances Restricting Plastics and/or Packaging

Locality	Description of legislation
Berkeley, Calif.	Banned use of polystyrene food packaging by local retailers
Capitola, Calif.	Banned use of polystyrene foam packaging by retail food outlets
Santa Cruz County, Calif.	Banned use of polystyrene foam packaging by retail food outlets
Sonoma County, Calif.	No longer purchasing polystyrene products
Broward County, Fla.	Banned county use of foam plastic containers
Minneapolis-St. Paul, Minn.	Banned use of food packaging that is not degradable, returnable, or collectible for recycling
Bergen County, N.J.	Phasing out use of nonbiodegradable plastic products
Cape May County, N.J.	Is no longer purchasing polystyrene products
Newark, N.J.	Banned use of polystyrene and PVC plastic food packaging at retail establishments. Retailers must place food in biodegradable packaging (either paper or plastic)
Sayreville, N.J.	Banned use of nonbiodegradable plastics by retail and fast-food outlets
Sea Bright, N.J.	Banned use of plastic bags, cups, and fast-food containers
Suffolk County, N.Y.	Banned use of polystyrene, PVC food packaging, and plastic grocery bags by local retailers. Banned use of polystyrene foam products at concession stands at county-owned beaches
Cuyahoga County, Ohio	Is no longer purchasing polystyrene containers
Portland, Oreg.	Banned polystyrene packaging
Port Townsend, Wash.	Banned use of polystyrene foam by fast-food outlets
Winslow, Wash.	Banned use of polystyrene foam by fast-food outlets

SOURCE: FIND/SVP, Inc.

keting activities. Both children and teachers are sensitive to environmental issues and therefore receptive to environmental communications.

Universities are a source of information, expertise, and research, and, therefore, are often appropriate to work with on a consulting basis. The University of Tennessee, for instance, has been working with the product certification organization Green Seal to help develop various product certification standards.

Universities are also increasingly incorporating environmental curricula at both the undergraduate and graduate levels. Tufts University (Medford, Massachusetts) has its widely respected Center for Environmental Management and was the first U.S. University to have a Dean of the Environment (Anthony Coretese). New York University in New York City has been in the forefront in encouraging environmental awareness among its graduate students in business administration. Many law schools have added environmental courses to their curriculum. Pace University (White Plains, New York) has a full-fledged environmental department plus an environmental certificate program. There is even a nonprofit organization, The Management Institute for Environment and Business (Arlington, Virginia), whose mission is to incorporate environmental materials into business school curricula around the country. (The Institute was established with grants from the U.S. EPA and from AT&T.)

The process is still in its early stages, but the country's educational institutions of higher learning are beginning to produce more environmentally aware students—and these people are both potential market targets *and* potential employees.

Scientific and Technical Institutions

Finally, the scientific/technical community also plays an important role in environmental marketing. If there is one single obstacle in the way of the rapid growth of the green-products movement, it is the lack of definitive scientific information on the environmental impacts of product development. Although the product certification organization Scientific Certification Systems claims to have cracked the life-cycle assessment nut, the consensus in the scientific community is that it will be several years before life-cycle assessment is a truly useful tool for analysis.

Enter the scientific community. The Society for Environmental Toxicology and Chemistry (SETAC) has emerged as the organizing force for the mainstream scientific community's explorations of life-cycle assessment. It is working with the EPA and other organizations, including the Battelle Memorial Institute (Columbus, Ohio) to advance life-cycle assessment.

Nor should we overlook the compelling issue of politically tainted science. Science has gotten a bad name in the environmental marketing arena, thanks to allegedly "objective" environmental-impact analyses which almost always seem to keep coming out in support of the position of the organization that funds the study.

The hard truth about science is that it cannot be relied upon in every case to produce incontrovertible, objective truths. Even our most hallowed scientific principles invariably get modified and expanded upon over time—which only tells us that there is no such thing as absolute scientific truth. If that is the case at the most theoretical levels of science, then how much less absolute are scientific truths in less theoretical domains like life-cycle assessment where the necessary information is not available and critically important value judgments about the relative importance of various environmental outputs must be made! We all want certainty, and in this century we tend to look to science for it. In the case of life-cycle assessment, that desire is misguided.

Which is not to suggest that it makes no sense to perform product life-cycle assessments. On the contrary, I believe that it is critically important to do so. But it is important to differentiate between the sort of absolute truths which we demand of hard science and the more probabilistic orientation of the current state of the art of life-cycle assessment.

Perhaps the best analogy I can make is to our jury system. No one claims that juries discover the truth. The best they can hope for is to draw the best possible conclusions based on the evidence presented them.

The same applies to product life-cycle assessment. We are not at a point where we can gain access to the truth, but the state of the art does permit us to have considered opinions. It does permit us, like a jury, to deal in *probabilities*.

And it is important that we deal in those probabilities. For all its flaws, no one seriously suggests that we do away with the jury system. Yet business has operated for years without a product-assessment jury. It is clearly in the interests of environmental justice to have such a system, i.e., to pursue life-cycle assessments, even if the system is something less than 100 percent reliable.

We are in an environmental crisis and cannot afford the luxury of staying in a holding pattern pending the attainment of the confidence levels we have grown to expect from hard science. It is the job of the scientific community to advance the level of knowledge about life-cycle assessment and other critically important areas of environmental impact as rapidly as possible. In the meantime, it is the business community's responsibility to take action.

Summary and Recommendations

In addition to consumers and environmental groups, a number of other players are important members of the environmental marketing infrastructure.

Retailers are on the environmental front line. They must respond daily to consumers' environmental concerns and complaints. With the exception of green products, where they have moved forward cautiously, retailers have responded strongly to environmental issues, laboring hard to respond to environmental issues across a range of fronts. They are extremely receptive to manufacturer-initiated environmental promotions, which give them a chance to improve their own environmental reputations at little or no cost.

Industry and trade associations are also key players in the environmental marketing infrastructure. They serve a particularly useful function for industries under heavy environmental fire, such as the oil and chemical industries. While there are certainly virtues in speaking with a common voice, companies should take care not to hide behind the skirts of industry associations when it comes to environmental initiatives. The existence of an industry or trade association is not a justification for inactivity.

A wide range of *regulatory bodies* is keeping tabs on environmental marketing. To date, most of the laws and enforcement activity have come from the state and local level. Although uniform guidelines for environmental labeling have been issued by the FTC, some states may be expected to hold manufacturers to their often stricter regulations.

Policy institutions help to chart the directions which environmental problem solving will take. Sometimes the recommendations of these organizations run against the tide of popular opinion, a fact that probably makes them all the more important. The information that these organizations provide can be enormously useful to companies as they plot their own strategic courses.

Educational institutions serve a double purpose. They are a source of expertise on environmental issues, and they also provide a forum for companies to make their own positions known.

Scientific and technical institutions help to differentiate the accurate from the specious in a domain where our expertise is all too limited. The actual environmental impacts of given processes are often unknown. This, of course, severely lowers the confidence level which can be placed in any given environmental strategy. One of the roles of scientific and technical institutions is to develop and disseminate the knowledge about environmental impacts that will allow corporate decision makers to raise their confidence levels to what truly qualifies as a comfort zone.

It is critically important for environmental marketers to stay in contact with all of these players. Only by making it a practice to maintain ongoing relations with these groups can an environmental marketer be confident that his environmental marketing strategy is resting on solid ground.

8

Green-Product Development

The Case for Green Products

Let's start with the most important point about green products: they represent a substantial product opportunity. In Chapter 5, we saw that there is a huge pool of consumers who are teetering on the edge of green consumerism. Green products are the wedge that could tap all that latent potential.

There are already numerous green-product success stories:

- Wal-Mart reports that its green labeling program, that was initiated in August 1989, contributed to an overall sales increase of 25 percent for the year.

- ARCO EC-1 emission control gasoline, introduced in Southern California in fall 1989, increased its share of market from 33 to 35 percent in seven months.

- Procter & Gamble's Downy Refill fabric softener went national in fall 1990 after reaching 20 percent of brand sales in test markets.

- Melitta Natural Brown unbleached coffee filters produces up to 50 percent of Melitta's filter business in some markets.

- Seventh Generation, a catalog merchandiser of green products, saw its sales climb from $1 million in 1988 to an estimated $10 million in 1991.

Overall, new products making green claims have grown to almost 13 percent of all new products, up from 9.5 percent in 1990 and 4.5 percent in 1989.[1]

Of course, it is not only for reasons of profit that it is important to move forward with green-product development. There's also the environment to consider. Businesses have an active obligation to work for the betterment of the environment. Green-product development is one way for companies to demonstrate their environmental commitment.

There's a third reason to develop green products, too. It's been one of the themes of this book that consumers are paying more and more attention to the companies behind the products. Green products offer companies a way to improve their *bona fides* with a populace that is demanding exemplary environmental performance from the corporate community.

Threshold Issues

Overcoming Management Resistance

Be forewarned: green-product development may not be an easy sell to senior management. There is a widespread perception that the introduction of a green-product line or lines will have a negative impact on sales. Typically, three separate concerns are voiced:

1. The introduction of environmentally superior alternatives will reduce the appeal—and sales—of core products or brands.
2. There will be inadequate demand for environmentally sensitive products, based on the assumption that people will not pay a premium or give up convenience and performance for environmental benefits.
3. There will be unacceptable costs for additional R&D and/or retooling.

Each of these perceptions is misguided. Let's look at each of them in turn.

Reduced Appeal of Core Products or Brands.   In my opinion, this is basically a red herring. Major consumer goods companies bring out new products all the time that cut into the sales of core products. That is what niche marketing is all about, after all. It's a curious fact about green products that they seem often to produce a paralysis of entrepreneurial will. Many managers seem compelled to bring a negative bias to the idea of green-product development: it's as if they're fixated on the consequences of failure. Yes, green-product development could go wrong—but it could go right, too. What about the upside? What about the potential financial payback of green products? What about their contribution to the quality of life? Considerations like these tend to get short shrift in many business analyses.

Why do so many businesses, which are premised on the principle of objective decision making, bring such a biased attitude to green-product development? The reason appears to be that many mainstream business managers are afraid of green products. They are afraid that green-product development could drive the examination process inward and force corporations to take a hard look at their environmental *bona fides*. They are also afraid that the extensive availability of green products in mainstream distribution channels could undermine the chemical-based product culture on which traditional consumer product business success has been based.

In short, they are afraid that green products could be the linchpin of radical change, both in their organizations and throughout the supermarkets of America. They say no to green products not because no is the right answer, but because they are concerned that by saying yes, they could be letting the genie out of the bottle.

Wrong. Not only are green products not as pernicious as many managers fear, they aren't pernicious at all. For one thing, green product development may drive internal change, but there is no rule that says it must. In the final analysis, it's up to management to determine how big an impact green-product development will have on the corporate culture. And where green-product development does accelerate corporate introspection, that's not necessarily bad. Change can be for the better. A case can be made that it's good to shake up the system from time to time, that such exercises in "corporate aerobics" trim off fat and get a company operating at peak efficiency.

The fears about the transformative potential of green products in the nation's supermarkets are just as overblown. Ours is a culture of niches, one that evolves by gradual and constant assimilation, not by radical change. Chemical-based products are too much a part of our culture to go the way of the dinosaur or the duckbilled platypus. Given a fair shake, green products may become a significant niche market, but that's not to say they will ever totally replace chemical-based products.

Many people *do* want alternatives to mainstream products. In short, green products aren't dangerous—they are a legitimate (indeed, substantial) niche opportunity. But it takes a willingness to think "out of the chemical box" to fully appreciate their potential.

Inadequate Demand   This is basically a self-fulfilling prophesy. We have already seen that there is substantial pent-up demand for green products. While it's true that consumers are currently hesitant to plunge into green products, that is in large measure due to the fact that the major consumer goods companies are not putting their marketing weight behind green products. The whole point about marketing is that it creates demand. If one or more major consumer goods companies wanted to make consumers more receptive to green products, they could, simply by launching an all-out marketing campaign. By electing to steer clear of green products, they're not responding to a marketplace reality so much as creating it.

R&D and/or Retooling Costs   The R&D and retooling costs will vary sharply from new product to new product. Clearly, these factors require close analysis. However, it is important to analyze these costs in the context of the potential returns. R&D and retooling costs are reasons for caution, but they are not grounds for ruling out green-product development from the start.

Additionally, the costs of retooling *on your schedule* may be significantly less costly than doing so on a schedule driven by government regulation or by the competition's having taken the lead. While management resistance is a frequent fact of life, you can't know how tough the management-resistance nut is until you've tried to crack it. Many managers assume that they won't be able to make headway and therefore don't even try. If a good business case can be made for moving forward with green-product development, and if senior management is competent enough to recognize a business opportunity that's staring them in the face, there's at least a fighting chance that green-product development will get the go-ahead.

Failing that, there's always the fallback position of greener product development. It's possible to improve products in modest ways that don't trigger alarms about retooling, the end of the chemical era, etc. Small steps are better than none.

Working with Suppliers

Once you've gotten management on your side, the next step is to win the support of your suppliers. This isn't always easy, either. Many suppliers resist green-product development because they have special products and processes to protect. But this shouldn't keep you from moving forward. It's important to maintain good relations with your primary suppliers, but it's also important to make sure that it's you and not your suppliers who are running the show. It's you, after all, who are bringing them the business, not vice versa.

In 1991, the privately held consumer goods company S.C. Johnson & Son, Inc. (Racine, Wisconsin) hosted a high-level conference with its suppliers which focused on the company's environmental commitment. In the keynote address, S.C. Johnson CEO Richard M. Carpenter stated, "I believe the 1990s will give birth to a broad-based technical revolution prompted by environmental needs and will result in unprecedented new business development." Suppliers were urged to review their own production processes and to participate as partners in S.C. Johnson's vision of an environmentally oriented product future. The conference was conducted in a positive, nonthreatening spirit. Still, the flip side was clear, if only by implication: Work with us on this—or we'll find someone else who will.[2]

Work with your own suppliers, if they're able and willing. If not, find suppliers you can work with. Supplier resistance isn't a reason to forgo green-product development. It's a reason to find new suppliers.

Obtaining Necessary Expertise

There is no getting around the fact that, when it comes to understanding a product's complete life-cycle impact, we are operating in an environment of incomplete information. It is not yet possible to develop green products in a context that allows us to measure environmental impact with 100 percent certainty.

But this does not justify steering clear of green products. The environment needs green products, and forward-thinking businesses need them, too. Moreover, the state of scientific knowledge *is* advanced enough to permit broad judgment calls about the relative merits of product offerings. We may not have absolute certainty, but we can have what I earlier called "jury-level" certainty.

It is quite another question whether the necessary scientific-technical and environmental product-development expertise exists to push the green-product development ball forward. Here, the answer is an unequivocal yes. Even if the required resources don't exist within your organization, they *are* available on a for-hire basis. Green-product development is rapidly becoming a specialty area for green consultancies.

The evolution of my own environmental marketing consultancy provides a case in point. Only a few years ago, most of our projects involved external marketing issues such as sales promotions and claims language. Today, 90 percent of our business is focused on internal and long-range issues—and that includes green-product development.

Green-Product Concept Generation

Not only do consumers want products that are green, they also are eager for help in managing their relatively new conservation and solid-waste responsibilities. Green products are one way in which companies can provide assistance. But of course consumer demand (and consumer need) aren't the only factors driving green-product development. Regulation creates its own set of pressures, more in some areas than in others. For instance, 30 percent of the United States is prohibited from using phosphated detergents, a fact that creates a powerful incentive to develop phosphate-free brands.

And then there is the reality of environmental degradation as well. Household cleaners account for 11 percent of municipal hazardous waste. Most household septic tanks contain over 100 traceable chemical pollutants which migrate into groundwater. Thus there is a strong environmental imperative to produce nontoxic household cleaners.

Happily, this matches consumer desire. In a Good Housekeeping Institute survey, 75 percent of consumers said they would be interested in purchasing household-cleaning products in environmentally friendly packages. In addition, as presented in Figure 8-1, household-cleaning products are the category of green product most frequently bought, with 38 percent of respondents in the Good Housekeeping Institute survey saying they had purchased green household-cleaning products. Household-cleaning products are one area where environmental necessity and consumer desire converge.

Consumer Needs

Green products most frequently bought:

1. Household-cleaning products (38%)
2. Paper products (33%)
3. Garbage and trash bags (24%)
4. Beauty products (21%)
5. Food products (12%)

Figure 8-1. Consumer Needs. (*Good Housekeeping Institute, August 1990*)

Where Good Ideas Come From

In order of frequency, good new product ideas (both green and non-green) come from the following sources: (1) competitive product analyses; (2) marketing and other non-R&D departments; and (3) R&D.

Most of the concepts for mass-marketable green products are already in the marketplace, although probably not in mainstream channels. If you want to come up with a list of viable green new-product ideas, go hunting in specialty shops and green- and nature-oriented direct-mail catalogs.

New green products have occasionally been found by the larger consumer products manufacturers in national distribution. In February 1991, *Supermarket News* reported on the introductions of four national green brands: (1) the Earth Rite line consisting of an all-purpose cleaner, a tub and tile cleaner, a toilet bowl cleaner, a surface floor cleaner and a counter cleaner; (2) Simple Green, an all-purpose cleaner (from appliances to laundry); (3) Earth Wise biodegradable, nontoxic cleaners; and (4) Natural Chemistry's Bioclean, Natural Chemistry glass cleaner, and Pet Care products.[3] Not too long afterward, Benckiser Consumer Products, seeking to gain a foothold in green products, bought the Earth Rite line of cleaning products.

Marketing and other non-R&D departments are likelier than R&D departments to come up with viable product ideas because they are more demand-oriented.

Three Legs to Stand On

In developing green-product concepts, three separate sets of issues must be addressed:

- *Concept issues.* A new product can be either a line extension, a reformulation of an existing product, or a completely new product offering.

- *Pipeline issues.* It is necessary to determine if the green new product or products will be compatible with current or available production capabilities, as well as with principles of sustainable development.

- *Strategic issues.* This involves such questions as: What competitive offerings are currently available? How will different green-product concepts position the company vis-à-vis the competition? How important is it to leverage existing brand recognition? What marketing strategies are appropriate?

Although they can be analyzed as conceptually distinct entities, all three sets of issues are closely connected. Tinker with the basic concept, and your pipeline and strategic issues will be affected.

Market Evaluation and Product Concept Testing

Some Research Axioms

How do you find out if the product concept you're so keen on actually has potential? You do market research—preferably through focus groups, which in my experience provide the best product feedback about green-product concepts.

Most consumers are confused about environmental issues. Unlike other research strategies, focus groups provide researchers with the opportunity to make sure that they have explained themselves clearly and that they truly understand the responses they have received.

Focus-group facilitators and other product-concept researchers need to be well versed, not only in their product and the environmental issues being addressed, but also in their target consumers' environmental attitudes (and confusions). Without this knowledge, they cannot draft questions intelligently, clarify points as required during the interviewing process, or correctly interpret the responses they receive.

It is surprising how often companies overlook this basic rule and wing their way through green-product–concept market research. As a rule of thumb, I recommend to marketers and researchers alike that they answer for themselves the following questions before going face-to-face with consumers:

- What issues are the most important or topical environmental issues in your target consumer's mind?

- What has been the response of your target consumer to local environmental issues?

- What community, government, or corporate programs have (or have not) been successful in getting your target consumer involved in proenvironmental activities?

- What has been your target consumer's prior exposure to the environmental issues that your product improvement addresses?

By getting answers in advance to questions like these, interviewers get better acquainted with their target markets, a fact that can only enhance the investigation and communication process.

The importance of educating the people who are being interviewed about relevant environmental issues is less obvious. At first glance, this may seem to violate a basic rule of market research. It is axiomatic that market-research subjects should be representative of the target market. Raising interviewees' environmental expertise above the norm would seem a surefire way to skew the findings.

These concerns notwithstanding, I believe that it is best to provide interviewees with a baseline understanding of relevant environmental issues.

The odds that a green product will sell well in the absence of accompanying consumer education are low. Green products are best marketed in conjunction with extensive consumer-education programs. Because of this, when focus group or other market-research interviewees are educated about environmental issues, they are put on the same footing as consumers who are in an actual buying situation. This makes the interviewees' context for understanding the product actually more rather than less "real-world."

A contextual green-product focus group of this sort will include the following steps:

- The *introduction*
- *Programming,* i.e., a cursory overview of relevant environmental issues, including how the issue affects participants now and how it may affect them (and their children) in the future
- The *proposition,* including: (1) a review of products in the market today that cause or contribute to the environmental problem; (2) a discussion of ways in which a product could be modified or designed to reduce or eliminate harmful effects; and (3) a discussion of your product and how it has been modified or designed to provide improved environmental performance
- *Input* (questions and feedback)

Another tip for focus groups: Don't just solicit feedback about the product concept. Focus groups are also excellent vehicles for learning more about associated consumer-education programs and strategic marketing partnerships.

Quantification

While research is at the heart of effective product-concept testing, it's also important to *quantify* one's analysis. Are similar products on the market and if so, how have they performed? What sales can be anticipated for the product throughout its life cycle? What sort of benchmarks is it reasonable to establish? I always recommend taking a very conservative approach to the product-quantification process. Even so-called cautious forecasts often prove overoptimistic. It has been my experience that if you take your worst-case scenario and reduce it by 10 percent, you'll wind up pretty close to on target.

Design for the Environment

Design for the Environment (DFE) is emerging as the term describing the philosophy of integrating environmental considerations into the design process. Here, from an article written by AT&T's Braden R. Allenby for the September 1991 issue of the *SSA Journal,* the periodical of the Semiconductor Safety Association, is a summary description of the nature and rationale for DFE:

> (We must recognize) the need for a fundamental reevaluation of the manner in which, and the manufacturing stage at which, we traditionally manage environmental issues. Two guiding principles apply here:
>
> - The firm must internalize environmental considerations and constraints.
> - The firm must evaluate environmental issues systemically, in conjunction with associated manufacturing, economic, regulatory, social and political factors.
>
> As a practical matter, this requires that environmental considerations and constraints must be driven into the product design process. Failure to adopt such an approach will entail increasingly greater costs for manufacturing firms relative to their more environmentally progressive competitors, with obvious results. Implementation of Design for Environment (DFE) practices provides the most practicable mechanism for integrating these two principles into modern . . . manufacturing activity. The idea behind DFE is to insure that all relevant (ascertainable) environmental constraints and considerations are brought into product and process engineering design procedures.[4]

No product can be considered genuinely green unless it is also manufactured in a manner that causes minimal environmental damage. An appraisal of the environmental impacts of the production process will include consideration of the following factors:

- *Raw materials usage.*   Are renewable resources being used whenever possible? How extensive is the demand for nonrenewable resources? How can the use of raw materials (both renewable and nonrenewable) be minimized? What sorts of alternatives are available?

- *Energy consumption.*   How much energy is consumed during the production process? Are there ways to reduce energy consumption? What are the energy sources? Might alternative, more environmentally benign energy sources be used?

- *Pollution prevention.*   Does the manufacturing process being used entail significant reductions in emissions into air and water? What is the quantity and composition of those emissions? Are appropriate technologies being used to minimize emissions?

- *Solid waste.*   Are raw materials being used completely, i.e., is there minimal scrap? What waste, if any, can be reused? Is solid waste disposed of in an environmentally desirable manner?

Designing for Disposal

Eventually, all products require disposal. We might say that they die. One goal of DFE is to minimize the environmental effects of product death by (1) minimizing the amount of waste by weight and by volume, thereby assuring that as little space as possible will be taken up in our filled-to-overflowing landfills, and (2) assuring that incineration will produce no toxic by-products.

Designing for "Nondisposal"

There's an alternative to product death. It's called recycling, and it's the product equivalent of eternal life. (Actually, it's less than eternal for most products, because constituent parts usually break down after a number of incarnations—then it's off to the landfill or incinerator with them).

Ideally, durable products should be designed for long life. This may require that products be designed so that they can be upgraded with new, improved parts or systems that further reduce the product's environmental impact and comply with new regulations.

The next preference is to design a product so that it is easily reusable or recyclable, i.e., so that it will have multiple lives before having to be shipped off for disposal. The difference between reusable and recyclable is quite simple. *Reusable* products are reused in their existing form, while *recyclable* products must be broken down into their constituent parts and then refabricated into new products. As a rule, it's environmentally preferable for a product to be reused rather than recycled, because the recycling and remanufacturing process usually consumes more natural resources than simple reuse.

Dr. Ian Boustead, a British physicist affiliated with Open University, Sussex, England, recommends that green-product designers establish both global-issue priorities and local-issue priorities, and has this to say about recycling:

> Once priorities are decided, the conclusions about the value of recycling may not be as expected. For example, suppose that the conservation of fossil fuels is placed as a top priority. Should materials made from renewable resources, such as paper, be recycled? If virgin

paper production consumes significant quantities of fossil fuels, as might be the case with nonintegrated paper mills, then it could be that recycling would lead to an overall saving in fossil fuels. However, if virgin paper is produced in an integrated plant so that waste wood products such as bark and waste materials produced during pulping are used to generate steam and electricity for paper production, then it is possible to envisage the situation where virgin paper can be produced with the use of little or no fossil fuel. Under these circumstances, we might reasonably question whether it is sensible environmental policy to recycle paper when the collection, de-inking, re-pulping and paper making would all require the consumption of fossil fuels. Better to use a fossil fuel free virgin paper than a second grade recycled product using fossil fuels.[5]

The above scenario is provided only to remind us that designing for the environment is a holistic exercise demanding integrated issues, considerations, and management. The conclusion drawn in the reasoning process also assumes, for example, that we are managing our forest resources for abundant supply and renewability.

Over the last several years, *product* (as distinguished from packaging) recycling has emerged as an important component of product design. The Design for Disassembly (DFD) and Design for Remanufacture (DFR) subsets of DFE describe approaches to product design that incorporate facilitated product dismantling and remanufacture into product design. Many auto manufacturers, with the Germans (BMW) in the lead, are beginning to design their cars for disassembly and remanufacture.

An example of design for disassembly comes from Shape, Inc. (Biddeford, Maine), a manufacturer of audio- and videocassettes, computer products, and compact disk packaging. The company reduced the number of parts in its videocassettes by about a third. It also molded the Society of the Plastics Industry (SPI) plastic number into each major component. In addition to reducing the amount of plastic used, these measures make it easier for Shape to disassemble defective videocassettes for subsequent reuse.

Designing for Pollution Prevention

As with the production process, DFE takes into consideration the environmental impact of the product's emissions into water and air, both as a function of use and disposal. Aerosols, for instance, contribute to smog formation; phosphate-containing detergents can lead to an overabundance of algae in ponds and streams.

DFE does not require *all* negative environmental impacts to be eliminated. Indeed, that is generally impossible: virtually every consumer product has a negative environmental impact, i.e., the planet is worse off by virtue of its existence than it would be if the product had never come into being. DFE does not foreclose, say, using aerosol packaging for a given product (especially if a pump version isn't possible, practical, or salable). However, DFE will attempt to minimize the environmental damage caused by aerosol usage, perhaps by using an aerosol that uses reduced levels of smog-causing volatile organic compounds, or by accompanying the product launch with a program to support the development of an aerosol recycling infrastructure.

Designing for Resource Conservation

DFE favors the use of recycled materials whenever possible. This is made easier when the recycled materials are readily and inexpensively available, as is the case with the plastic waste-bag industry, where second-tier suppliers Carlisle Plastics (Ruffies) and Webster Industries (Good Sense, Renew) are both using extensive amounts of recycled materials in their plastic waste bags—and using that fact to market to consumers' environmental consciousness.

Collateral Damage

The above categories are something less than completely comprehensive. Green-product developers should also take care to assess the impact of their product on a host of collateral environmental issues such as biodiversity (i.e., habitat preservation so that species are not rendered extinct) and rain-forest destruction.

Figure 8-2 is a planning guide developed by Coddington Environmental Management, Inc. as part of a design process that considers *environmental management issues* in addition to marketing management issues.

The United States Environmental Protection Agency, Office of Pollution Prevention and Toxics, has recently introduced *its* Design for the Environment (DfE) Program. To quote their promotional literature:

> By using long term research investments and model industry examples, the Design for the Environment Program seeks to bring about a basic paradigm shift in the way that companies approach the design of their products. It is a partnership between the public and private

Key Development Areas ▶	Opportunity	Feasibility	Design	Preproduction	Production	Sales/Distribution	Education/Regulation	Promotion
Research & Development	Identify Alternative Products and/or Applications	Assess Existing and Alternative Products' Environmental Impact (LCA)	Design for: * Least Impact * Long Life * Secondary Use * Recycling * Maintenance and Repair * Disposability	Weigh Animal Testing versus Alternative Testing	DEVELOP PRODUCT RECYCLING INFRASTRUCTURES			CERTIFY GREEN PRODUCTS AND PROCESSES
Manufacturing/Technology	Identify Alternative Materials, Energy Sources, Processing Methods	Assess Extraction, Transporting, Processing and Waste Disposal Environmental Impact	DESIGN FOR POLLUTION PREVENTION AND ZERO WASTE	Comply with Federal and State Regulations and Local Environmental Ordinances	PRACTICE QUALITY ENVIRONMENTAL MANAGEMENT	GREEN AUDIT PACKING MATERIALS, TRANSPORT VEHICLES, STORAGE FACILITIES, ET AL.	ESTABLISH STAKEHOLDER ALLIANCES WITH ADVOCACY GROUPS, GOVERNMENT AGENCIES, EDUCATION AND RESEARCH INSTITUTIONS, RETAILERS, ET AL.	TRANSFER GREEN TECHNOLOGY
Finance/Economics	Compare the Cost of Managing for Conformance vs. Managing for Assurance	Project the Cost of Impact on: * Human and Environmental Health * Liability * Resource Supply	INSTITUTE SUSTAINABLE DEVELOPMENT PLANNING	Investigate Energy Savings and Resource Conservation Incentives	Consider Product Development Partnerships and Joint Business Ventures	LOBBY FOR FREE MARKET ENVIRONMENTALISM		Budget for Environmental Education, Purchase Incentives and Stakeholder Alliance Programs
Market	Conduct Consumer/Customer Environmental Marketing Research	Conduct Product Purchase, Usage and Performance Research	Satisfy Consumers'/Customers' Basic Needs such as Value Price and Performance	Engage Support of Green Suppliers, Ecopreneurs and Environmentalists	BE ATTENTIVE TO COMMUNITY RELATIONS AND COMMUNITY RIGHT-TO-KNOW	Support Trade with Environmental Education Community Outreach Programs	PROMOTE CONSUMER ENVIRONMENTAL EDUCATION AND EMPOWERMENT	COMPLY WITH STATE GREEN LABELING REGULATIONS AND FTC GUIDELINES

Figure 8-2. Green product design: environmental management considerations.

sector which transfers EPA's experience in chemical problem evaluation to industry and the public so that self-generated assessments of
alternatives and sharing of information will ensure safer design and
use of chemicals and products.[6]

Companies and industries who wish to participate in the EPA's DfE
Program begin by applying DfE tools and participating in a cycle of actions as set forth in Figure 8-3.

Green-Packaging Development

The same generic set of environmental considerations enters into both
packaging and product design—designing for disposal (and nondisposal), designing for pollution prevention, and designing for resource
conservation. Beyond that, packaging presents its own unique array of
design and related issues.

Tradeoffs

Helping the environment inevitably involves tradeoffs. In late 1991, for
instance, Procter & Gamble began offering its Sure and Secret deodorants without any cardboard packaging, a move that cut production
costs by 20 percent while reportedly increasing sales by 4 percent.
Curiously, some consumers I spoke with about Procter & Gamble's initiative were critical of the move. "Why did it take Procter & Gamble
years of study to decide to do something as simple as eliminating cardboard packaging?" one consumer asked. "What could be more obvious?
Talk about bureaucratic deadweight!"

This person failed to appreciate the multiple roles played by packaging. The cardboard layer was not simply extraneous. It helped to prevent tampering. With the outer layer eliminated, it became necessary for
P&G to redesign the deodorant stick itself to make it tamper-resistant.

A separate safety issue arises in conjunction with the use of recycled
materials that come into direct contact with foods and beverages. The
concern here is that the original containers will be used to store poi-
sonous materials, and that these materials will not be purged from the
containers during the recycling process. The Food and Drug
Administration has issued no-objection letters for several PET plastic recycling processes which depolymerize the plastic, thereby rendering it
"effectively virgin" again. The FDA has also okayed the use of recycled
polystyrene in egg cartons. By and large, however, there continue to be

Figure 8-3. U.S. Environmental Protection Agency DfE Program Cycle.

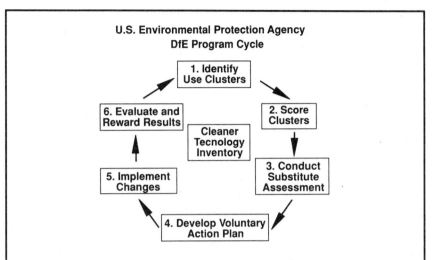

- *Use Cluster Identification.* The DfE program cycle begins in an industry or company by identifying "use clusters" in the industry. A "use cluster" is a set of chemicals, processes, and technologies that can substitute for one another in order to perform a specific function. For example, in the paint-stripping industry three "use clusters" exist: paint stripping for maintenance, paint stripping in household and commercial purposes, and paint stripping for original equipment manufacturing. Each of these use clusters has several alternative chemicals or technologies that can perform the paint-removal function.

- *Use Cluster Scoring System.* After the identification of use clusters, a comparative risk-scoring system is administered to assist in prioritizing use clusters for substitutes assessments. This streamlined scoring system incorporates such factors as human and ecological risks, EPA program office interest, and pollution-prevention opportunities to rank clusters for further work. Prioritizing the clusters for further work, however, depends on additional factors, such as the availability of lower-risk substitutes and the amount of waste or pollution associated with chemicals in the cluster. If, for example, the more widely used chemicals in a cluster present relatively high risks and lower-risk alternatives are available, the cluster would be a good candidate for a substitutes assessment.

(*Continued*)

- *Cleaner Technology Substitutes Assessment (CTSA).* A substitutes assessment is conducted for prioritized use clusters. The substitutes assessment compares the trade-off issues associated with alternatives including risk, releases, performance, cost, energy impacts, resource conservation, and pollution-prevention opportunities.

- *Voluntary Action Plan.* Based upon the results of the substitutes assessment, companies and industries develop a voluntary action plan. A printing company's plan, for instance, could include a commitment to change to water-based inks. The EPA will publicly recognize all participants in the DfE project.

- *Cleaner Technology Inventory.* Information collected throughout the cycle will be reported to PIES for inclusion in the cleaner technology inventory. The inventory will (1) identify safer substitutes for use in existing industry operations; (2) identify opportunities for incorporating pollution-prevention principles into the development of new chemicals and technologies; and (3) assist other companies and industries who wish to conduct substitutes assessments.

Figure 8-3. (*Continued*)

sharp regulatory constraints on the use of recycled materials in packaging that comes into direct contact with food and beverage products.

Environmental considerations can also bring tradeoffs in packaging *efficacy*. A modest reduction in efficacy may be an acceptable price to pay for improved environmental performance, but there clearly comes a point beyond which further declines in performance are unacceptable.

Over the last several years, a number of environmentally friendly alternatives to polystyrene loose fill have been introduced to the market. Some of these alternatives are paper-based; others involve the use of popcorn (yes, popcorn!). When polystyrene-bashing was at its height, some pundits delightedly predicted that the arrival of these eco-alternatives would lead to drastic declines in market share for polystyrene. Things haven't worked out that way. Why? In a word, *performance*. The majority of product shippers, including those open-minded enough to have tested the alternatives, have stayed with polystyrene because they are persuaded that it is a substantially superior product.

Nor has their choice of polystyrene necessarily been environmentally detrimental. More and more shippers are using *recycled* polystyrene, an option that combines excellent performance and environmental desirability.

Benefits, Hidden and Otherwise

Tradeoffs occur when the incorporation of environmental considerations into packaging design reduces performance in other areas. But bringing heightened environmental awareness into the design process can also produce benefits:

- *Reduced production costs.* Use less packaging material, and your costs go down. As noted above, when Procter & Gamble eliminated the outer cartons of its Sure and Secret deodorants, its production costs were reduced by 20 percent.

- *Increased shelf space.* By reducing packaging, suppliers also free up valuable shelf space. This does wonders for retailer relations. It can also increase product sales, assuming the retailer uses that extra space to sell other product offerings from the same supplier.

Nor should we overlook the most obvious business advantage of environmentally improved packaging. It offers a significant marketing opportunity. As we've mentioned before, the environment is a tiebreaker, even among consumers whose buy decisions are driven largely by price and convenience. By improving a package's environmental performance—and by publicizing that improved performance, often on the packaging itself—a company can boost product sales.

Keeping One Eye on the Infrastructure

Recycling infrastructures are evolving constantly. Today's unrecyclable packaging material is tomorrow's somewhat recyclable material; today's somewhat recyclable material will be universally recyclable tomorrow. Because of the shifting reach of recycling infrastructures, the environmental desirability of packaging types such as polyethylene terephthalate (PET), high-density polyethylene (HDPE) and low-density polyethylene (LDPE) requires constant reexamination.

Given these conditions, I recommend to green-product and package designers that they keep their eye on the long-term ball, i.e., that they make a point of assessing recycling *trendlines* as well as the current state of the art. If widely recyclable, would a given packaging material be environmentally desirable? If so, what if any steps might the supplier take to help make widespread recyclability a reality? Green-packaging issues are best examined in the context of recycling infrastructures—where they are now, where they're headed, and how the supplier's own marketing and educational strategies can contribute to their formation.

Not Just Product Packaging

When packaging is mentioned, most people think of the product container and nothing more. But green-packaging design involves other types of packaging, too—shipping containers, for instance. The Food and Drug Administration has approved the use of recycled polyethylene and polypropylene harvesting crates, while Chep USA (Park Ridge, N.J.) offers a pallet-pooling program in which customers rent pallets which are then maintained and tracked by Chep. These are just two examples of ways in which environmental efficiencies are being introduced to packaging types that never make it onto supermarket shelves. Consumer-product packaging has more visibility and therefore is more easily used as a marketing tool, but back-room packaging improvements have significant environmental impact and should not be overlooked.

We noted in the beginning of this chapter that extensive marketing planning is an intrinsic part of green-product development. Such an approach requires product developers to incorporate a DFE approach into planning for marketing materials such as in-store promotional displays. Although promotional displays are not, strictly speaking, packaging, like product packages they are highly visible consumer-communications vehicles. If a company chooses to promote a green product using a promotional display that is made out of virgin materials, that won't speak well for the company's environmental sensitivity.

A Case Study

The 1990 redesign of the famous L'Eggs package demonstrates how one company leveraged consumers' environmental concerns to convert a potentially disastrous packaging makeover into an enormous success.

Of all the product and packaging concepts ever developed, few have enjoyed the widespread and instant brand recognition of the L'Eggs pantyhose plastic egg. L'Eggs brand's distinctive package hit the streets in the early 1970s and, fueled by availability and reasonable price, soon became the biggest-selling hosiery in the world. The ubiquitous eggs, packed tightly in their paperboard bases, were in every supermarket and drugstore in America. The plastic egg—soon the darling of the arts-and-crafts set and a popular kiddie sandbox toy—wasn't cheap to produce, but it was worth every penny to the firm's marketers.

Then L'Eggs began to come under criticism for its ovoid box. The eggs were made of durable polyethylene, a plastic difficult to recycle at best. Nor was the paperboard base recyclable in most communities.

Consumers and environmentalists criticized Sara Lee Corp., L'Eggs parent company, for adding to the nation's mounting garbage crisis. What was once the product's trademark was turning into a liability.

In a bold marketing move, L'Eggs decided to replace its famous package. The company opted for a paperboard-only carton with a rounded, egg-shaped top, sporting bold new lettering on a brightly colored background. Although clearly risky—L'Eggs brand identity was part and parcel of its unique box—from another perspective, the move made good business sense. The graphics were updated and the labeling information improved. Because the new packages are slightly smaller than the old design, almost a third more containers can fit into the same display space. And because the new box uses 38 percent less packaging material than its predecessor, it saved the company money.

Most observers believed that the new package would have a neutral impact on the product's marketing and advertising. They were wrong. Within weeks of the unveiling of the new package, L'Eggs was being hailed as visionary in the popular and trade press. True, most stories mentioned the benefits of the smaller container size and clearer labeling. But praise was also lavished on this "green visionary" and "environmentally proactive" company's "eco-friendly" box. Made of 100 percent recycled paperboard and printed with water-based inks, the new carton catapulted L'Eggs and Sara Lee Corp. into the environmental limelight.

Executives had been optimistically but cautiously hoping for a nonnegative consumer response. Now, they found that the company was being touted as "environmentally caring" and a leader in responsible and environmentally sound repackaging and environmental marketing. With its new package, L'Eggs pulled off a major marketing coup and turned a potentially risky move into the stuff public relations dreams are made of.

Summary and Recommendations

Green-product development is an essential component of a comprehensive environmental marketing strategy. While an aggressive green-product development program may encounter resistance from senior management, that doesn't necessarily make it a bad idea. Nor does it preclude a more conservative green-product strategy involving the improvement of existing product lines rather than the development of entirely new product lines.

It's important to secure the support of your suppliers in developing green products. In the final analysis, however, you're in charge of the relationship. If a supplier isn't willing to work with you, you can and should be willing to go out and find a replacement.

In addition to resistance from suppliers and from your own senior management, a third possible obstacle involves insufficient in-house expertise. Don't let this stand in your way. Expert assistance is available on a for-hire basis.

Extensive market evaluation and product-concept testing is an absolute prerequisite to product development and launch. This may seem self-evident, but it is surprising how many companies overlook this critically important step. At our firm, we have found focus groups to be particularly effective tools for helping to evaluate green-product concepts.

Regarding green-product and packaging design, the state of the art of life-cycle analysis is not yet sufficiently advanced to permit definitive analyses of the total environmental impacts of a given product or package. However, one can have enough of a sense of what is better and what is worse to enable one to move forward. The emerging science of design for the environment (DFE) calls upon product designers to factor the following considerations into their planning (the same considerations, of course, also apply to packaging design):

- *The production process.* Among the issues to address are: (1) raw-materials usage; (2) energy consumption; (3) pollution prevention; and (4) solid-waste implications.

- *Designing for disposal.* What are the environmental impacts of the product once it reaches the end of its useful life?

- *Designing for nondisposal.* To what extent is the product reusable or recyclable?

- *Designing for pollution prevention.* What are the implications of manufacture and use for air and water quality?

- *Designing for resource conservation.* Are recycled materials used whenever possible?

9
Green-Product Positioning

The Environmental Imperative

Most Americans live lives that are out of touch with the natural world. The ground beneath our feet is often covered with concrete or asphalt, our water is piped to us from who knows where, and we get our food and other "necessities" from characterless warehouses. Little of what we consume bears any physical resemblance to what it came from originally, and it comes packaged in materials that will outlive all of us.

In his book *Lame Deer—Seeker of Visions*, John Lame Deer, a Sioux Indian, provides a glimpse of how our relationship with nature has changed:

> You can't understand about nature, about the feeling we have toward it, unless you understand how close we were to the buffalo. That animal was almost like a part of ourselves, part of our souls. The buffalo gave us everything we needed. Our tipis were made of his skin. His hide was our bed, our blanket, our winter coat. Out of his skin we made our water bags. Not the smallest part of it was wasted. His stomach . . . became our soup kettle. His horns were our spoons, our bones, our knifes, our women's awls and needles. Out of his sinews we made our bowstrings and thread. His ribs were fashioned into sleds for our children. . . .

I would venture to say that most Americans today have no idea what their shoes are made of! We live inside an industrial-age cocoon, with little or no sense of being connected to the natural world. It is almost as if there are two separate universes: the universe of the natural environment, which is suffering from pollution, global warming, deforestation, and a host of other ailments and the universe of the consuming public, which is insulated from the natural world by those very commodities that have helped wreak havoc on it—air-conditioned homes, overpackaged and overprocessed goods, gasoline-powered vehicles, endless electrical gadgets, etc.

Ultimately, these twin realms of experience are going to have to be merged if we are to achieve significant, long-term improvements in the condition of the environment, as well as a business environment predicated on sustainable development. People must come to the realization that they do not live separated from the environment, but that they are part and parcel of it. Until people learn to see beyond their synthetic environment to the larger world of nature that surrounds (and, indeed, embraces) it, improvements in our environmental lot will be incremental at best.

As environmentally responsible citizens, product marketers have an obligation to help move consumers beyond the insular mindset that is so commonplace in today's world. Green products can help to do this. But mindset changes of this magnitude cannot be expected to occur overnight. One can't reasonably expect to make a difference by saying, or even implying, that "You should buy green products because it's the right thing to do." Consumers are not yet ready to take action on that basis. In the words of a focus-group participant, "I need a product that will clean my grease-encrusted stove, not my conscience."

The best way for product marketers to help make consumers more aware of the "environmental environment" that surrounds the "consumer environment" they inhabit is by positioning green attributes as one appealing element among others such as price and performance. This is a far better stratagem than attempting to sell green products on the basis that "They're green and that's enough."

The Green Joker in the Parity Deck

Boiled down to its essentials, a product is a very simple thing, an assemblage of materials whose function is to meet people's needs (or perceptions of what they need). One of the marketer's jobs is to let people know that the product exists and how it will help them. But there is more to marketing than that. It is also about creating an identity, a personality, for a product. It is about making a product seem to "live."

With parity among products the rule rather than the exception, it is often a product's unique image that brings it success or failure in the marketplace. This is why green-product positioning is so important. In an age of parity products, highlighting a product's environmental attributes can provide that critical marketing edge.

The Elements of Green-Product Positioning

A green-product–positioning strategy requires marketers to address the following issues: (1) user features and benefits; (2) the price point; (3) distribution channels; (4) labeling; (5) environmental benefits; (6) environmental performance; and (7) the corporate environmental policy.

Figure 9-1 examines each of these issues in the context of the planning or design and communications issues they raise. Let's consider each of these in turn.

User Features and Benefits

This is product positioning at its most fundamental. How can the consumer use the product? What is it good for? What are the benefits it offers? The product's *application* is thus the key design issue—and the *unique selling point* (commonly known as the USP) is the core point of differentiation around which a marketing strategy is constructed.

It can be problematic to position a product's environmental benefits as the USP because many consumers operate on the knee-jerk assump-

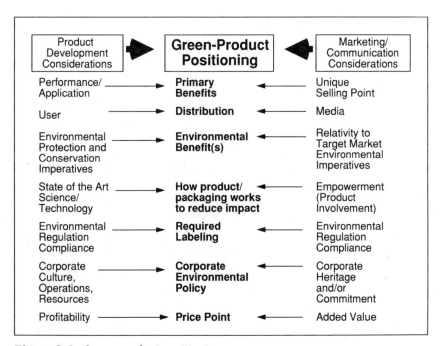

Figure 9-1. Green-product positioning.

tion that if a product's identity is based on its green attributes, its performance in other key areas such as efficacy will be inferior. This assumption is not always correct, but it is widespread. As a result, it is often more advisable to position a product's basic reason for being first and its green attributes second.

Some companies have gone so far as to deemphasize their products' green virtues entirely. Miles Labs (Chicago, Illinois) took this approach with its SOS Kitchen-Safe All-Purpose Cleaner. This product is both environmentally sensible and nontoxic because it is made with natural lemon oil, baking soda, and no phosphorus. It is safe to use where food is being prepared. Given the choice between emphasizing the product's environmental and safety benefits, Miles chose to stress the latter, in accord with consumers' prioritization of desired benefits.

Was discretion the better part of valor? In Miles' case, perhaps. Although the company isn't using the product to get the word out about environmental issues, SOS Kitchen-Safe is an environmentally superior product, and it is also doing well in the marketplace. What is really important is not that companies *market* green, but that they *be* green. Even without being environmentally marketed, SOS Kitchen-Safe is a noteworthy example of successful green-product development. Nor has anything ruled out the possibility of the product's being marketed on the basis of its environmental strengths sometime in the future.

Distribution Channels

To a significant degree, a product's positioning is a function of its channels of distribution. Distribute a product at a Bloomingdale's, and it's likely to have one identity. Distribute it at a K mart, and it will probably have another.

Distribution channels also affect how a product is positioned environmentally. The higher the income level, the likelier it is for people to be well informed about environmental issues—and willing to buy green. Because of this, environmental promotions are likely to be more effective in upscale distribution channels than in mass outlets. Another implication of this fact is that, where a decision is made to accentuate a product's environmental virtues in mass channels, a more extensive educational program will be needed to support the product's positioning.

It may also be desirable to vary the content of the environmental messages that are being delivered, depending on the distribution channel and the demographics (and psychographics) of the groups who shop there. Lower-income buyers tend to have more of a "use" orientation towards the environment, i.e., their concerns about it are premised largely on the use they get out of the environment for hunting, fishing, boating, and so on. An upscale audience in, say, northern California would be likely to have less use-oriented and more conservation concerns about the environment. Sharply contrasting environmental messages would be appropriate for these two groups.

Environmental Benefits and Performance

Since most consumer packaged products have, at some point in their life cycle, an adverse effect on the environment, we tend to call any correction of that negative impact an environmental benefit. Thus, environmentally friendly may be something of a misnomer: environmentally better might be the more accurate term.

Semantic niceties aside, marketers who wish to position their products as green must at a minimum communicate two discrete sets of information: (1) the nature of the problem; and (2) how the product in question contributes to the solution.

1. *The nature of the problem.* The environmental situation addressed by the product or package must be identified and explained in as much detail as is necessary to communicate the nature and scope of the problem. As a rule, the more complex the environmental problem, the more explanation required. Of course, there are limits on how much explaining can be done on a product package—which is precisely why an essential component of a green-product positioning strategy can be an accompanying environmental education program.

2. *The contribution to the solution.* It's also necessary to relate that general explanation back to the product-packaging combination, i.e., to explain how and to what extent the green product in question addresses the problem. This explanation will often have a scientific, technical cast to it. This is okay, so long as it's comprehensible. Techno-babble will persuade readers that you've got something to hide, not that you're really green.

These are the two axes around which environmental product positioning is based. Leave out one of these two components—the characterization of the problem and the connecting of the problem to the solution—and your message will fall short of the mark.

This general set of operating principles leaves room for a broad range of strategic options. Marketers can be minimalist, i.e., they can limit themselves basically to top-line descriptions of the problem. For instance, the front panel of Lever Brothers' environmental labeling language reads simply, "SUPPORT PLASTIC RECYCLING—See Back Panel," and the back panel states, "PLEASE HELP! We are now using technology that can include recycled plastic in our bottles at levels between 25 percent and 35 percent. But to do so consistently, we need more recycled plastic. So please encourage recycling in your community. For more information, please call 1-800-544-2002." Alternatively, environmental labeling language can be maximalist, i.e., it can serve up detailed explanations. Similarly, marketers can keep their discussions of how their product addresses the problem to a few choice words, or they can go into elaborate detail. Either way, the fundamental rule remains the same: explain both the issue *and* how your product addresses it.

Other issues to keep in mind as you develop your green-product positioning strategy include: (1) relating the environmental benefits to your target market; and (2) the principle of empowerment.

Environmental Benefits and Your Target Market.   It is important to tailor your environmental communications to the demographic and psychographic characteristics of your target market. Where does your target market fit in the Roper/Johnson segmentation? How sophisticated is your target market about the environmental issue that your product addresses? You will want to address questions like these as you map your strategy for communicating the environmental implications of your green product.

Green-Product Positioning and Empowerment.   In our mass society, many people, including large numbers of apparently successful individuals, feel effectively foreclosed from the corridors of power and influence. Odd as it may seem, green products can do something about this—about the feelings if not the fact of alienation. Green products work because they empower people who want to make a difference. The availability of environmentally-oriented products which they can choose to buy or not buy allows them to feel as if they are gaining control over their environmental destinies.

In the final analysis, green-product positioning is about *relationship-building*. It is about having the product function as more than a commodity, as more than a mere "thing." It is about positioning the product so that it meets an emotional need that goes beyond its basic functionality. In this day and age, *that means giving consumers a sense that they can make a difference, that their fate is not entirely out of their hands.*

Labeling

In considering the impacts of labeling on product positioning, it is important to keep in mind that there are two levels of labeling: *mandatory* labeling, i.e., labeling that is required by law, and *optional* labeling.

Unlike mandatory labeling, optional labeling can have a substantial impact on product positioning. All environmental labeling currently falls into the optional category. Currently, at no level in the United States—not at the federal, state, or local level—do regulations require the environmental assets of products or their packaging to be disclosed. What regulations and guidelines *do* exist require certain rules to be followed for those companies that choose to communicate their product-packaging combinations' environmental attributes.

It is useful to draw a further distinction between theoretically optional and actually optional labeling. No law or regulation currently requires companies to put the Society of the Plastics Industry (SPI) plastic codes on the bottom of their plastic packaging, but the company that neglects to do so puts itself so far behind the environmental curve that it almost cannot help but attract attention. Using the SPI codes is only theoretically optional: as a business reality, it's effectively mandatory.

It is in the area of actually optional (as distinguished from theoretically optional) labeling that all the controversy about environmental labeling lies. Neither formal regulation nor the more subtle pressure to keep up with the business mainstream currently requires companies to use terms like recyclable or even recycled-content on their labeling. There are good business reasons both for and against using optional labeling of this sort. On the positive side, it educates consumers and can also provide a competitive edge. On the negative side, it can attract regulatory scrutiny and bad publicity. Any company that calls its product recyclable without going into substantial detail on the extent of that recyclability risks getting a great deal of unwanted attention.

I happen to believe that carefully drafted environmental labeling language, when combined with a genuine effort to be environmentally responsible as a corporation, can be an effective educational and marketing strategy.

The boundary separating theoretically optional from actually optional labeling will shift over time as more and more companies add environmental information to their labels. As this happens, much environmental labeling will take on the character of a defensive strategy, i.e., it won't be used to position a company as ahead of the pack so much as to establish that it isn't lagging.

Corporate Environmental Policy

As we have mentioned before, there was a time when consumers weren't particular about the companies behind the products they consumed, but that is no longer the case. Increasingly, corporations' reputations are affecting consumers' buy decisions. As a result, marketers must factor their corporations' environmental reputations, as well as their actual practices and policies, into their green-product positioning.

How does one tie the corporate environmental reputation in with the green product? One proceeds very carefully. I strongly recommend *specificity* in your communications: "X Co. cares about the environment" is an intrinsically less credible statement than "X Co. has pledged to reduce the weight of its packaging by 15 percent by 1995."

Another way to promote a positive corporate image is by encouraging consumers to behave in an environmentally responsible fashion. Such a strategy creates the impression that the corporation is committed to the environment without the sort of self-promotional claims that automatically invite distrust.

Green Private-Label Products

In May 1991, Frank Mayes, vice-president of planning and development at Topco Associates, a cooperative owned by supermarket chains and grocery wholesalers, was quoted by *Private Label* magazine as saying,

> If we were a General Foods or a Procter & Gamble and therefore able to extrapolate our sales numbers on a national basis, GreenMark [the company's green private-label brand] would be a $300 million brand. It was certainly our most successful new brand introduction in several years.[1]

Loblaw International Merchants, the Toronto-based supermarket chain that dominates Ontario, witnessed consumer demand turn their President's Choice G.R.E.E.N. line of private-label products into over a $100 million business in less than two years.

This track record hasn't been duplicated throughout the green private-label business. Many retailers found that consumers initially responded enthusiastically to their green private-label offerings, and that demand thereafter became sluggish. The green private-label business can best be described as spotty.

It is much easier for large, financially healthy retailers, wholesalers, and distributors to take the green product plunge than it is for manufacturers. Retailers don't necessarily need to pay for product development or retooling, nor do they have to go through the complex and time-consuming process of persuading their channels of distribution to support their green products. Retailers can get in and out of green (and other) new product launches relatively quickly and painlessly through private-label programming.

The ability of retailers to compete with their trade partners while also working with them (and indeed continue to be perceived as *trade partners!*) is one of the wonders of modern business. How far can retailers go in expanding their own private-label lines without being perceived as biting the hand that feeds them? Farther than they've gone to date, it seems, for they clearly haven't yet alienated their trade partners. Which is surprising, given that the share of market for private-label products now is in the 20 percent range.

Here are some private-label rules of thumb:

- Carry a large selection of products in a variety of sizes, weights, flavors, etc. To get the most out of their private-label investment, retailers usually must carry 300 or more items across different product categories (some merchants carry as many as 3000 private label items!). And of course the same principle applies to green private-label products: private-label lines should be end-to-end, not just the miscellaneous green product here and there.

- Expand the product category, don't cannibalize it. As a rule, consumers prefer national brands over store brands. Until this situation changes (and there are no indications it's going to), retailers cannot afford to have customers come to their stores for store brands only. Whether green or nongreen, private-label products must be positioned as alternatives to rather than substitutes for national brands (herein lies the secret to being perceived as a trade partner, not a competitor!).

- Look for long-range potential. When introducing private-label lines (green or otherwise), select the product categories that are likeliest to create the largest—and longest-term—response.

- Take care that your private-label products perform as well as national brands—and that product quality is consistently excellent, too.

- Actively promote your private-label lines.

- Private-label products should be more profitable than national brands.

Not only do these principles apply equally to green and nongreen private-label offerings, but with one exception (the requirement that private-label lines be more profitable than national brands), they also apply to green-branded offerings. Let us now examine how these principles apply to branded offerings.

Develop Complete Lines. Retailers have become accustomed to the marketing efficiencies and profitability of multiproduct marketing. National brand marketers are likelier to get meaningful retailer support for a full line of green products than for the occasional, stand-alone green product. Indeed, the sporadic character of nonprivate-label–green-product offerings has been a major reason for their only middling success.

Expand, Don't Cannibalize. Just as retailers must take care to position their private-label lines (green or otherwise) as alternatives to (rather than replacements for) national brands, so must national marketers take care to position green-product lines as alternatives to their established product lines. Consumers are favorably disposed to this approach; they have always supported variety.

Choose Your Category Carefully. According to Greg Phillips, President of Ashdun Industries, a private-label marketer, private-label products traditionally fare well where there are two or more leading brands. Why? Because, where no brand has a stranglehold on the market, consumers are likelier to switch brands—and therefore to be more amenable to private-label lines.

The same appears to hold true for green products. The 1990 study conducted by the Good Housekeeping Institute, which was cited in Chapter 8 found that the most frequently purchased green products are in categories where there is no clear market leader: (1) cleaning products (38 percent); (2) paper products (33 percent); (3) garbage or trash bags (24 percent); (4) beauty products (21 percent); and (5) food products (12 percent).

With the exception of beauty products, private-label product sales skew similarly.

Don't Stint on Performance. While both *quality* and *consistency* of green-product performance are always extremely important, they are particularly so for green products because consumers assume the worst about how green products will perform.

Promote Your Green Products! Like private-label lines, green products will not simply jump off the shelves into consumers' shopping carts. As we have stressed at various points in this book, they have considerable potential, but only if they are marketed on a foundation of (1) environmental education, and (2) inducements to purchase.

Summary and Recommendations

The key points in this chapter may be summarized as follows.

The Prominence of the Environmental Factor. In a time of parity products, a product's environmental attributes can serve as the critical differentiator between a product and its competitors. However, this is not to suggest that marketers should position their product's environmental attributes as their unique selling point (USP). With many consumers assuming that green products underperform their less green competitors, it can be counterproductive to give primacy to a product's environmental attributes. It is better to use a product's environmental assets as a collateral strategy, i.e., to position green qualities as an *added* benefit rather than as the *central* one.

Distribution Channels. The environmental profile of consumers varies from distribution channel to distribution channel. If you are distributing your green product through upscale department stores, one communications strategy may be indicated. If mass merchandisers are your outlet, a different approach will be warranted.

Environmental Benefits/Performance. Green-product positioning requires marketers to discuss both (1) the nature of the particular environmental problem in question, and (2) how the product addresses it. This strategy allows marketers to achieve the twin psychographic goals of green-product positioning—education and empowerment.

Labeling. Currently, all environmental labeling is optional, but some types are more optional than others. Marketers, for example, who fail to put the SPI plastic code on their plastic packaging invite a perception that they are environmentally backward. Now that the ground rules for environmental labeling are becoming more clearly established, more types of environmental labeling will become only theoretically optional, as distinguished from actually optional.

Corporate Environmental Policy. Marketers' green-product positioning will inevitably be affected by their company's environmental positioning. In the great majority of cases, when a company's environmental reputation is somewhere between wonderful and terrible, care should be taken not to seem to be making unjustifiable claims about a company's environmental *bona fides*.

Private-Label Lessons.   Green private-label products are one of the success stories of the green-product marketplace. National marketers can draw some valuable lessons from the rollout of green private-label products. Among them:

- Develop complete green-product lines rather than just the occasional product.
- Aggressively promote green products—their success is built on a foundation of education and awareness.

10
Strategic Alliances and Environmental Marketing Partnership Planning

The Types of Strategic Alliance

Environmental strategic alliances are informal or formal relationships with other organizations to further corporate goals. They are usually entered into with one *or more* of the following three objectives in mind: (1) promotion; (2) consumer education; and (3) research (solid-waste management and pollution prevention).

Let's briefly examine each of these three types of strategic alliance.

Promotion-Based Strategic Alliances

Also known as environmental cause–marketing partnerships, these arrangements constitute a popular (if often ill-understood) strategy. In its most simple form, this environmental marketing partnership takes the form of a straightforward donation to an environmental advocacy group in exchange for the actual or implied endorsement by the group of a company's product or other environmental initiative. Environmental Group X gets a contribution of $Y for each $Z of product sold. Environmental cause–marketing programs of this sort are a viable strategy (although, as we shall see, not without their pitfalls), but they are only the tip of the promotional iceberg (and certainly not the best product movers). The more interactive the marketing partnership, the better.

The dollars-only approach can be pretty thin. Although some sort of financial contribution is usually at the heart of promotion-based strategic alliances, there are other ways in which environmental groups and corporations can work together.

For instance, a 1992 arrangement between Conservation International and Bank of America called for cooperation across a number of fronts, including: (1) the donation of $2 million in Brazilian loans to fund Conservation International programs in Brazil; (2) a new Conservation International environmental check series—among the first on recycled paper—for Bank of America customers; and (3) a variety of other cooperative efforts aimed at international environmental education.

Table 10-1 presents examples of business and environmental-group–partnered marketing programs.

Environmental marketing partnerships need not be limited to environmental groups. It is one of the themes of this chapter that strategic alliances, whatever their objective, are best served by including a wide range of stakeholders in the project or ongoing program.

Consumer Education

Consumer education is a primary or secondary goal of most environmental strategic alliances. Consumers need to learn more about environmental issues in order for them to appreciate the value of green products and other environmental management initiatives of business. This is a major reason why many companies are underwriting school and consumer–environmental education efforts.

Of course, that's not the only reason why corporations underwrite consumer education efforts. The fact that they are doing so gets publicly noted, and that produces public relations benefits.

Table 10-2 briefly describes a number of corporate environmental education programs.

Environmental education–stakeholder alliances can also prove to be a fast track to commercial business development as the following example illustrates.

"Scrubco" has two lines of business, a consumer products division and a specialty products and technology division. The company has a strong environmental profile and a track record of fostering environmental education. Its products and technology are not only environ-

Table 10-1. Business and Environmental Organization Partnerships

Business organization	Environmental organization	Type of tie-in program
Procter & Gamble Co.	Keep America Beautiful	Educational program
General Electric	National Audubon Society	Audubon TV specials
Citibank Corp.	National Park Foundation	Credit card usage and donation
S.C.Johnson & Son	World Wildlife Fund	Purchase and donation promotion
RJR Nabisco	The Nature Conservancy	Employee matching gift
Hallmark Cards	Heartland All-Species	Community and school education
McDonald's Corp.	Global ReLeaf	Plant-a-tree promotion
Toyota Motor Sales USA	Chesapeake Bay Foundation	Educational centers
Johnson & Johnson	World Resources Institute	Corporate information exchange
United Telecommunications	Wilderness Society	Usage and contribution promotion
Ford Motor Co.	Tread Lightly	Vehicle-owner education
Church & Dwight Co.	Clean Water Fund	Home Safe Home

mentally benign, they are also used to clean up, reduce, and in some cases prevent environmental pollution.

Scrubco was invited by a federal government agency to be the main sponsor of a multimedia exhibit that would promote the principles of environmental education and highlight the initiatives in that area by various government and world environmental organizations.

Scrubco welcomed the opportunity to work with the government on this project for three reasons: (1) the project fit Scrubco's business objective of environmental education; (2) the project would become the basis for a more meaningful relationship between Scrubco and environmental regulators; and (3) the project provided a great opportunity to involve media organizations (for promotion) and other businesses (for cosponsorship) that the company wanted to get closer to.

During the project development, Scrubco had the opportunity to interface with many government organizations and NGOs that heretofore had not been easily accessible or amenable to Scrubco or to its salespeople.

Table 10-2. Corporate Environmental Education Programs

Company	Program name	Age group	Description
Browning-Ferris Ind. (Houston, Tex.)	Moebius	Grades 4–6	Curriculum plus cartoon character teaching about recycling and waste disposal
Chevron Corporation (San Francisco, Calif.)	Reasoning & Risk	High school	Introduces concepts of risk and analysis in relation to environment
Dow Chemical Company (Midland, Mich.)	Recyclesaurus	Elementary school	Coloring book, games, songs, mazes on recycling
	Recycle This	High school	Staged presentation on recycling
Exxon Corporation (New York, N.Y.)	The Energy Cube	Secondary school	Video and print material library and science and energy educational materials
First Brands Corp. (Danbury, Conn.)	What Does it Do? Where Does It Go?	Upper elementary	Educational materials on plastics and the environment
HDR Engineering, Inc. (White Plains, N.Y.)	Mister Roger's Neighborhood Talks About the Environment	Preschool	Pro bono distribution of Mister Roger's Neighborhood TV program on environment plus associated materials
J. C. Penney Co., Inc. (Dallas, Tex.) and Fiber Industries, Inc. (New York, N.Y.)	Help the Environment	Children 10 and under	Essay and poster contest on the environment
McDonald's Corp. (Oak Brook, Ill.)	Environmental Action Pack	Grades 3–6	Deals with ecology and recycling. Developed with the Field Museum of Natural History
	WEcology	Grades 6–10	Magazine addressing environmental issues. Has asserted that polystyrene is "environmentally better than the present alterna-

Company	Program	Audience	Materials
National Polystyrene Recycling Company (Lincolnshire, Ill.)	Recycling Riddles/Do the Right Thing; Recycle	Elementary and Middle school	Video and print materials on plastics, packaging, and the environment
Procter & Gamble (Cincinnati, Ohio)	Planet Patrol Decisions on Product Safety	Upper-elementary and Secondary school	Solid waste solutions program Information on product testing, storage, and disposal of hazardous household products
Scott Paper Co. (Philadelphia, Pa.)	Everybody's Talking about the Environment	Secondary school	Video on polystyrene food packaging
Sebastian International (Woodland Hills, Calif.)	Little Green	Elementary school	Information about the rainforest
Target Stores (Minneapolis, Minn.)	Kids for Saving Earth	Children of all ages	Environmental clubs
Weyerhaeuser Co. (Tacoma, Wash.)	Educational Resource Packet	Upper elementary and Middle school	Material on wood, trees

SOURCES: Green MarketAlert, Naidus Group, Coddington Environmental Management.

**Research (Solid-Waste
Management and Pollution
Prevention)**

Although not uncommon, strategic alliances of this sort tend to be less well publicized than those focusing on consumer education or environmental cause-related promotions. Of course, there are exceptions, as with the heralded partnership between the Environmental Defense Fund and McDonald's Corp. This initiative, which a McDonald's executive described as "letting the camel into the tent," led to a decision by the fast food giant to abandon the polystyrene clamshell in favor of a quilted paper wrap. It also produced a comprehensive waste-reduction plan which included: (1) pressuring McDonald's 600 suppliers to improve their environmental performance; and (2) testing such initiatives as recycling postconsumer, paper-based food packaging; assessing the feasibility of composting organic and paper waste; and testing a starch-based material for consumer cutlery to evaluate its functionality and compostability.

More recently, General Motors and the Environmental Defense Fund (EDF) announced that they have agreed to hold formal discussions on environmental issues. As Joseph Goffman, a lawyer with EDF, put it, "Over the last 20 years, it has been each side preaching to the heathen on the other side. We've decided to skip the great conversion speeches and talk about what we can talk about."[1]

In addition to a program for scrapping old cars, the two groups will discuss gasoline alternatives, emissions measurement, cost-effectiveness of new-fuel and new-vehicle emissions standards, cost effectiveness, the role of vehicles in global warming, and the impact of regulatory requirements on vehicle design.

The Strategic Importance of the Strategic Alliance

The adage "The whole is greater than the sum of the parts" definitely applies to the strategic alliance. By working with complementary allies, a range of objectives can be achieved that could not be attained by a company working on its own.

Extension of Reach

Strategic alliances expand the reach of product marketers. The most direct way to achieve this is by partnering with the media, but alliances with other corporate partners can achieve the same effect. Let's say a food company partners with an automobile company. That gives the food company access to everyone who comes into the auto manufacturer's dealerships, and vice versa.

Ancillary Benefits

In addition, strategic alliances offer a host of ancillary benefits.

Access to Expertise.   Strategic alliances often provide access to expertise that wouldn't be available in-house. In one instance, a leading consumer goods company hired a management consulting firm to critique a product's environmental performance. For a second opinion, the consumer goods company went to an environmental group with which it had an ongoing relationship. That group, which has an excellent reputation for analyzing the particular type of product involved, wound up disagreeing with the management consulting firm's conclusions. If it hadn't been for its prior relationship with the environmental group, the consumer goods company would have been stuck, in this case, with the incorrect information of the management consultancy.

Access to Intelligence.   In Chapter 3, we discussed the importance of environmental intelligence. Strategic alliances offer marketers a way to keep their hands in the information cookie jar on a nonstop basis.

Entrée.   Sometimes, strategic partners are also prospective customers. Whether with the government, another corporation, or even an environmental group, establishing a relationship of trust can pave the way for future sales. For instance, in the Scrubco case study presented above, the Scrubco environmental campaign enabled the company to establish closer relationships with the Environmental Protection Agency, the Department of Defense, and other government agencies, all potentially heavy users of their services.

Influence.   Many corporations enter into partnerships with government agencies in the hope of tilting policy decisions in their direction. I am not talking about bribes or anything else illegal here. But, it is a fact of life that you're likelier to be treated better when you're inside the door than when you're outside it.

The same holds true for corporate relationships with environmental advocacy groups. Ask any corporation that has made a donation to an environmental group, and they'll tell you that (Heavens no!) they haven't done it to influence the environmental group's policy. Meanwhile the environmental group will tell you that, yes, they accepted Corporation X's money, but they absolutely will not let it affect policy, and they told Corporation X as much just before they were handed the check.

All true enough: yet there's a dog here, and a hand here, and it's reasonable to wonder how many dogs will dare to bite the feeding hand—and if so, how hard they'll be willing to chomp. It's for precisely this reason that a debate is currently raging in environmental advocacy group circles over the propriety of accepting corporate donations. More and more environmental groups are saying yes, but they're nervous about any constraints that feeding at the corporate trough may place, consciously or unconsciously, on their behavior.

There's a saying: "Stay close to your detractors." Strategic alliances are a way to do just that.

The Range of Partners

Appropriate candidates for an environmental strategic alliance include: (1) environmental groups; (2) government agencies; (3) retailers; (4) media; (5) trade associations; (6) academic institutions; and (7) other companies.

Environmental Groups

With over three decades' experience on the environmental firing line, mainstream environmental organizations are extremely knowledgeable about environmental issues. Rather than view them as adversaries, businesses can and should look to them for environmental information, research, and technical and scientific support.

Cooperation between environmental groups and corporations can take one of three general forms: (1) corporate giving; (2) joint business ventures; and (3) nonfinancial collaborations, including information exchanges.

Corporate Giving.   Increasingly, environmental groups are loosening their guidelines to permit contributions from a broader array of corporations. Historically, this has been the main avenue for corporate/environmental-group involvement, with contributions typically in the $5000 to $10,000 range. There are usually no restrictions on how this money may be spent by the environmental group. Nor is there much interaction between the donor and donee, or much leveraging of the relationship by either the group or the sponsor.

Joint Business Ventures. Many environmental groups are shifting their sights to corporate marketing departments because, in the immortal words of Willie Sutton, that's where the money is. These joint business ventures include joint sponsorships, cause-related educational promotions, and licensing arrangements. Environmental cause–marketing deals are growing particularly rapidly. Cause-related marketing burst onto the U.S. marketing scene in 1988 with a program by American Express on behalf of the Statue of Liberty, which led to a 20 percent increase in American Express card usage. Environmental groups are ardently pursuing such arrangements, with many organizations creating positions for the express purpose of developing such relationships. Examples of corporate–environmental-group strategic alliances abound. Table 10-3 provides an overview of environmental cause–marketing deals that were inked in 1991.

Information Exchange Partnerships. An example of such a program comes from Procter & Gamble, which in 1992 teamed up with the National Audubon Society in a demonstration project to find out how much compostable waste is produced in a typical American household. The project was conducted in two upscale Connecticut communities where recycling levels were already at an impressive 40 percent. Other participants in the project included McDonald's, which agreed to collect "behind-the-counter" compostable wastes at local shops, and Fuji Photo Film USA, which provided project funding to the National Audubon Society.

Government Agencies

A program called "Bartlett Recycles!" provides an example of the role government agencies can play in an environmental strategic alliance. As the name suggests, the purpose of the program was to develop a community recycling and environmental education program in Bartlett, Tennessee, a Memphis suburb of 27,500. Partners in the project included The Kroger Company (a major retailer), Lever Brothers, Bartlett city government, the Shelby County Environmental Improvement Commission, the Bartlett Schools, the Bartlett Chamber of Commerce, Leadership Bartlett, and Smurfit Recycling, a division of Jefferson-Smurfit Inc., one of Lever's largest packaging suppliers. The aim of the project was to establish a voluntary drop-off recycling infrastructure,

Table 10-3. Green-Cause Marketing Deals: 1991

Sponsor	Amount	Sponsee
Beatrice Cheese, Inc. (Country Line)	$50,000	America the Beautiful Fund
Citicorp	$500,000	National Parks Foundation
Conoco	$500,000	National Parks Foundation
Fuji Photo Film Canada, Inc.	CD20,000	Canadian Wildlife Federation
General Mills, Inc. (Gorton's)	$100,000	Ocean conservation groups
Leica Cameras	$120,000	National Audubon Society
Mars Inc. (Kal Kan)	$100,000+	World Wildlife Fund
Mobil (U.K.)	£127,000	Living Earth and Greensight
Nabisco (Cream of Wheat)	$75,000	National Parks Foundation
Natural Wonders	$50,000+	Conservation International
Procter & Gamble Co.	$300,000	Keep America Beautiful
Ramada International Hotels & Resorts	$83,000	The Nature Conservancy
Reckitt & Coleman (French's, Woolite, Easy-Off, Airwick)	$100,000	National Park Service/ National Park Foundation
W.H. Smith	CD70,000+	Global Releaf
The Stroh Brewery	$20,000	Five Minnesota wildlife groups
Warner-Lambert Co. (Listerine, Listermint, Efferdent)	$100,000	The Nature Conservancy
Hewlett-Packard, Canon	$10,000+ (contributions running at $45K/quarter	Nature Conservancy
U.S. Sprint	$100,000+	Earthshare

SOURCES: Special Events Report, Green MarketAlert

encourage consumer participation, and educate the public as to alternative solutions to the solid-waste problem, including source reduction, waste-to-energy, and landfilling. A Kroger parking lot served as the community collection center. At the end of the program, plans were for Lever and Kroger to produce a how-to guide for communities nationwide in an effort to spark similar recycling and education programs.

It would be very difficult—and even more foolish—to try to implement a program like Bartlett Recycles! without the active support of local government. Because the program operated as a de facto extension of municipal solid-waste management, the cooperation of local authorities was indispensable.

A noteworthy feature of this program was that it worked with such a wide array of local government and civic organizations. Talk about multiple stamps of approval!

Retailers

The Bartlett program demonstrates the central role retailers can play in a strategic alliance. In that initiative, Kroger provided the drop-off site—which, in addition to being environmentally responsive, helped bring shoppers into the store, given that the drop-off site was located only steps away from the company's supermarket.

It's important to note that there are two types of supplier–retailer strategic alliance. The first involves product merchandising and promotion, and the second involves image and awareness building.

The difference is important for legal as well as for conceptual reasons. Under the Robinson-Patman Act, manufacturers are required to offer promotional campaigns for specific products to all retailers within a given geographic area. They are not allowed to play favorites by offering a promotional program to one chain but not another. But this requirement is limited to programs that involve specific product promotions. Where the program is not about a specific product or products, but is more general and softer in focus, manufacturers are not barred from cutting deals with single retailers. Bartlett Recycles! is an example of such a program. Had incentives to buy a specific product been involved, Lever Brothers would not have been legally permitted to make a deal with just one retailer.

Media

It is advisable wherever possible to pull both print and broadcast media into the environmental alliance mix. It goes without saying that a media partner can provide extension of reach in the form of free or discounted air time or space. In a noteworthy recent example, *Business Week* provided inexpensive advertising to Globe '92, a major environmental trade show. The magazine ran three full-page color ads in its international edition in return for a small percentage of the trade show's attendance revenues. Globe '92 estimates that the ads cost about 25 percent as much as they would have if they had paid the standard rate.

Public broadcast stations such as PBS make particularly good partners because they are always looking for programming yet don't have the money to produce the programs themselves. Their name makes a program more credible in the same way that association with an environmental organization does.

Sometimes, it's the media organization that is the primary organizer of the strategic alliance. Times-Mirror Magazines sponsors a program called Partnership for Environmental Education in which the publisher pledges to contribute (to a variety of environmental projects and causes) 2.5 percent of the net revenues it derives from advertising in its special-interest magazines that includes an environmental message of at least 15 words. One of the recipients of the contribution is the National Environmental Education and Training Foundation, established by President Bush and the EPA as part of the 1990 National Environmental Education Act.

Trade Associations

Companies and trade associations often have common interests that lead to collaboration. For instance, because 90 percent of Del Monte Foods' products come in steel cans, the company is an ardent supporter of the Steel Can Recycling Institute, which is the trade association for the steel can industry. Del Monte has run ads encouraging consumers to recycle steel cans with a tag line inviting people to contact the Steel Can Recycling Institute for further information. According to a Del Monte spokesperson, the ads generated "thousands of inquiries" from consumers. Del Monte and the Steel Can Recycling Institute also collaborate on lobbying and related information-exchange activities.

Academic Institutions

Schools of business administration are increasingly interested in environmental marketing and are eager to develop or acquire case studies for their students. Corporations can provide this service, and in so doing, provide a service to themselves. Most promotional programs have a short life: they have their moment in the sun and are then forgotten. Not so with case studies: they endure, through generation after generation of students.

Providing support for business-school curriculum development has another advantage, too, albeit a soft one. Business students are consumers, and they are also prospective employees. Both of these qualities make them particularly appropriate targets for corporate public relations activities.

Another way for corporations to work with universities involves technical research. As mentioned earlier, many universities are offering their services to corporations on a donated or for-hire basis to do research in environmental management and related areas, including environmental marketing. The examples of this sort of collaboration are legion. For instance, AT&T is working with the National Pollution Prevention Center at the University of Michigan to develop models for industrial ecology, a management philosophy that involves incorporating ecological principles into business management.

Corporate Partners

Some prospective corporate partners will have excellent environmental reputations; others, not so excellent. Although some companies have such bad environmental reputations that it never makes sense to partner with them, it is sometimes appropriate to work with companies whose environmental reputations are mixed. Automobile and oil companies, for instance, don't enjoy great environmental reputations, but this doesn't necessarily rule them out for strategic alliances.

Another consideration is a prospective partner's channels of distribution. If the candidate company distributes through different retail channels, the reach of the program will be broadened. However, having a car manufacturer as a partner will not make a consumer packaged-goods promotional program any more appealing to the supermarket retailers whose collaboration is essential. In short, both choices have pluses and minuses.

Happily, you're not stuck with making an either/or choice. Nothing stands in the way of having a mix of partners, some that work the same distribution channels (and therefore make the program that much more appealing to retailers) and some that use different distribution channels (thereby expanding the program's reach).

Finally, it's worth keeping in mind that there are additional possibilities for environmental strategic alliances. Church groups and civic groups, the Boy Scouts, for example, can provide both personnel and public relations benefits.

General Principles

Choose the Right Partners

It goes without saying that it's critically important to choose the right partners. But what is a right partner? I recommend to my clients that they examine the following criteria:

- *Noncontroversial.* Does the prospective partner have a questionable environmental reputation? Is its reputation dubious in any other ways? Obviously, the less controversial, the better.

- *Noncompetitive.* On rare occasions, it can make sense to work with a direct competitor. In general, however, it is best to partner with organizations that are complementary rather than competitive.

- *Add value.* What special strengths can the prospective partner contribute to the enterprise? Does it have special scientific or technical expertise? Is it prepared to reach deep into its pockets for the project (deep pockets are without question a special strength!)?

- *Compatible.* Will I be able to get through to the prospective partners' key decision makers easily? Will I have to put up with interminable red tape before critical decisions get made? Do I have good "vibes" about the people I'll be working with, i.e., what are the odds that significant tensions will develop—or even a falling-out?

- *Extend reach.* To what extent will the partner expand the number of people who will be reached by the program?

- *Extend life.* Most promotions have a relatively short life. The right partner can change that. I noted earlier how working with a school of business administration to create business case studies can extend the life of a promotion. So can partnering with a television station to develop programming that will be played many times.

Do Your Homework

Choose the wrong partner, and you've got a program that's in trouble. It's important to be selective in choosing your strategic allies. Not only that, but you should know them so well before signing the contract that you can say with a high degree of certainty that these are organizations you can be comfortable with over the long term.

It's not only your partners that require close scrutiny. There's also the proposed program. More than a few programs have backfired because their sponsors made the critical mistake of not "walking around them" several times in advance, i.e., by not checking, double-checking and triple-checking how they would play in the marketplace. Role playing is a necessary skill. Unless a program's sponsors can view the campaign through the eyes of consumers, environmental organizations, and other potential detractors, they risk getting a rude shock when the program goes public.

In 1990, Coca-Cola Foods ran a promotion in which consumers were asked to mail Minute Maid proofs of purchase plus 75 cents to Coca-Cola. The company pledged to match the contribution and, in conjunction with the National Parks and Conservation Association, to have a tree planted in California's Redwood National Park in any family member's name.

All well and good—except that the Minute Maid products being promoted used aseptic packaging, which is widely viewed as environmentally undesirable. During the promotion, the Minute Maid In-a-Box even received a highly publicized "Wastemaker Award" from the office of Representative Frank Pallone of New Jersey and the United States Public Interest Research Group.

By playing the environmental card in conjunction with an environmentally controversial product, Coca-Cola overplayed its hand. Had the company asked in advance the hard question, "How will this play?", chances are it wouldn't have launched the program in the first place.

The Role of Role Playing

Role playing is not only important in helping a sponsor to anticipate the marketplace response to an environmental promotion or program. It also plays a central role in putting together a strategic alliance. How do you recruit partners? By understanding what their needs are, i.e., by role playing. Once you understand how they will benefit from participation, you increase the probability of meeting with a favorable response when you make your approach.

Think Long-Term Relationships

The best strategic partners are the ones you work with again and again and again. Whether you are in the process of identifying appropriate partners or are already working with them, it's important to do so against a backdrop of long-term thinking. Is the prospective strategic partner someone with whom you wish to establish a long-term relationship? Will the actions you are about to take enhance the long-term relationship? Questions like these should animate the nature of your relationship with prospective and actual strategic partners.

Determining in Advance What
Your Partners' Needs Are

As discussed earlier in this chapter, analyzing what your partners will get out of the promotion requires you to role-play. Table 10-4 provides a planning tool for this activity. The rows indicate the various sectors from which to draw partners. The columns indicate the types of benefits that can potentially be derived from the program:

- *Awareness and image enhancement.* Every organization wants to increase consumer and public awareness of its activities and to enhance its public image.

- *Issue communication and education.* Organizations also want to educate consumers and the public about issues that they view as important.

- *Build franchise base.* Organizations are always seeking to expand their core constituencies.

- *Reward current franchise base.* If you have loyal customers, it's a good idea to reward them.

- *Franchise involvement and continuity.* Another way to keep customers on board is to involve them in product-related activities. It's one thing simply to get them to take a product off the shelf and pay for it, and another to get them clipping coupons, redeeming proofs of purchase for premium offers, etc.

- *Increased income.* This speaks for itself. In the final analysis, the bottom line usually drives the partnership.

The challenge is to make sure that the partnership program delivers at least two or three benefits to each party.

Summary and
Recommendations

Strategic alliances and environmental marketing partnerships are essential elements of an environmental marketing strategy. They provide the following direct benefits to participating companies:

- Additional expertise, authority, credibility, objectivity
- Additional resources
- Additional audience reach
- Additional program life
- New business development contacts

Table 10-4. Creating WIN, WIN Marketing Partnerships
(Satisfying the Needs of Each Partner)

	Enhance awareness and image	Communicate issues and education	Build franchise base	Reward current franchise base	Involve franchise base continuity	Increase income
Environmental advocacy groups						
Government agencies						
Retailers						
Media						
Trade associations						
Academic institutions						
Other companies						

Although complexity has no value in and of itself, strategic alliances do tend to provide strength in numbers. The ideal strategic alliance will include participants from the public sector (including environmental groups, government, and academia), the media, and other corporations. Retailers should also be directly involved on a sponsorship level where legally appropriate. Their cooperation is essential—whatever the program. It simply makes no sense to go it alone when excellent collaborators are available. (There is, of course, a prerequisite—the partners must be wisely chosen.)

Another key: create a win-win-win situation. It is critically important to plan in advance how each of the partners stands to benefit from the relationship—and then to make sure that the partnership delivers on that promise.

11

Environmental Communication Strategies

Introduction

If there is one point that I had hoped to make in this book, it is that environmental marketing is not simply about increasing sales by coloring a product or products green. Environmental marketing is about much more than that. Seen most broadly, it entails far-reaching changes in attitude—about the role of the environment in corporate management practices and product planning, and also about the role of the marketer in environmental management.

When conceptualized more narrowly as the set of practices directly related to increasing green-product demand, environmental marketing still remains a complex, multilayered enterprise calling for the construction of an ongoing network of strategic alliances within which a range of individual promotional, advertising, and labeling strategies are pursued.

In Chapters 9 and 10, we discussed two major strands of the environmental marketing web—product positioning and strategic alliances, respectively. In this chapter, we discuss environmental communication strategies: (1) advertising; (2) promotion; (3) public relations; and (4) consumer affairs. We preface these discussions with an examination of how consumers get their information about environmental issues—and about the extent to which consumers (and also journalists) find corporations to be trustworthy sources of information about the environment.

Consumers, Corporations, and Environmental Information

Corporations rank low among consumers as a source of environmental information, in terms of both the extent to which they are relied on and the credibility of their information.

Corporations as a Source of Environmental Information

Let's start with the extent to which consumers look to corporations for environmental information. The 1990 survey conducted by The Roper Organization for S.C. Johnson & Son (see Chapter 3) found the following about consumers' sources of environmental information:

> In terms of continuing education—that is, keeping abreast of current environmental developments—both the electronic and print media are the public's main sources of information. A 75 percent majority say TV news is a major source of information, followed by newspapers (65%) and TV news magazine programs (61%). No other source of information is considered "major" by a majority.
>
> Radio and magazines are important secondary sources of information for a plurality of people, as are environmental groups, federal and local government, friends and other personal contacts. Local schools, one's children, and civic groups are somewhat less important as information sources.
>
> But local businesses and large corporations are the only two entities which are reported by a majority as "not an information source" about the environment, ranking at the bottom of the list of sources.

Roper also found, not surprisingly, that

> More information usually translates into less confusion about environmental issues. By nearly two-to-one margins, the True-Blue and Greenback Greens [the most environmentally aware of the five Roper segments] say they are *not* confused about "what's good and what's bad for the environment." By similar margins—but tilting in the other direction—the Grousers and Basic Browns say they *are* confused.

Roper drew two conclusions from these findings. First,

> The dissemination of more information about the environment—especially, perhaps, "how-to" information—could be a key to encouraging stronger beliefs in the effectiveness of the individual, and hence to more voluntary behavioral changes by individual consumers.

Second,

> [T]he media clearly have a leading role—perhaps even primary re-
> sponsibility—in educating the public about environmental issues.
> The media are far and away the main sources of information about
> the environment for most Americans—easily surpassing other
> sources, such as environmental groups, government, the schools,
> and business—and this seems unlikely to change. As the debate
> about complex environmental issues continues and the search for so-
> lutions intensifies, the media will be the primary channel through
> which citizens become better informed.[1]

For corporate strategists, this suggests that the best way to a consumer's heart is through the media. If corporate messages can get delivered via the fourth estate rather than through clearly biased channels
such as advertising and labeling, they are that much likelier to be favorably received.

(And if you think that journalists don't know how eager corporate
communications strategists are to have them deliver corporate messages, think again. In late 1991, the business newsletter *TJFR Business
News Reporter* polled environmental journalists about corporate communications. Among the findings: "Fifty-three percent of the journalists
said they believe that "public relations are more nuisance than help."[2]

Figure 11-1 presents the Roper findings on consumers' sources of environmental information.

The Credibility of Corporate Communications

Corporate communications are neither relied on nor generally trusted
as sources of environmental information. Earlier, we noted that in a
1992 environmental marketing study, the Hartman Group, based in
Newport Beach, California, found that only 13 percent of respondents
believe that corporations are "trustworthy sources of information about
environmental matters." The Hartman Group went on:

> The government fares slightly better, and universities and private re-
> search groups, the media, and environmental groups are the most
> trusted. Nevertheless, even the best source barely succeeds in garner-
> ing the trust of a majority of consumers. People are very skeptical.[3]

As with Roper/Johnson, the Hartman Group found a sharp discrep-
ancy between consumers who are inclined to buy green and those who
are not (Figure 11-2):

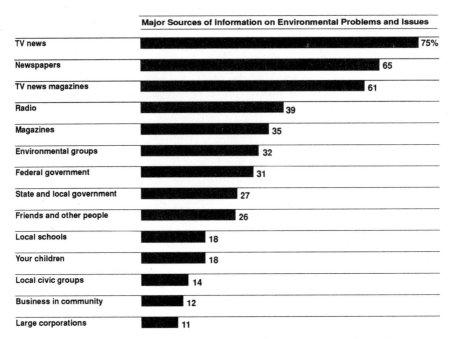

Figure 11-1. Major sources of information on environmental problems and issues. (*The Roper Organization*).

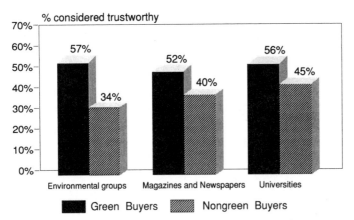

Figure 11-2. Trusted sources of environmental information: green vs. nongreen buyers. Green buyers are more likely to trust complex environmental information sources. (*Hartman Group Survey*)

Consumers who said they are giving more emphasis to environmental purchase considerations favor certain sources by a healthy margin over the `non-green' buyers. In general, green buyers are more likely to favor in-depth, complex sources of information such as that provided by environmental groups, universities, and private research groups, as well as by magazines and newspapers. These statistics are supported by the comments made in Hartman focus groups, where the most environmentally-committed among the participants invariably were more knowledgeable on environmental issues and more demanding of hard data to substantiate environmental claims of any kind.

Similarly, better- and less well-educated groups differed sharply on their perceptions of which environmental information sources were trustworthy—hardly a surprise, since educational levels correspond closely with green-ness. The well-educated trusted universities and research groups highly, while the less well-educated put their faith in television and radio news.

Figure 11-3 identifies the perceived trustworthiness of various sources of environmental information across all segments of society, as per the Hartman Group. Figures 11-4 and 11-5 present the environmental information sources that are most trusted by better- and less well-educated groups, respectively.

The Hartman Group findings remind us that corporate communicators have an uphill battle when it comes to delivering environmental messages. The findings also suggest that the choice of media for disseminating environmental information depends largely on the particular audience being targeted. When a company gets the word out

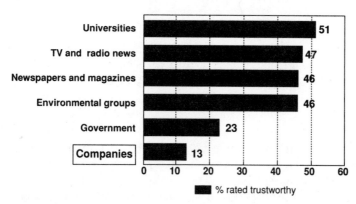

Figure 11-3. Trustworthy sources of general environmental information. Companies are the least trusted source of environmental information. (*Hartman Group Survey*)

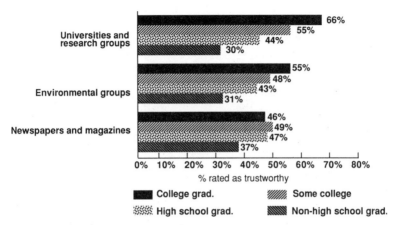

Figure 11-4. Environmental information sources trusted by the well-educated. Well-educated consumers trust in-depth information sources on environmental matters. (*Hartman Group Survey*)

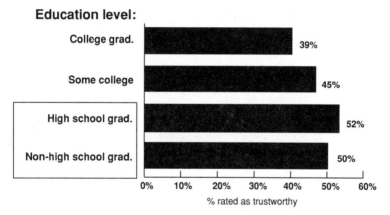

Figure 11-5. Environmental information sources trusted by the less well-educated. The less-educated tend to trust television and radio most. (*Hartman Group Survey*)

through an environmental group, it is likely to reach a relatively upscale and green audience. Television and radio news are likelier outlets for less well-educated consumers.

Consumers are also skeptical about environmental labels. In a 1991 Cambridge Reports/Research International survey, a modest 55 percent of respondents agreed with the statement that "[w]hen a product is labeled as environmentally friendly, [it] really is better for the environment." The same study found that 42 percent of the people who say they read environment labels don't generally find them credible.[4]

Another 1991 survey, this one by the New York–based Gerstman & Myers, also uncovered a substantial amount of skepticism about environmental claims, with only 3 percent of respondents saying they were "extremely believable" and 12 percent saying they were "very believable." (Sixty-three percent said they were somewhat believable, sixteen percent said they were "not too believable," and six percent said they were "not at all believable.")[5]

It's not only consumers who distrust corporate communications. The *TFJR Business Newsletter* survey found that,

> (G)iven a choice of putting their trust in environmental groups, government officials, scientists, other news organizations or business executives, environmental reporters overwhelmingly rank Corporate America last.

TJFR went on to note,

> Given their mistrust of Corporate America, it isn't surprising that relatively few environmental journalists use corporate sources to help them formulate their stories. Fewer than half of the 50 journalists questioned say they rely even periodically upon interviews with corporate executives as sources for their reports.

Implications for Marketers

Is distrust of corporate environmental communications so severe as to require environmental marketing to be avoided entirely? Not at all. Let's start with the fact that a substantial majority of consumers feel that environmental labeling is appropriate: in the above-mentioned 1991 Cambridge Reports/Research International survey, 70 percent of consumers stated that it is appropriate for corporations to make environment-related claims.

Just as importantly, environmental communications can be effective. When the Cambridge Reports/Research International survey asked consumers if "(I)n just the last week [italics added], (they had) really read the label on a product to find out whether or not it is better for the environment," 47 percent of respondents (68 percent of greens and 44 percent of nongreens) answered in the affirmative. And in the 1990 Roper/Johnson survey, 29 percent of respondents answered "yes" when asked if they had "ever bought a product because the advertising or the label said the product was environmentally safe or biodegradable."

The issue isn't *if* one should pursue environmental advertising and labeling, but *how*. This is the topic we take up in the following pages.

Advertising

Different Ad Categories, Different Strategies

There are four basic categories of green advertisement: (1) public service announcements (PSAs); (2) image advertising; (3) labeling; and (4) product-related ads. Each has its own strategies and rules.

Public Service Announcements. PSAs perform a laudable educational function. They also provide an excellent way for companies to communicate their concern about the environment in the understated way that best circumvents the distrust of corporations that is endemic among consumers.

But even PSAs can backfire. If a PSA throws the spotlight too much on the sponsoring corporation and too little on the cause, a PSA quickly becomes an exercise in self-congratulation. Unless the corporation remains quietly in the background, with the cause in front and center stage, a PSA will be perceived as self-serving and hypocritical.

Environmental Image Advertising. Strategically, this is the riskiest type of advertising because image advertising plays directly into consumers' distrust of corporations.

A corporation's environmental image will often be better enhanced by indirect rather than by direct advertising. If a company improves a product and informs consumers of those improvements, the corporate image is *indirectly* enhanced. If that same corporation sponsors a public service announcement and attaches its name to that PSA in a small-print (but visible) way, its image is similarly enhanced. That is a more subtle (and therefore more effective) strategy than beating the corporate breast and shouting out, "How green I am!"

To the extent that corporate image advertising is deemed necessary or desirable, it is best tied in to information about specific products or projects. "We've made Product X more environmentally sensitive by reducing the packaging by 30 percent. That's one way our company is working to be more environmentally responsive" is a much better approach than "Corporation X—We Care." The more general a claim is, the likelier it is to meet with derision.

Labeling. In Chapter 6, we provided an overview of current environmental labeling guidelines and regulations. Here, we examine strategies for making sure that a company's environmental labeling practices meet all regulatory requirements—and make good business sense, too.

1. *Err on the side of caution.* If there are any doubts about the appropriateness of a labeling claim, it shouldn't be made.

2. *Be as specific as possible.* Many states are concerned about *misleading* environmental claims. You can't mislead if you use language that cannot reasonably be misconstrued.

For instance, when used without further clarification, the term recycled is clearly subject to being misunderstood. We have already seen how confused consumers are about labeling language. The term recycled is so vague that it practically begs to be misconstrued.

But if you say, for example, "Product (or package) contains a minimum of 30 percent recycled material, of which at least 25 percent is postconsumer," there is much less room for misinterpretation. While one can technically differ on what constitutes postindustrial (i.e., preconsumer) waste, such a claim will not run afoul of regulators because it does not violate the spirit of environmental labeling guidelines—which are, as we said, to prevent deception.

It's relevant to this discussion that many state labeling laws define the conditions under which the state's recyclable and recycled-content labeling *logos* may be used. Here, too, the states are addressing the issue of specificity. Precisely because they are so abstract, logos are subject to abuse unless clear limitations are placed on their use.

3. *Use the FTC environmental marketing guidelines as your overall benchmark!*

4. *Obey the laws of the strictest state.* One often hears from national marketers the complaint that the current crazy quilt of state environmental labeling legislation makes environmental labeling so complex that is it hardly worth the trouble. National marketers, the standard argument goes, can't reasonably be expected to generate different labels for different states. It would be too expensive—and besides, national marketers often don't know where specific product lots are going to end up.

As I pointed out before, this is something of a specious argument. Even in a balkanized environmental labeling marketplace, there is a straightforward way to cut through the clutter. Simply take all the environmental labeling laws that are on the books, compare them on a term-by-term basis (recyclable, recycled-content, compostable, and so on), and then conform to the requirements of the strictest state. If a stricter statute comes along, you will usually have a grace period of one to two years to comply.

Regarding life-cycle assessments, *Green Report II* notes the curious coincidence that "the few product life assessments that have been conducted by the business community have come out in favor of the manufacturer who paid for the assessment," and recommends that

> the results of [these assessments] . . . not be used to advertise or promote specific benefits until uniform methods for conducting such assessments are developed and a general consensus is reached among government, business, environmental, and consumer groups on how this type of environmental comparison can be advertised nondeceptively.[6]

Product-Related Ads.   We recommend to environmental marketers that they apply four rules of thumb to product-related ads.

1. *Comprehensiveness.*   Address both the environmental problem and how the product being advertised helps to address it, i.e., discuss both the problem and the benefit (this is discussed in greater detail in Chapter 10).

2. *Specificity and clarity.*   Be as specific as possible—and when discussing scientific or technical issues, use plain English.

3. *Keep your categories distinct.*   Bear in mind the distinction between image and product advertising. If you're going to mix the two in a single advertising package, do so carefully. The image message should be subordinated to the product message. Flip the balance and your product ad could backfire.

4. *Play into empowerment.*   Repeat over and over again the mantra: Empowerment. Consumers are looking for ways to help clean up the environment. Your product advertising should establish roadmaps for their doing so.

Metaphors That Do (and Don't) Work

A 1991 study by J. Walter Thompson's Greenwatch provides an interesting perspective on current trends and future directions in green-advertising strategies. Entitled *The Meaning of Green—How Environmental Advertising Works*, the study analyzed a pool of green ads by the type of authority invoked and found that three types of authority—"Mother Nature," "science," and "ordinary people"—were generally drawn upon.

These authority figures, in turn, were matched against the stage in the product life cycle on which the ad focused—*extraction, manufacture, use,* and *disposal.* This matching process established that extraction-stage ads use Mother Nature as the source of authority. JWT Greenwatch explained this as follows:

The average consumer has little firsthand experience with extraction. Many early stage processes—like mining and oil drilling—are conducted remotely, and are so technical as to seem mysterious. And, although we love Mother Nature, most of us don't have much firsthand knowledge with her, either.... That's why ... extraction is almost always associated with Mother Nature in green commercials.

At the *manufacture* and *use* stages, science provides the necessary authority. According to JWT Greenwatch, this is because these "in-between" stages "are symbolized by a language well-suited to informing consumers of improvements in processing and in products themselves, that of Science."

At the *disposal* stage, ordinary people take over. "Given the day-to-day proximity of the disposal stage," writes JWT Greenwatch, "the most likely way to talk to consumers is through a language that feels colloquial and familiar, like ordinary people messages."

Based on its analysis, J. Walter Thompson concluded that green advertising that invokes Mother Nature or science is losing its effectiveness:

> Consumers catch on quickly to advertising conventions. That, plus the seriousness of the environmental issue, may account for their resistance to the metaphors of Mother Nature and Science.... [C]onsumers would like marketing advice from an environmental authority that is both objective and committed. The heavy use of metaphor in environmental advertising may be seen as an attempt to create a substitute authority through imagery and emotion. We believe that, as consumers grow more sophisticated about the environment, purely emotional green advertising will provide diminishing returns. This will work to the advantage of messages which convey a pragmatic tone, or are spoken in what we call the language of Ordinary People.... [W]e think the successful green brands of the future will have to demonstrate closeness-of-fit with consumer experience. "Why-use-it" and "how-to-dispose-of-it" demonstrations are likely to become more common elements in green commercials.... As consumers better understand the environmental consequences associated with the Use and Disposal stages of the product life cycle, what we have called Ordinary People messages will proliferate.

As for Mother Nature and science,

> [They] will remain viable advertising images if they're not used gratuitously, as is often the case now. We see Mother Nature becoming more closely identified with the backyard than the national park, and Science moving from the laboratory to the household.[7]

I agree with J. Walter Thompson's analysis. It is important to steer clear of metaphors that play into consumers' assumptions that corporations are hypocritical and exploitative. To the extent that Madison Avenue catches on to this fact, the environmentally-related advertising of the future will focus increasingly on hands-on issues that strike close to home for consumers. Extraction- and manufacture-stage ads will fade slowly from the scene, while use and disposal ads will become more prominent. As that happens, ordinary-people ads will become more widespread, and appeals to Mother Nature and science will become correspondingly infrequent.

If we approach this situation from a different conceptual angle, we find that once again the theme of *empowerment* has reemerged. Consumers need to be related both about subjects and in ways that enable them to feel as if they can make a difference. Use and disposal ads—and ordinary-people metaphors—do just that. For example, First Brands, makers of Glad plastic bags, focuses on people cleaning up their neighborhoods, and using Glad bags to do so. Communications like this position solid-waste management at the level of the individual citizen, thereby combining effective advertising with good corporate citizenship.

Sales Promotion

For a long time now, the only thing that has differentiated parity products from one another (apart from the packaging) has been the type of sales promotion incentives (e.g., plush dolls, trips, bonus packs, etc.) offered with proof of purchase.

Today, however, *environmental attributes* can help distinguish one product from another, and, while we have recommended considered restraint in promoting environmental attributes on packaging and in advertising, we believe that sales promotion is a marketing arena well suited to more aggressive positioning of a product's environmental attributes.

This is not to say that we should throw environmental-claims caution and environmental education principles to the wind. Because sales promotion marketers have accustomed consumers to no-frills, here's-what's-in-this-for-you communications, the approach "it cleans the same, it costs the same, but *it's safer for the environment* (see details on back of package)" is pretty powerful to a growing number of consumers that want to know what they can do to make a difference *now!*

Environmental Promotion Objectives. Environmental (sales) promotion objectives include: (1) awareness and trial of a new product's environmental attributes; (2) conversion from an environmentally insensitive–competitive product to an environmentally responsible product; and (3) cultivating brand loyalty based on the manufacturer's commitment to protect the environment.

Environmental Promotion Strategies. Several currently used promotional strategies and tactics have environmentally beneficial attributes or impact. Repeat-purchase and product-loading strategies, such as refillable packaging and larger package sizes, are inherently good for the environment since they reduce the total amount of packaging (and natural resources) utilized, packaging that would have eventually ended up in a landfill.

Bonus packs, some two-in-one packs, and no-frills packaging can also have an environmental advantage over much of the regular packaging (and can and should be promoted to retailers as such!).

Certain merchandising tools such as permanent displays and electronic (and therefore programmable) signage have environmental advantages over a proliferation of semipermanent and use-one-week-and-throw-away floorstand displays and header cards.

All aspects of the design and implementation of an environmental promotion program (or any promotion program for that matter) should involve the consideration or application of the principles and recommended practices set forth in this book: TQEM, environmental intelligence, claims-regulations compliance, stakeholder alliances, and even-handed communications.

Product. Assuming that your company already has and has demonstrated a corporate environmental policy that reflects a commitment to environmental improvement, it is best to build your program around a product that clearly has an environmental advantage over other mass-marketed products in the category or a product that has always been environmentally benign. Recycled or easily recyclable product and/or packaging; less toxic or nontoxic product formulation; made with less energy and/or less natural resources; made from renewable resources; made from recycled materials—these are a few attributes that represent environmentally beneficial product features or improvements.

Message. As we know from consumer research, issue- or product-related environmental communication is more credible when it comes from an environmental group or authority. This being the case, most (but not necessarily all) environmentally related product promotion is more credible (and, therefore, potentially more successful) when fashioned and implemented with the involvement of an independent environmental expert or organization.

Planning. The following environmental product–promotion planning process often begins with an environmental education proposal brought to you by an environmental advocacy group or other outside party. The flow and nature of evaluation and planning activities should generally follow the steps listed in the box that follows.

Step 1. Evaluate the environmental education proposal against the numerous other proposals received. Criteria: (1) environmental issue relevance to company or product environmental issue(s), corporate environmental education objectives, and other corporate environmental education programs; (2) environmental group's reputation, credibility, and comfort level with company's products, processes, and environmental track record and/or policies; (3) cost of program and environmental-group fee or donation; (4) environmental group's interest and ability to participate in all aspects of the *product* promotion and communications portion of the program; (5) environmental group's interest in and suitability for long-term partnership.

Step 2. Develop a preliminary promotion-program proposal to review with other or potential partners (e.g. the media, government, other corporations, etc.), company sales and brand managers, and upper management. The preliminary program plan covers the following:

- Rationale for environmental marketing
- Corporate environmental business and education objectives
- Environmental marketing opportunity overview (executive summary)
- Environmental group profile and agenda
- Environmental educational objectives
- Company product(s) promotion objectives
- Target market
- Detailed program description
- Consumer-promotion incentive program
- Trade-promotion incentive [to participate] program
- Media support
- Potential additional sponsors list and profiles
- Timing
- Budget
- Next Steps

Step 3. Confer with company sales and brand managers to determine their interest in selling and funding the program. (If the sales and/or brand managers are not interested, and you can't convince them otherwise, stop now!)

Step 4. Run the basic concept by several respected retail representatives for their "unofficial" input and approval.

Step 5. Secure upper management's approval to proceed with program development and implementation.

Step 6. Begin the partnership solicitation process.

Step 7. Simultaneously test (via focus groups of educators) the program's educational content. Also test product-sell copy and promotion incentives (with panels of consumers from various green and not-so-green markets around the country).

Step 8. Finalize program design with the input of all partners.

At the core of an environmental promotion program that my firm helped to develop was a one-hour TV special produced by an environmental group and an independent coproducer. The family-oriented special explored specific environmental problems and advised consumers on how to improve the situation through their product-purchasing behavior. A number of celebrities donated their services on the basis that all promotional applications of the show and their involvement would contribute in some way to the support of the environmental group. The show was aired on a national cable channel that did not accept advertising. Various companion program elements were created, therefore, to extend the reach of the message and provide opportunities for the sponsors to directly promote their products. The elements include a multipage national consumer magazine insert, a Sunday newspaper FSI (free-standing insert), a school kit containing a videocassette of the TV special and a teacher's guide, and in-store promotional materials.

The in-store consumer promotion carried the theme of the TV special along with the environmental group's signature and celebrity visuals. Consumer purchase incentives included product coupons, the TV show home video discounted with proofs of purchase, and a special environmental group membership offer.

Retail participation incentives included the donation of educational videocassettes and viewer's guides (the school kits) to community schools in the store name; free radio PSAs featuring environmental tips and sponsor and retailer (customized) tags; heavy television, print, and couponing support; and free in-store–environmental education materials. Additionally, local chapters of the environmental organization agreed to work with participating retailers to facilitate community outreach education and store and product promotion activities.

Because this was an in-store product promotion, no retailers were involved as program development partners. (Under the Robinson-Patman Act such in-store promotional programs must be made equally available to all retailers.) However, the support of the retailing community was a linchpin of the overall strategy.

Public Relations

The best approach to environmental public relations is nicely captured in the phrase, "sustainable communications." Here is how Bruce Harrison, president of E. Bruce Harrison Associates (Washington, D.C.) defined the term in the February 1992 issue of *Inside PR:*

> I define sustainable communications as a process-driven approach, not a problem-driven approach. It must be continuous, open, interactive and consistent. Its values must be understanding, concern and commitment. It must draw deeply on intimate knowledge—research data—about specific publics who are impacted by a company's environmental programs and can help shape them.[8]

Corporate–environmental issue public relations must continually track and evolve with corporate environmental policy and practice developments, not just react to corporate environmental crises.

Ongoing environmental public relations activities are targeted first to employees who, in addition to having personal health- and safety-oriented needs to know, are often unofficial company environmental spokespersons.

Externally, ongoing environmental public relations should be targeted to the following audiences:

- Stockholders
- Vendors
- Community residents
- Allied environmental groups
- Media
- Regulatory agencies

- Industry associations
- Consuming public

Guidelines for environmental information reporting are covered in your corporate environmental communications plan (Chapter 2). Official corporate environmental spokespersons are designated on your environmental communications flowchart (Chapter 2).

Books have been written on the subjects of risk and crisis communications. I did, however, want to include this observation by James Lindheim and Frederick Wodin of the public relations firm Burson-Marstellar on the subject of "blame."

> While lawyers will argue that a corporation must avoid unnecessary liability that may come from accepting blame, there is an important distinction between "blame" and "responsibility" in any crisis. That distinction is essential to effective environmental communications.
>
> In any media encounter in an environmental crisis, there will be three fundamental questions that a spokesperson must be prepared to address: "What happened?" "Why" and "What are you going to do about it?" The first two questions are concerned with blame and, in most instances, are unanswerable in the first several days of a crisis. The third question has to do with responsibility and should be, as much as possible, the focus of corporate action and the primary focus of corporate communication. The more the crisis team is focused on actions to solve the problem and the more environmental communications are focused on information about commitment to solve the problem, the more confidence will be created. And, from a legal perspective, a corporation's effort to assume responsibility for solving an environmental problem usually will not add to liability but rather will create an atmosphere that is far more favorable to successful liability settlements.[9]

On the legislative front, company lobbyists are discovering that providing regulators with pollution-prevention solutions is much more productive than debating the pros and cons of hundreds of environmental regulation proposals—state by state. Not only does the government welcome industry expertise, but many branches have committed themselves to be more environmentally responsible and therefore need industry cooperation to help them meet their commitments. Figure 11-6, letter from the Department of the Navy, illustrates this point.

Consumer Affairs

The corporate consumer affairs professional is on the front line when it comes to dealing with consumers' protests, concerns, and general in-

DEPARTMENT OF THE NAVY
NAVY RESALE AND SERVICES SUPPORT OFFICE
NAVAL STATION NEW YORK STATEN ISLAND
STATEN ISLAND, N.Y. 10305-5097

AN OPEN LETTER TO SUPPLIERS,

The Navy Resale System has embarked on an important program of strong and continuing commitment to be a responsible environmental retailer. While I am encouraged by the wide range of efforts at our exchanges, commissaries and lodges, you will begin to see a sharper corporate focus that reaches through our product lines and gives priority to products which favor the environment. Through-out the Navy Resale system, you will see an environmental program committed to the goal of fostering, supporting and participating in appropriate solutions to the solid waste problems, leading to clean air and clean water. Our program will be implemented under the theme "Navy Exchange Earth Friendly," and promotionally supported with an environment logo.

We will be innovative and pro-active in our merchandising efforts. Not <u>only will our buyers seek out and give preference to products promoting a better environment</u>, but a campaign will be initiated to increase customer awareness and encourage environmental concerns. Our program focus will review packaging, verify environmental promotional statements, assure the use of recycled materials, and the use of environmentally safe materials. As you discuss your products with our buyers, you should raise these points and point out how they apply to your products.

One person, or even one firm, cannot solve the environmental concerns faced by our country and the world. However, concerned companies, working toward a common goal, can contribute and help solve these problems. We are encouraged that with your help, we can improve our environment and make a healthier world for ourselves and future generations.

I trust my concern corresponds with yours.

Sincerely,

H. D. WEATHERSON
Rear Admiral, SC, USN
Commander

♻ PRINTED ON 100% RECYCLED PAPER

Figure 11-6. Government commitment to environmental responsibility.

quiries about the environment. Hesitation, uncertainty, or a no comment–no answer response can be collectively disastrous. Marketers should work with the consumer affairs department to establish credible and satisfying response scripts and communication mechanisms. At the very least, companies should have general statements about environmental initiatives or policy available for distribution. These documents should address the most common and important questions that consumers have about a company's products or other aspects of its environmental performance, such as those regarding packaging, recycling, hazardous-waste management, and air and water emissions.

An alternative to having your company consumer affairs, product, or environmental representatives handle more detailed inquiries is to refer callers to environmental groups or other organizations. Table 11-1 lists a few environmental and industry organizations that have fielded inquiries (according to their area of specialization) for corporations.

My work with consumer affairs professionals has constantly uncovered two areas of primary concern or frustration: (1) getting management to take seriously (or anticipate) the complaints or concerns of environmentally sensitive consumers and to allocate sufficient funds to address those concerns; and (2) environmental education—dealing with consumer misinformation.

Table 11-1. Directing Consumer Inquiries to other Companies, Environmental Groups, and Industry Associations

Issue	Organization
Recycling/packaging:	
Glass	Glass Packaging Institute
Plastic	Council for Solid Waste Solutions
Paper	American Paper Institute
Aluminum	Alcan Aluminum Corporation
Steel	The Steel Can Recycling Institute
Composting	Keep America Beautiful
Toxic/hazardous waste	The National Toxics Campaign
Global warming	The Alliance for Environmental Education
Ozone depletion	The Alliance for Environmental Education
Rain forests	The Alliance for Environmental Education
Life-cycle analysis	The Alliance for Environmental Education
Environmental groups	The Environmental Exchange
Labeling certification	Green Seal and Green Cross
Woodlands clearcutting	Siskiyou Action Project
Proenvironment politicians	League of Conservation Voters
Green Legislation	Sierra Club

The best way I have found to get management's attention is to position environmentally related issues such as communication and research needs in terms of dollars (cost of nonresponse and missed opportunity). Here, case histories work well. Find out how other companies have suffered in terms of negative image and loss of distribution or market share when consumer interest were ignored. (These examples do not have to be environmentally related). Present management with the latest environmental consumer research. Get employees to openly express their environmental concerns; the process of environmental education, so critical to the success of green processes and products, begins within.

And, on the subject of environmental education, it is time to correct the staggering amount of misinformation circulating among consumers, teachers and students, investors, and regulators. Having relied on the media for its environmental information (often because it distrusts manufacturers) the public has suffered the effects of education by soundbite. Sensational environmental-issue or environmental-event coverage is not generally synonymous with a balanced and comprehensive presentation. Consumer affairs professionals have their work cut out for them in this area of environmental education and they need management's full support and commitment. Their mission is not to follow the propensity of certain media and other special-interest groups for biased or rating-driven communications. Rather they must *lead the charge* of environmental education.

Summary and Recommendations

Advertising and labeling are central components of an environmental marketing strategy. However, these are only subsets of a comprehensive strategy that posits a more central role for the environment in the corporate management mix—and also for the marketer in the environmental management structure.

Because consumers are deeply distrustful of corporate communications, it is advisable to deliver corporate messages through more credible sources, such as environmental groups and the print and broadcast media.

Despite the negative bias that consumers bring to corporate communications and environmental advertising and labeling, both constitute viable business strategies. However, certain rules of thumb should be applied to both practices.

Public service announcements (PSAs) are an excellent environmental communications strategy because they allow a corporation to demonstrate its concern about the environment while avoiding the self-congratulatory horn-tooting that inspires disdain among much of the population.

Environmental *image advertising* is strategically more problematic because it travels directly into the headwind of consumers' distrust of corporate communications. Generally, *indirect* image-enhancement strategies are preferable. Among the options: PSAs and a focus on specific projects such as environmental improvements in product or packaging design.

Regarding *product-related* ads, we recommend the following:

1. Address both the environmental problem and how the product or package addresses it.

2. Be as specific as possible about how the product or package addresses the environmental problem—and use plain English.

3. Keep your emphasis on the product or the package. Keep the corporate image in the background—corporate image messages should never be allowed to dominate the presentation.

4. Communicate how the product *empowers* consumers to help improve the environment.

Regarding labeling, we also have several rules of thumb:

1. Err on the side of caution. If you're uncertain about how a labeling claim will play with regulators, don't use it.

2. As with advertising, make sure that your communications are as specific as possible.

3. Begin with the FTC guidelines for environmental marketing, but for any given claim type, obey the laws of the strictest state.

Sales Promotion

Sales promotion objectives are short-term oriented, aimed at stimulating product sales and merchandising support. As such, sales promotion programs for environmentally oriented products must (and can) work harder than environmental advertising. Sales promotions typically utilize price to distinguish one product from its competition and get the attention of retailers and consumers who care about profit and value respectively. Environmental benefits can be utilized to serve the same function for retailers and consumers who care about the environment. It is doubtful that an environmental-claim-only promotion (without a price-value offer) will break incremental sales records, but retailers are looking for and willing to support meaningful environmental-promotion programs with strong environmental-education value.

Public Relations

Just as sustainable development expresses the notion that businesses should make special efforts to ensure that the planet's ecosystems can continue to support economic growth, so should public relations be sustainable, i.e., they should be designed so as to foster a long-term relationship of trust between a company and its various constituencies.

Consumer Affairs

Consumer affairs personnel should be carefully briefed on the appropriate responses to common environmental inquiries. One excellent strategy is to refer people to environmental groups with recognized expertise in the areas being asked about.

Lack of management support and consumer misinformation are two conditions best remedied with internal and external environmental education, respectively.

12
Summary: The Right Approach to Environmental Marketing

Why Environmental Marketing?

Environmental marketing is more than good, sound business. Environmental marketing is the strategy that the times demand. If the health of the planet is to be restored, it is industry that must play the leading role. True, businesses have been the parties largely responsible for our environmental predicament in the first place, but my reasons for saying this are pragmatic, not reparations-oriented. Unless businesses commit earnestly to cleaning up the environment, our planet is doomed.

Happily, what is good for the environment is good for business, too. In survey after survey, consumers have expressed strong concerns about the environment, along with a willingness to purchase products that they believe will contribute to a healthier planet. Although much of this concern is still latent, which is to say that consumers often don't put their money where their mouths are, the potential is strong. Green consumerism is already a substantial movement, and it promises to become even more significant with the passage of time.

Not only do environmental marketing strategies often provide a short-term competitive edge, but they also offer solid long-term benefits in the form of goodwill and market positioning.

The Right Approach to Environmental Marketing

There are two basic approaches to environmental marketing. One approach—let's call it shallow environmental marketing—does not involve any basic changes in attitude on the part of marketing management or other corporate executives. The environment is treated as simply one more weapon in the marketing arsenal. Shallow environmental marketing is business-as-usual, colored green.

The other approach, which is the one we have espoused in this book, is more complex, more comprehensive, and ultimately more effective. Conceptually, the *right approach* to environmental marketing implies a fundamental change in attitude about the right role of the corporation vis-à-vis the environment. It asks companies to have a much stronger sense of fiduciary responsibility than is embodied in the extractive or exploitative relationships they have traditionally enjoyed with the environment. It calls for companies to think beyond the short-term bottom line, i.e., to factor the environment into all of their strategic planning.

The right approach to environmental marketing operates at several levels and entails additional responsibilities and strategies for environmental marketers.

The Alliance. The most effective environmental marketing strategy builds on a host of long-term alliances. As a rule, going it alone is less effective than working in collaboration with partners drawn from (among others) government agencies, environmental groups, retailers, other corporations, and the media.

Strategic alliances offer many advantages. They extend an environmental marketing program's reach. They also increase the flow of information coming in to the marketer, and information is the lifeblood of intelligent business planning. So long as one's partners are carefully chosen, the more, the better.

Environmental Education. As we noted above, much of green consumerism's potential is still latent. It is a movement still in the making. While green-product positioning can and often does supply a short-term marketing edge, much of the payoff will come down the road. Long-term thinking and the right approach to environmental marketing go hand in hand.

Unfortunately, long-term thinking isn't all that common. Short-termitis is endemic in the United States. As a rule, managers are so preoccupied with churning out profits that they tend not to see the middle term, much less the long term. Japan reportedly is developing a 100-year plan for certain aspects of its environmental strategy. In the United States, such a strategy is unimaginable.

The right approach to environmental marketing calls for a transition from a preoccupation (obsession?) with the short-term bottom line to an awareness of the advantages in incorporating multiple time frames into the planning process. The right approach to environmental marketing assumes that the long term is as important as the short term.

The right approach to environmental marketing is about market-building as well as about activating short-term demand, and the key to market-building is *education*. The seeds that are sown under the right approach to environmental marketing are the seeds of environmental education.

The strategic alliance is the first core concept of right-approach environmental marketing. Environmental education is the second.

Not all environmental marketing programs do (or for that matter should) roll out under the shadow of either a strategic alliance or an environmental education program. Labeling and advertising, for instance, are both central environmental marketing strategies, yet too often they have been executed on a stand-alone basis. And, our basic point holds true, namely, that strategic alliances and environmental education are at the core of the right approach to environmental marketing.

The Environmental Marketer as Environmental Manager

As discussed in Chapter 2, right-approach environmental marketing also drives the marketer's responsibilities inward, in the direction of environmental management. Without a genuine commitment to the environment, an environmental marketing program is not only *not* the right approach, it is a sham. It is the marketer's responsibility to help ensure the ethical consistency of a corporate marketing program. This is done by working to ensure that the corporation's internal behavior is consistent with the pledges it is making in its environmental marketing campaigns.

The Role of Partnership

At the heart of the right approach to environmental marketing is the notion of partnership. When the marketer approaches the consumer with an environmental marketing campaign, what is being proposed, in essence, is a partnership on behalf of the environment.

But that partnership extends beyond the corporation's relationship with consumers. Earlier in this chapter, we identified strategic alliances as one of the core tenets of the right approach to environmental marketing. And what is a strategic alliance but a partnership, pure and simple? Thus a business's relationships with its consumer base are partnerships within partnerships, i.e., relationships for mutual long-term benefit that are embedded within an overarching set of business relationships, also for mutual benefit.

Nor does the partnership end with the corporation's strategic alliances. Under the right approach to environmental marketing, it also extends to the environment. Environmental education is about what happens when you enter into an implied partnership with the environment. Environmental education is premised on the assumption that if we are good to the environment, the environment will be good to us.

Thus the concept of the partnership is pervasive. When the approach to environmental marketing is the *right* one, partnerships are involved—in a business's relationships with its customers, with its strategic allies, and, ultimately, with the environment itself.

Industry, Trade, and Professional Associations that Are Active in the Environmental Arena

Aluminum Recycling Association
1000 16th St. NW, Ste. 603
Washington, DC 20036
202/785-0550

American Association of
  Advertising Agencies
666 3rd Ave., 13th floor
New York, NY 10017-4011
212/682-2500

American Marketing Association
250 S. Wacker Dr., Ste. 200
Chicago, IL 60606
312/648-0536

American Paper Institute
260 Madison Ave.
New York, NY 10016-2439
212/340-0600

American Petroleum Institute
1220 L St. NW
Washington, DC 20005-4070
202/682-8000

Association of National Advertisers
155 E. 44th St., 33rd floor
New York, NY 10017-4201
212/697-5950

Chemical Manufacturers
  Association
2501 M St. NW
Washington, DC 20037-1342
202/887-1100

Chemical Specialties Manufacturers
  Association
1913 Eye St. NW
Washington, DC 20006
202/872-8110

Consumer Aerosol Products Council
1201 Connecticut Ave. NW, Ste. 300
Washington, DC 20036
202/833-9471

Cosmetic, Toiletry and Fragrance
  Association
1101 17th St. NW, Ste. 300
Washington, DC 20036
202/331-1770

The Partnership for Plastic Progress
(formerly Council for Solid Waste
  Solutions)
1275 K St. NW
Washington, DC 20005
202/371-5319

Council on Plastics and Packaging
  in the Environment
1001 Connecticut Ave. NW
Washington, DC 20036
202/331-0099

Degradable Plastics Council
1000 Executive Pkwy., Ste. 105
St. Louis, MO 63141-6397
314/576-5207

Direct Marketing Association
11 W. 42nd St., 25th floor
New York, NY 10036-8096
212/768-7277

Flexible Packaging Association
1090 Vermont Ave. NW, Ste. 500
Washington, DC 20005-4960
202/842-3880

Food Marketing Institute
800 Connecticut Ave. NW
Washington, DC 20006-2701
202/452-8444

Glass Packaging Institute
1801 K St. NW, Ste. 1105-L
Washington, DC 20006
202/887-4850

Grocery Manufacturers of America
1010 Wisconsin Ave. NW, Ste. 800
Washington, DC 20007
202/337-9400

Institute of Packaging Professionals
11800 Sunrise Valley Drive
Reston, VA 22091-5302
703/620-9380

National Association for Plastic
  Container Recovery
4828 Parkway Plaza Blvd., Ste. 260
Charlotte, NC 28217
704/357-3250

National Association of Diaper
  Services
2017 Walnut St.
Philadelphia, PA 19103
215/569-3650

National Association of
  Manufacturers
1331 Pennsylvania Ave. NW, Ste.
  1500N
Washington, DC 20004-1703
202/637-3000

National Association of
  Professional Environmental
  Communicators
P.O. Box 8352
Chicago, IL 60661
708/918-4129

National Food Processors
  Association
1401 New York Ave. NW
Washington, DC 20005
202/639-5900

National Forest Products
  Association
1250 Connecticut Ave. NW, Ste. 200
Washington, DC 20036-2615
202/463-2700

National Oil Recyclers Association
2266 Bellfield Ave.
Cleveland, OH 44106
216/791-7316

National Recycling Coalition
1101 30th St. NW, Ste. 305
Washington, DC 20007
202/625-6406

National Solid Wastes Management
    Association
1730 Rhode Island Ave. NW, Ste.
    1000
Washington, DC 20036
202/659-4613

Paperboard Packaging Council
1101 Vermont Ave. NW, Ste. 411
Washington, DC 20005
202/289-4100

Polystyrene Packaging Council, Inc.
1025 Connecticut Ave. NW
Washington, DC 20036
202/822-6424

Soap and Detergent Association
475 Park Ave. South, 27th floor
New York, NY 10016-6947
212/725-1262

Society of the Plastics Industry
1275 K St. NW, Ste. 400
Washington, DC 20005
202/371-5200

Solid Waste Composting Council
214 South Pitt St.
Alexandria, VA 22314
703/739-2401

Steel Can Recycling Institute
Foster Plaza 10
680 Anderson Drive
Pittsburgh, PA 15220
800/876-SCRI

The Vinyl Institute
155 Route 46 West
Wayne Interchange Plaza II
Wayne, NJ 07470
201/890-9299

Appendix **B**

FTC Guides for the Use of Environmental Marketing Claims

**The Application of Section 5
of the Federal Trade Commission Act
to Environmental Advertising
and Marketing Practices (July 1992)**

Table of Contents

A. Statement of Purpose:

These guides represent administrative interpretations of laws administered by the Federal Trade Commission for the guidance of the public in conducting its affairs in conformity with legal requirements. These guides specifically address the application of Section 5 of the FTC Act to environmental advertising and marketing practices. They provide the basis for voluntary compliance with such laws by members of industry. Conduct inconsistent with the positions articulated in these guides may result in corrective action by the Commission under Section 5 if, after investigation, the Commission has reason to believe that the behavior falls within the scope of conduct declared unlawful by the statute.

B. Scope of Guides:

These guides apply to environmental claims included in labeling, advertising, promotional materials and all other forms of marketing, whether asserted directly or by implication, through words, symbols, emblems, logos, depictions, product brand names, or through any other means. The guides apply to any claim about the environmental attributes of a product or package in connection with the sale, offering for sale, or marketing of such product or package for personal, family or household use, or for commercial, institutional or industrial use.

Because the guides are not legislative rules under Section 18 of the FTC Act, they are not themselves enforceable regulations, nor do they have the force and effect of law. The guides themselves do not preempt regulation of other federal agencies or of state and local bodies governing the use of environmental marketing claims. Compliance with federal, state or local law and regulations concerning such claims, however, will not necessarily preclude Commission law enforcement action under Section 5.

C. Structure of the Guides:

The guides are composed of general principles and specific guidance on the use of environmental claims. These general principles and specific guidance are followed by examples that generally address a single deception concern. A given claim may raise issues that are addressed under more than one example and in more than one section of the guides.

In many of the examples, one or more options are presented for qualifying a claim. These options are intended to provide a "safe harbor" for marketers who want certainty about how to make environmental claims. They do not represent the only permissible approaches to qualifying a claim. The examples do not illustrate all possible acceptable claims or disclosures that would be permissible under Section 5. In addition, some of the illustrative disclosures may be appropriate for use on labels but not in print or broadcast advertisements and vice versa. In some instances, the guides indicate within the example in what context or contexts a particular type of disclosure should be considered.

D. Review Procedure:

Three years after the date of adoption of these guides, the Commission will seek public comment on whether and how the guides need to be modified in light of ensuing developments.

Parties may petition the Commission to alter or amend these guides in light of substantial new evidence regarding consumer interpretation of a claim or regarding substantiation of a claim. Following review of such a petition, the Commission will take such action as it deems appropriate.

E. Interpretation and Substantiation of Environmental Marketing Claims:

Section 5 of the FTC Act makes unlawful deceptive acts and practices in or affecting commerce. The Commission's criteria for determining whether an express or implied claim has been made are enunciated in the Commission's Policy Statement on Deception.[1] In addition, any

---

[1]*Cliffdale Associates, Inc.*, 103 F.T.C. 100, at 176, 176 n.7, n.8, Appendix, *reprinting* letter dated Oct. 14, 1983, from the Commission to The Honorable John D. Dingell, Chairman, Committee on Energy and Commerce, U.S. House of Representatives (1984) ("Deception Statement").

party making an express or implied claim that presents an objective assertion about the environmental attribute of a product or package must, at the time the claim is made, possess and rely upon a reasonable basis substantiating the claim. A reasonable basis consists of competent and reliable evidence. In the context of environmental marketing claims, such substantiation will often require competent and reliable scientific evidence. For any test, analysis, research, study or other evidence to be "competent and reliable" for purposes of these guides, it must be conducted and evaluated in an objective manner by persons qualified to do so, using procedures generally accepted in the profession to yield accurate and reliable results. Further guidance on the reasonable basis standard is set forth in the Commission's 1983 Policy Statement on the Advertising Substantiation Doctrine. 49 Fed. Reg. 30,999 (1984); *appended to Thompson Medical Co.*, 104 F.T.C. 648 (1984). These guides, therefore, attempt to preview Commission policy in a relatively new context—that of environmental claims.

F. General Principles:

The following general principles apply to all environmental marketing claims, including, but not limited to, those described in Part G below. In addition, Part G contains specific guidance applicable to certain environmental marketing claims. Claims should comport with all relevant provisions of these guides, not simply the provision that seems most directly applicable.

1. *Qualifications and Disclosures:* The Commission traditionally has held that in order to be effective, any qualifications or disclosures such as those described in these guides should be sufficiently clear and prominent to prevent deception. Clarity of language, relative type size and proximity to the claim being qualified, and an absence of contrary claims that could undercut effectiveness, will maximize the likelihood that the qualifications and disclosures are appropriately clear and prominent.

2. *Distinction Between Benefits of Product and Package:* An environmental marketing claim should be presented in a way that makes clear whether the environmental attribute or benefit being asserted refers to the product, the product's packaging or to a portion or component of the product or packaging. In general, if the environmental attribute or benefit applies to all but minor, incidental components of a product or package, the claim need not be qualified to identify that fact. There may be exceptions to this general principle. For example, if an unqualified "recyclable" claim is made and the presence of the incidental compo-

nent significantly limits the ability to recycle the product, then the claim would be deceptive.

Example 1: A box of aluminum foil is labeled with the claim "recyclable," without further elaboration. Unless the type of product, surrounding language, or other context of the phrase establishes whether the claim refers to the foil or the box, the claim is deceptive if any part of either the box or the foil, other than minor, incidental components, cannot be recycled.

Example 2: A soft drink bottle is labeled "recycled." The bottle is made entirely from recycled materials, but the bottle cap is not. Because reasonable consumers are likely to consider the bottle cap to be a minor, incidental component of the package, the claim is not deceptive. Similarly, it would not be deceptive to label a shopping bag "recycled" where the bag is made entirely of recycled material but the easily detachable handle, an incidental component, is not.

3. *Overstatement of Environmental Attribute:* An environmental marketing claim should not be presented in a manner that overstates the environmental attribute or benefit, expressly or by implication. Marketers should avoid implications of significant environmental benefits if the benefit is in fact negligible.

Example 1: A package is labeled, "50% more recycled content than before." The manufacturer increased the recycled content of its package from 2 percent recycled material to 3 percent recycled material. Although the claim is technically true, it is likely to convey the false impression that the advertiser has increased significantly the use of recycled material.

Example 2: A trash bag is labeled "recyclable" without qualification. Because trash bags will ordinarily not be separated out from other trash at the landfill or incinerator for recycling, they are highly unlikely to be used again for any purpose. Even if the bag is technically capable of being recycled, the claim is deceptive since it asserts an environmental benefit where no significant or meaningful benefit exists.

Example 3: A paper grocery sack is labeled "reusable." The sack can be brought back to the store and reused for carrying groceries but will fall apart after two or three reuses, on average. Because reasonable consumers are unlikely to assume that a paper grocery sack is durable, the unqualified claim does not overstate the environmental benefit conveyed to consumers. The claim is not deceptive and does not need to be qualified to indicate the limited reuse of the sack.

4. *Comparative Claims:* Environmental marketing claims that include a comparative statement should be presented in a manner that makes the basis for the comparison sufficiently clear to avoid consumer

deception. In addition, the advertiser should be able to substantiate the comparison.

Example 1:   An advertiser notes that its shampoo bottle contains "20% more recycled content." The claim in its context is ambiguous. Depending on contextual factors, it could be a comparison either to the advertiser's immediately preceding product or to a competitor's product. The advertiser should clarify the claim to make the basis for comparison clear, for example, by saying "20% more recycled content than our previous package." Otherwise, the advertiser should be prepared to substantiate whatever comparison is conveyed to reasonable consumers.

Example 2:   An advertiser claims that "our plastic diaper liner has the most recycled content." The advertised diaper does have more recycled content, calculated as a percentage of weight, than any other on the market, although it is still well under 100% recycled. Provided the recycled content and the comparative difference between the product and those of competitors are significant and provided the specific comparison can be substantiated, the claim is not deceptive.

Example 3:   An ad claims that the advertiser's packaging creates "less waste than the leading national brand." The advertiser's source reduction was implemented sometime ago and is supported by a calculation comparing the relative solid waste contributions of the two packages. The advertiser should be able to substantiate that the comparison remains accurate.

G. Environmental Marketing Claims:

Guidance about the use of environmental marketing claims is set forth below. Each guide is followed by several examples that illustrate, but do not provide an exhaustive list of, claims that do and do not comport with the guides. In each case, the general principles set forth in Part F above should also be followed.[2]

1. *General Environmental Benefit Claims:*   It is deceptive to misrepresent, directly or by implication, that a product or package offers a general environmental benefit. Unqualified general claims of environmental benefit are difficult to interpret, and depending on their context, may

---

[2]These guides do not address claims based on a "lifecycle" theory of environmental benefit. Such analyses are still in their infancy and thus the Commission lacks sufficient information on which to base guidance at this time.

convey a wide range of meanings to consumers. In many cases, such claims may convey that the product or package has specific and far-reaching environmental benefits. As explained in the Commission's Ad Substantiation Statement, every express and material, implied claim that the general assertion conveys to reasonable consumers about an objective quality, feature or attribute of a product must be substantiated. Unless this substantiation duty can be met, broad environmental claims should either be avoided or qualified, as necessary, to prevent deception about the specific nature of the environmental benefit being asserted.

Example 1: A brand name like "Eco-Safe" would be deceptive if, in the context of the product so named, it leads consumers to believe that the product has environmental benefits which cannot be substantiated by the manufacturer. The claim would not be deceptive if "Eco-Safe" were followed by clear and prominent qualifying language limiting the safety representation to a particular product attribute for which it could be substantiated, and provided that no other deceptive implications were created by the context.

Example 2: A product wrapper is printed with the claim "Environmentally Friendly." Textual comments on the wrapper explain that the wrapper is "Environmentally Friendly because it was not chlorine bleached, a process that has been shown to create harmful substances." The wrapper was, in fact, not bleached with chlorine. However, the production of the wrapper now creates and releases to the environment significant quantities of other harmful substances. Since consumers are likely to interpret the "Environmentally Friendly" claim, in combination with the textual explanation, to mean that no significant harmful substances are currently released to the environment, the "Environmentally Friendly" claim would be deceptive.

Example 3: A pump spray product is labeled "environmentally safe." Most of the product's active ingredients consist of volatile organic compounds (VOCs) that may cause smog by contributing to ground-level ozone formation. The claim is deceptive because, absent further qualification, it is likely to convey to consumers that use of the product will not result in air pollution or other harm to the environment.

2. *Degradable/Biodegradable/Photodegradable:* It is deceptive to misrepresent, directly or by implication, that a product or package is degradable, biodegradable or photodegradable. An unqualified claim that a product or package is degradable, biodegradable or photodegradable should be substantiated by competent and reliable scientific evidence that the entire product or package will completely break down and return to nature, *i.e.,* decompose into elements found in nature within a reasonably short period of time after customary disposal.

Claims of degradability, biodegradability or photodegradability should be qualified to the extent necessary to avoid consumer deception about: (a) the product or package's ability to degrade in the environment where it is customarily disposed; and (b) the rate and extent of degradation.

Example 1: A trash bag is marketed as "degradable," with no qualification or other disclosure. The marketer relies on soil burial tests to show that the product will decompose in the presence of water and oxygen. The trash bags are customarily disposed of in incineration facilities or at sanitary landfills that are managed in a way that inhibits degradation by minimizing moisture and oxygen. Degradation will be irrelevant for those trash bags that are incinerated and, for those disposed of in landfills, the marketer does not possess adequate substantiation that the bags will degrade in a reasonably short period of time in a landfill. The claim is therefore deceptive.

Example 2: A commercial agricultural plastic mulch film is advertised as "Photodegradable" and qualified with the phrase, "Will break down into small pieces if left uncovered in sunlight." The claim is supported by competent and reliable scientific evidence that the product will break down in a reasonably short period of time after being exposed to sunlight and into sufficiently small pieces to become part of the soil. The qualified claim is not deceptive. Because the claim is qualified to indicate the limited extent of breakdown, the advertiser need not meet the elements for an unqualified photodegradable claim, *i.e.*, that the product will not only break down, but also will decompose into elements found in nature.

Example 3: A soap or shampoo product is advertised as "biodegradable," with no qualification or other disclosure. The manufacturer has competent and reliable scientific evidence demonstrating that the product, which is customarily disposed of in sewage systems, will break down and decompose into elements found in nature in a short period of time. The claim is not deceptive.

3. *Compostable:* It is deceptive to misrepresent, directly or by implication, that a product or package is compostable. An unqualified claim that a product or package is compostable should be substantiated by competent and reliable scientific evidence that all the materials in the product or package will break down into, or otherwise become part of, usable compost (*e.g.*, soil-conditioning material, mulch) in a safe and timely manner in an appropriate composting program or facility, or in a home compost pile or device.

Claims of compostability should be qualified to the extent necessary to avoid consumer deception. An unqualified claim may be deceptive: (1) if municipal composting facilities are not available to a substantial majority of consumers or communities where the package is sold; (2) if the claim misleads consumers about the environmental benefit provided when the product is disposed of in a landfill; or (3) if consumers misunderstand the claim to mean that the package can be safely composted in their home compost pile or device, when in fact it cannot.

Example 1:   A manufacturer indicates that its unbleached coffee filter is compostable. The unqualified claim is not deceptive provided the manufacturer can substantiate that the filter can be converted safely to usable compost in a timely manner in a home compost pile or device, as well as in an appropriate composting program or facility.

Example 2:   A lawn and leaf bag is labeled as "Compostable in California Municipal Yard Waste Composting Facilities." The bag contains toxic ingredients that are released into the compost material as the bag breaks down. The claim is deceptive if the presence of these toxic ingredients prevents the compost from being usable.

Example 3:   A manufacturer indicates that its paper plate is suitable for home composting. If the manufacturer possesses substantiation for claiming that the paper plate can be converted safely to usable compost in a home compost pile or device, this claim is not deceptive even if no municipal composting facilities exist.

Example 4:   A manufacturer makes an unqualified claim that its package is compostable. Although municipal composting facilities exist where the product is sold, the package will not break down into usable compost in a home compost pile or device. To avoid deception, the manufacturer should disclose that the package is not suitable for home composting.

Example 5:   A nationally marketed lawn and leaf bag is labeled "compostable." Also printed on the bag is a disclosure that the bag is not designed for use in home compost piles. The bags are in fact composted in municipal yard waste composting programs in many communities around the country, but such programs are not available to a substantial majority of consumers where the bag is sold. The claim is deceptive since reasonable consumers living in areas not served by municipal yard waste programs may understand the reference to mean that composting facilities accepting the bags are available in their area. To avoid deception, the claim should be qualified to indicate the limited availability of such programs, for example, by stating, "Appropriate facilities may not exist in your area." Other examples of adequate qualification of the claim include providing the approximate percentage of communities or the population for which such programs are available.

Example 6:   A manufacturer sells a disposable diaper that bears the legend, "This diaper can be composted where municipal solid waste composting facilities exist. There are current [X number of] municipal solid waste composting facilities across the country." The claim is not deceptive, assuming that composting facilities are available as claimed and the manufacturer can substantiate that the diaper can be converted safely to usable compost in municipal solid waste composting facilities.

Example 7: A manufacturer markets yard waste bags only to consumers residing in particular geographic areas served by county yard waste composting programs. The bags meet specifications for these programs and are labeled, "Compostable Yard Waste Bag for County Composting Programs." The claim is not deceptive. Because the bags are compostable where they are sold, no qualification is required to indicate the limited availability of composting facilities.

4. *Recyclable:* It is deceptive to misrepresent, directly or by implication, that a product or package is recyclable. A product or package should not be marketed as recyclable unless it can be collected, separated or otherwise recovered from the solid waste stream for use in the form of raw materials in the manufacture or assembly of a new package or product. Unqualified claims of recyclability for a product or package may be made if the entire product or package, excluding minor incidental components, is recyclable. For products or packages that are made of both recyclable and non-recyclable components, the recyclable claim should be adequately qualified to avoid consumer deception about which portions or components of the product or package are recyclable.

Claims of recyclability should be qualified to the extent necessary to avoid consumer deception about any limited availability of recycling programs and collection sites. If an incidental component significantly limits the ability to recycle the product, the claim would be deceptive. A product or package that is made from recyclable material, but, because of its shape, size or some other attribute, is not accepted in recycling programs for such material, should not be marketed as recyclable.

Example 1: A packaged product is labeled with an unqualified claim, "recyclable." It is unclear from the type of product and other context whether the claim refers to the product or its package. The unqualified claim is likely to convey to reasonable consumers that all of both the product and its packaging that remain after normal use of the product, except for minor, incidental components, can be recycled. Unless each such message can be substantiated, the claim should be qualified to indicate what portions are recyclable.

Example 2: A plastic package is labeled on the bottom with the Society of the Plastics Industry (SPI) code, consisting of a design of arrows in a triangular shape containing a number and abbreviation identifying the component plastic resin. Without more, the use of the SPI symbol (or similar industry codes) on the bottom of the package, or in a similarly inconspicuous location, does not constitute a claim of recyclability.

Example 3: A container can be burned in incinerator facilities to produce heat and power. It cannot, however, be recycled into new products or packaging. Any claim that the container is recyclable would be deceptive.

Example 4: A nationally marketed bottle bears the unqualified statement that it is "recyclable." Collection sites for recycling the material in question are not available to a substantial majority of consumers or communities, although collection sites are established in a significant percentage of communities or available to a significant percentage of the population. The unqualified claim is deceptive since, unless evidence shows otherwise, reasonable consumers living in communities not served by programs may conclude that recycling programs for the material are available in their area. To avoid deception, the claim should be qualified to indicate the limited availability of programs, for example, by stating, "Check to see if recycling facilities exist in your area." Other examples of adequate qualifications of the claim include providing the approximate percentage of communities or the population to whom programs are available.

Example 5: A soda bottle is marketed nationally and labeled, "Recyclable where facilities exist." Recycling programs for material of this type and size are available in a significant percentage of communities or to a significant percentage of the population, but are not available to a substantial majority of consumers. The claim is deceptive since, unless evidence shows otherwise, reasonable consumers living in communities not served by programs may understand this phrase to mean that programs are available in their area. To avoid deception, the claim should be further qualified to indicate the limited availability of programs, for example, by using any of the approaches set forth in Example 4 above.

Example 6: A plastic detergent bottle is marketed as follows: "Recyclable in the few communities with facilities for colored HDPE bottles." Collection sites for recycling the container have been established in a half-dozen major metropolitan areas. This disclosure illustrates one approach to qualifying a claim adequately to prevent deception about the limited availability of recycling programs where collection facilities are not established in a significant percentage of communities or available to a significant percentage of the population. Other examples of adequate qualification of the claim include providing the number of communities with programs, or the percentage of communities or the population to which programs are available.

Example 7: A label claims that the package "includes some recyclable material." The package is composed of four layers of different materials, bonded together. One of the layers is made from the recyclable material, but the others are not. While programs for recycling this type of material are available to a substantial majority of consumers, only a few of those programs have the capability to separate out the recyclable layer. Even though it is technologically possible to separate the layers, the claim is not adequately qualified to avoid consumer deception. An appropriately qualified claim would be, "includes material recyclable in the few communities that collect multi-layer products." Other examples of adequate qualification of the claim include providing the number of communities with programs, or the percentage of communities or the population to which programs are available.

Example 8:   A product is marketed as having a "recyclable" container. The product is distributed and advertised only in Missouri. Collection sites for recycling the container are available to a substantial majority of Missouri residents, but are not yet available nationally. Because programs are generally available where the product is marketed, the unqualified claim does not deceive consumers about the limited availability of recycling programs.

5. *Recycled Content:*   A recycled content claim may be made only for materials that have been recovered or otherwise diverted from the solid waste stream, either during the manufacturing process (pre-consumer), or after consumer use (post-consumer). To the extent the source of recycled content includes pre-consumer material, the manufacturer or advertiser must have substantiation for concluding that the pre-consumer material would otherwise have entered the solid waste stream. In asserting a recycled content claim, distinctions may be made between pre-consumer and post-consumer materials. Where such distinctions are asserted, any express or implied claim about the specific pre-consumer or post-consumer content of a product or package must be substantiated.

It is deceptive to misrepresent, directly or by implication, that a product or package is made of recycled material. Unqualified claims of recycled content may be made only if the entire product or package, excluding minor, incidental components, is made from recycled material. For products or packages that are only partially made of recycled material, a recycled claim should be adequately qualified to avoid consumer deception about the amount, by weight, of recycled content in the finished product or package.

Example 1:   A manufacturer routinely collects spilled raw material and scraps from trimming finished products. After a minimal amount of reprocessing, the manufacturer combines the spills and scraps with virgin material for use in further production of the same product. A claim that the product contains recycled material is deceptive since the spills and scraps to which the claim refers are normally reused by industry within the original manufacturing process, and would not normally have entered the waste stream.

Example 2: A manufacturer purchases material from a firm that collects discarded material from other manufacturers and resells it. All of the material was diverted from the solid waste stream and is not normally reused by industry within the original manufacturing process. The manufacturer includes the weight of this material in its calculations of the recycled content of its products. A claim of recycled content based on this calculation is not deceptive because, absent the purchase and reuse of this material, it would have entered the waste stream.

Example 3: A greeting card is composed 30% by weight of paper collected from consumers after use of a paper product, and 20% by weight of paper that was generated after completion of the paper-making process, diverted from the solid waste stream, and otherwise would not normally have been reused in the original manufacturing process. The marketer of the card may claim either that the product "contains 50% recycled material," or may identify the specific pre-consumer and/or post-consumer content by stating, for example, that the product "contains 50% total recycled material, 30% of which is post-consumer material."

Example 4: A package with 20% recycled content by weight is labeled as containing "20% recycled paper." Some of the recycled content was composed of material collected from consumers after use of the original product. The rest was composed of overrun newspaper stock never sold to customers. The claim is not deceptive.

Example 5: A product in a multi-component package, such as a paperboard box in a shrink-wrapped plastic cover, indicates that it has recycled packaging. The paperboard box is made entirely of recycled material, but the plastic cover is not. The claim is deceptive since, without qualification, it suggests that both components are recycled. A claim limited to the paperboard box would not be deceptive.

Example 6: A package is made from layers of foil, plastic, and paper laminated together, although the layers are indistinguishable to consumers. The label claims that "one of the three layers of this package is made of recycled plastic." The plastic layer is made entirely of recycled plastic. The claim is not deceptive provided the recycled plastic layer constitutes a significant component of the entire package.

Example 7: A paper product is labeled as containing "100% recycled fiber." The claim is not deceptive if the advertiser can substantiate the conclusion that 100% by weight of the fiber in the finished product is recycled.

Example 8: A frozen dinner is marketed in a package composed of a cardboard box over a plastic tray. The package bears the legend, "package made from 30% recycled material." Each packaging component amounts to one-half the weight of the total package. The box is 20% recycled content by weight, while the plastic tray is 40% recycled content by weight. The claim is not deceptive, since the average amount of recycled material is 30%.

Example 9:   A paper greeting card is labeled as containing 50% by weight recycled content. The seller purchases paper stock from several sources and the amount of recycled material in the stock provided by each source varies. Because the 50% figure is based on the annual weighted average of recycled material purchased from the sources after accounting for fiber loss during the production process, the claim is permissible.

6. *Source Reduction:*   It is deceptive to misrepresent, directly or by implication, that a product or package has been reduced or is lower in weight, volume or toxicity. Source reduction claims should be qualified to the extent necessary to avoid consumer deception about the amount of the source reduction and about the basis for any comparison asserted.

Example 1:   An ad claims that solid waste created by disposal of the advertiser's packaging is "now 10% less than our previous package." The claim is not deceptive if the advertiser has substantiation that shows that disposal of the current package contributes 10% less waste by weight or volume to the solid waste stream when compared with the immediately preceding version of the package.

Example 2:   An advertiser notes that disposal of its product generates "10% less waste." The claim is ambiguous. Depending on contextual factors, it could be a comparison either to the immediately preceding product or to a competitor's product. The "10% less waste" reference is deceptive unless the seller clarifies which comparison is intended and substantiates that comparison, or substantiates both possible interpretations of the claim.

7. *Refillable:*   It is deceptive to misrepresent, directly or by implication, that a package is refillable. An unqualified refillable claim should not be asserted unless a system is provided for: (1) the collection and return of the package for refill; or (2) the later refill of the package by consumers with product subsequently sold in another package. A package should not be marketed with an unqualified refillable claim, if it is up to the consumer to find new ways to refill the package.

Example 1:   A container is labeled "refillable x times." The manufacturer has the capability to refill returned containers and can show that the container will withstand being refilled at least x times. The manufacturer, however, has established no collection program. The unqualified claim is deceptive because there is no means for collection and return of the container to the manufacturer for refill.

Example 2:   A bottle of fabric softener states that it is in a "handy refillable container." The manufacturer also sells a large-sized container that indicates that the consumer is expected to use it to refill the smaller container. The manufacturer sells the large-sized container in the same market areas where it sells the small container. The claim is not deceptive because there is a means for consumers to refill the smaller container from larger containers of the same product.

8. *Ozone Safe and Ozone Friendly:* It is deceptive to misrepresent, directly or by implication, that a product is safe for or "friendly" to the ozone layer. A claim that a product does not harm the ozone layer is deceptive if the product contains an ozone-depleting substance.

Example 1: A product is labeled "ozone friendly." The claim is deceptive if the product contains any ozone-depleting substance, including those substances listed as Class I or Class II chemicals in Title VI of the Clean Air Act Amendments of 1990, Pub. L. No. 101-549, or others subsequently designated by EPA as ozone-depleting substances. Class I chemicals currently listed in Title VI are chlorofluorocarbons (CFCs), halons, carbon tetrachloride and 1,1,1-trichloroethane. Class II chemicals currently listed in Title VI are hydrochlorofluorocarbons (HCFCs).

Example 2: The seller of an aerosol product makes an unqualified claim that its product "Contains no CFCs." Although the product does not contain CFCs, it does contain HCFC-22, another ozone depleting ingredient. Because the claim "Contains no CFCs" may imply to reasonable consumers that the product does not harm the ozone layer, the claim is deceptive.

Example 3: A product is labeled "This product is 95% less damaging to the ozone layer than past formulations that contained CFCs." The manufacturer has substituted HCFCs for CFC-12, and can substantiate that this substitution will result in 95% less ozone depletion. The qualified comparative claim is not likely to be deceptive.

Notes

Preface

1. Eldon D. Enger and Brad F. Smith, *Environmental Science: A Study of Interrelationships*, 4th ed. Wm. C. Brown, Dubuque, Iowa, 1992, p. 48.

2. Dr. Neils Skakkebaek, Univ. of Copenhagen Study cited by *Greenwire*, American Political Network, Inc., volume 2, no. 93, Sept. 11, 1992.

Chapter 1

1. Carl Frankel, *The Green Consumer*, FIND/SVP, New York, 1990, p. 37.

2. Alice Tepper Marlin, Jonathan Schorsch, Emily Swaab, and Rosalyn Will, *Shopping For A Better World*, Council on Economic Priorities, 1991, p. 110.

Chapter 2

1. George M. Carpenter, "Evolution of Total Quality Environmental Management," *Corporate Quality—Environmental Management II: Measurement and Communications Conference* (symposium), Arlington, Va., March 16, 1992.

2. Philip B. Crosby, *Quality Without Tears*, McGraw-Hill Book Company, New York, 1984.

3. Ernest Callenbach, Fritjof Capra, and Sandra Marburg, *The Elmwood Guide to Eco-Auditing and Ecologically Conscious Management*, The Elmwood Institute, Berkeley, Calif., 1990, pp. 21–22.

4. *Corporate Environmental Policy*, Church & Dwight Co., Inc., Princeton, N.J., 1992.

5. Chris FitzGerald, "Selecting Measures for Corporate Environmental Quality: Examples from TQEM Companies," *Total Quality Environmental Management*, Executive Enterprises Publications Co., Inc., New York, Volume 1, Number 4, Summer 1992, p. 332.

Chapter 3

1. William Rathji, "Rubbish," *The Atlantic*, The Atlantic Monthly Company, Boston, December 1989, p. 106.

Chapter 5

1. "Influential Americans in the 1990s," a Roper Organization report cosponsored by *The Atlantic Monthly*, 3rd Edition, September 1992, New York, p. 105.
2. *Wall Street Journal/NBC News Report* (on the environment), New York, July 1991.
3. "The Environment: Public Attitudes and Behavior," a report by The Roper Organization and S.C. Johnson & Son Inc., New York, 1990, pp. 31–47.
4. Archie Comic Publications, Inc., Mamaroneck, N.Y., June 11, 1992 press release.
5. "The Power of Children," INFOCUS Environmental, Princeton, N.J., 1992.
6. Stanislav Grof, *Beyond the Brain: Birth, Death and Transcendence in Psychotherapy*, SUNY Press, Albany, N.Y., 1985, p. 195.
7. Abraham Maslow, *Motivation and Personality*, Harper & Row, New York, 1954.
8. Cited in *Green MarketAlert*, The Bridge Group, Bethlehem, Conn., January 1991, p. 10.
9. *JWT Greenwatch*, J. Walter Thompson USA, Consumer Behavior Department, New York, Volume 1, Number 2, Autumn 1990.
10. *The Green Shopping Revolution: How Solid Waste Issues Are Affecting Consumer Behavior*, Food Marketing Institute (Washington) and *Better Homes and Gardens* (New York), 1990, p. 23.
11. *Advertising Age* poll conducted by Yankelovich Clancy Shulman, *Advertising Age*, Crain Communications, Inc., Chicago, June 29, 1992, Special Section p. 4.
12. American Opinion Research, Princeton, N.J.
13. Brenda J. Cude, Ph.D., "Comments Prepared for the July 1991 FTC Public Hearings on Environmental Marketing and Advertising Claims," University of Illinois at Urbana-Champaign, June 1991 and expanded September 1991.
14. "Peter Kim, ed., The Meaning of Green: How Environmental Advertising Works," *JWT Greenwatch*, New York, Number 3, Spring/Summer 1991, p. 3.
15. "The Changing Mood of America," *The Good Housekeeping/Roper Survey*, The Roper Organization and The Hearst Corporation, 1991, New York, p. 8.
16. *The Hartman Environmental Marketing Report*, The Hartman Group, Newport Beach, Calif., January 1992, p. 83.

17. Jane Barnett (for the American Marketing Association), testimony before the Environmental Protection Agency meeting on recycling labeling, Washington, November 13, 1991, p. 4.

Chapter 6

1. *Green Report II.* Task Force of State Attorneys General, May 1991, p. 25.
2. *Summary of the FTC Environmental Marketing Guidelines,* The Federal Trade Commission, Washington, July 1992.
3. Robert Viney, personal interview, September 1991.
4. Good Housekeeping Institute Survey on Women's Environmental Consumerism, Good Housekeeping Institute, New York, July 1990 cited in *Green MarketAlert,* The Bridge Group, Bethlehem, Conn., May 1991, p. 9.
5. James Salzman, "Environmental Labeling in OECD Countries," OECD, Paris, 1991, p. 50.
6. *The European Community's Environmental Policies and Practices: Assessing the Business Implications of EC Environmental Regulations,* symposium presented by The European-American Chamber of Commerce and Baker & McKenzie, New York, July 7, 1992.

Chapter 7

1. "The Tellus Institute Packaging Study," Tellus Institute, Boston, 1992.
2. Terry L. Anderson and Donald R. Leal, *Free Market Environmentalism,* Pacific Research Institute for Public Policy, San Francisco, Calif., 1991.

Chapter 8

1. Marketing Intelligence Service, Naples, N.Y., 1991.
2. Richard M. Carpenter, quote from keynote address to S.C. Johnson & Son, Inc. suppliers as cited in an S.C. Johnson press release, Racine, Wis., February 1991.
3. Susan E. Lordi, "Green Brands Clean Up," *Supermarket News,* Fairchild Fashion & Merchandising Group, New York, February 4, 1991, p. 22.
4. Braden R. Allenby, *SSA Journal,* Semiconductor Safety Association, Washington, September 1991, pp. 5–9.
5. Dr. Ian Boustead,"The Relevance of Re-use and Recycling Activities for the LCA Profile of Products," reprinted in *Life Cycle Inventory and the Environmental Report Card Draft Copy,* Scientific Certification Systems, Inc., Oakland, Calif., May 5, 1992, Appendix 5.

6. "Design for the Environment: Cleaner Technologies for a Safer Future," Economics and Technology Division, Office of Pollution Prevention and Toxics, U.S. Environmental Protection Agency, Washington. For more information call (202) 260-0686.

Chapter 9

1. "Economic Slowdown Pinpoints Opportunities in the 1990s," *Private Label*, Private Label Publishing Co., Fort Lee, N.J., May/June 1991, p. 86.

Chapter 10

1. Matthew L. Wald, "G.M. Signs an Accord With Environmentalists," *The New York Times*, July 9, 1992, p. D4.

Chapter 11

1. "The Environment: Public Attitudes and Behavior," a report by The Roper Organization and S.C. Johnson & Son Inc., New York, 1990, pp. 53–55.

2. *TJFR Business News Reporter*, TJFR Publishing, Co., Ridgewood, N.J., January 1992, as cited in *Green MarketAlert*, The Bridge Group, Bethlehem, Conn., April 1992, p. 9.

3. *The Hartman Environmental Marketing Report*, The Hartman Group, Newport Beach, Calif., January 1992, p. 83.

4. "Green Consumerism Update: Environmentalism and Its Impact on American Consumers," Cambridge Reports/Research International, Cambridge, Mass., 1990, as cited in *Green MarketAlert*, The Bridge Group, Bethlehem, Conn., December 1991, p. 7.

5. "Consumer Solid Waste: Awareness, Attitude and Behavior Study III," Gerstman + Meyers Inc., New York, N.Y., 1990, Question 15.

6. *Green Report II*. Task Force of State Attorneys General, May 1991, p. 11.

7. Peter Kim, ed., "The Meaning of Green: How Environmental Advertising Works," *JWT Greenwatch*, New York, Number 3, Spring/Summer 1991, as cited in *Green MarketAlert*, The Bridge Group, Bethlehem, Conn., September 1991, pp. 4–5.

8. Bruce Harrison, "Green Has to Run More than Skin Deep," *Inside PR*, Editorial Media Marketing International, Inc., New York, February 1992, pp. 26–27.

9. James B. Lindheim and Fredrick E. Wodin, "Communicating in the New Environmental Age," a special report originally produced by Burson-Marsteller, New York, 1990, p. 5.

Index

About the Author

Walter Coddington is the founder of Coddington Environmental Management, Inc., the first marketing consultancy dedicated solely to providing clients with strategic planning and program managemet services in the sensitive and quickly evolving environmental arena. Formerly, as president of the marketing agency Coddington, Chadwick & Meyerson, Mr. Coddington developed business and marketing plans for many major consumer packaged goods and service companies. A graduate of the functionally oriented Bauhaus School (Illinois Institute of Technology, Institute of Design, Chicago), Mr. Coddington's holistic approach to situation analysis and business development planning has proven particularly effective in managing the market impact and growth potential of companies engaged in environmental improvement and "clean(er)" product marketing.

Mr. Coddington joined industry in its appeal to the Federal Trade Commission (FTC) to issue guidelines on environmental marketing, labeling, and advertising, and on July 17, 1991 he testified on the subject of "consumer perception." In an historically short period of time, the FTC issued those guidelines on July 28, 1992. They are included in this book.